THE WORLD'S BEST INDOOR GAMES

THE WORLD'S BEST INDOOR GAMES

GYLES BRANDRETH

794
B

Pantheon Books, New York

Library of Congress Cataloging in Publication Data

Brandreth, Gyles Daubeney, 1948–
   The world's best indoor games.

   1. Games.   I. Title.
GV1229.B67   794   81-18929
ISBN 0-394-52477-2   AACR2
ISBN 0-394-71001-0 (pbk.)

Manufactured in the United States of America
First American Edition

About the Author

Gyles Brandreth was educated at Oxford and, at present, lives and works in England. He is the author of many game books, including *Games for Rains, Planes, and Trains; Brain-Teasers and Mind-Benders;* and *Great Puzzle Mountain.* He is also, at thirty-two, a past president of the Oxford Union and former European Monopoly champion.

CONTENTS

4 Card Games

5 Board Games

6 Domino Games

7 Dice Games

8 Matchstick Games

9 Games of Chance

10 Allsorts

11 Solo Games

12 Children's Party Games

13 Children's Card Games

INTRODUCTION

You may not have noticed, but over the past decade or so a quiet revolution has been sweeping the Western world. It is a social revolution which gradually has been gathering momentum and, though no-one has yet paid much attention to it, before long everyone will be talking about it, television producers will be devoting prize-winning documentary films to it, and earnest post-graduate students will be exploring its ramifications in heavy doctoral theses.

I refer, of course, to the Indoor Games Revolution. People – of all ages, of all classes and of most nationalities – are playing games now as never before. And the games they are playing – parlour games, card games, board games, games of chance – are assuming an increasingly important part in the leisure pattern of their lives.

I am not asserting this simply because I have written this book, nor even because I happen to be an unrepentant Snakes and Ladders fanatic who is never happier than when sitting in a festive party hat making a small fortune at Tiddlywinks – or losing one at Bridge. It's a fact. While the European and American toy industries have been going through hard financial times of late, the sale of *games* of all kinds continues to show a steady increase. And, according to Dr Gallup, while watching television remains our number one pastime, games-playing in all its manifestations has moved from eighth place to fourth place in the league table of our leisure activities. It appears that in the austere 1980s we are falling back on our own resources, staying at home and doing our best to entertain ourselves.

In my own family we have been indoor games enthusiasts for generations. A century ago, in New York, my great-great-grandfather published *Brandreth's Puzzle Book*, a compendium of his favourite games, pastimes and brainteasers. The book was really intended to promote the sales of Brandreth's Pills – 'a medicine that acts directly on the stomach, bowels and liver, and through them purifies the blood: they cure rheumatism, headache, biliousness, constipation, dyspepsia and liver complaint' – but having been to Sing Sing, the bizarre location of the Brandreth Pill Factory, and both tasted the medicine and read the book, I am inclined to think my ancestors were better games players than they were pharmacists.

My own parents met over the Monopoly board. In the winter of 1936 my father bought the then very novel board game and took the box back to his lodgings where he asked his landlady if she fancied a game. She didn't, but she said that the Canadian lady and her daughter on the top floor might – and they did. Forty years later when that Monopoly tyro and the Canadian lady's daughter were celebrating their ruby wedding anniversary, I was in New York doing my best to uphold the family honour by coming third in the World Monopoly Championships. (I love games, but I am not very good at winning them. That is why I founded and now organise the British National Scrabble Championships. I am happy presiding over the competition: were I to take part I would never reach even the semi-finals!)

Naturally there is nothing new in man playing games. Many of the games which are enjoying a vogue at the moment have been popular for thousands of years. Take, as an example, a particular favourite of mine, Blind Man's Buff, perhaps the oldest party game of all. A blindfolded player rushes about the room trying to catch hold of the other sighted players who dodge out of his way. When the blindfolded player catches his victim he has to guess who it is, and if he is right to change places. In its origins the game is almost certainly connected with the early rites of human sacrifice and undoubtedly dates back to the time of the blind god Odin, chief deity of Norse mythology. Through the centuries it has been known as Billie Blind, Hoodle-cum-Blind and Blind Harrie, but it's an entertaining romp for all its gruesome history.

Some games, like Blind Man's Buff and Grandmother's Footsteps (which originally involved children daring one another to run up and touch an old lady on the back without her noticing!), spring from cruel beginnings, but most seem to me to be a mark of civilisation. After all, it was the eighteenth-century German poet Schiller who took time off from *Wilhelm Tell* to observe: 'Man only plays when in the full meaning of the word he is a man, and he is only completely a man when he plays.'

Someone who was without doubt 'completely a man' (and highly civilised with it) was Samuel Pepys. He thoroughly approved of games-playing. Just over three hundred years ago he noted in his diary, 'from thence to the Hague, again playing at Crambo in the wagon.' Crambo is played still and you will find the modern rules on page 37. A game which pre-dates Pepys, but which he never recalls having had the good fortune to enjoy, is Postman's Knock. It is an engaging domestic entertainment that is at least as historic as the first postman (1529) and, if you don't already know how to play the game, turn to page 20 and you will find you are in for a real treat.

My own favourite parlour game recently celebrated its bicentenary. The name Charades is derived from the Spanish *charrada*, meaning the chatter of clowns, but it came to England and was transformed into an after-dinner amusement in 1776. As a parlour game it really came into its own in the late nineteenth century, during the Victorian heyday of home entertainment when no house party was complete without a session of Charades or Sardines – or Apple Ducking, a particular royal favourite. When you play the latter game today (page 16) you set apples bobbing in a washing-up bowl of water and attempt to remove them with your mouth without losing either your teeth or your dignity. King Edward VII, as Prince of Wales, played the game but he had his apples bobbing in an ice-bucket filled to the brim with champagne!

Nowadays, alas, there are very few house parties and most contemporary homes don't have the size or number of rooms which made rambling Victorian country manors the perfect setting for party games. After a hard day's huntin', shootin', or fishin', the company would recharge themselves with a huge tea, then assemble in one of the downstairs living rooms and play games – word games in the library, card games in the billiards room, play-acting games in the drawing room – until it was time to change for dinner. In its way, it was an idyllic existence, but difficult to recapture or recreate in modern, urban surroundings. Difficult, but not impossible, for, as you'll know if you have ever played the game called Proverbs (page 39), where there's a will there's a way.

As I see it, the real revolution is not so much the extent to which people of all ages are now playing games, as the extent to which games playing has now become socially acceptable again. If you want to suggest a session of Beetle (page 199) or a round of Battleships (page 56) or even a hand of Brag (page 114), you no longer have to apologise first. But you do have to know the rules.

That's why I have written this book.

Almost everyone knows the rules of a handful of their favourite games, but there are scores of others equally entertaining that are rarely played today simply because no-one knows how. In producing this international games compendium, what I have tried to do is introduce in as straightforward a way as possible the rules of the world's best indoor games: from the simple (such as the parlour games I have just been discussing) to the sophisticated (such as some of the card games that appear in Chapter 4), from the obvious (Tiddlywinks, Darts) to the obscure (Gioul, Mu-Torere, Plakato), from the classic (Chess, Draughts, Backgammon) to the juvenile (Pass the Parcel, Hunt the Slipper, Musical Chairs), from games with curious names borrowed from the famous (Moriarty, Guggenheim, Botticelli) to games that don't come from the West and with which you may be unfamiliar (Achi, Four Field Kono, Wari), from paper and pencil games to gambling games, from games involving dice and dominoes and matchsticks to games you can play on your own or with the children.

Curiously, while no-one disputes that play is vital to children, a lot of people are reluctant to admit that it can also be of immense value to adults. The importance of games-playing was powerfully underlined by the German historian and philosopher, Johan Huizinga, in his book *Homo Ludens*, which is one of the few serious studies of the place of play in culture. 'Play', according to Professor Huizinga, 'adorns life, amplifies it and is to that extent a necessity, both for the individual – as a life function – and for society by reason of the meaning it contains, its significance, its expressive value, its spiritual and social associations, in short, as a cultural function. The expression of it satisfies all kinds of cultural needs.'

To say that 'play adorns life' does sound absurdly grandiose, yet having played – though by no means mastered – every one of the games you will find here, I think it is true. And by the time you finish the book I hope you will agree.

1

Yes and No
Odd or Even
Shopping List
Pan Tapping
Apple Ducking
Execution
Moriarty
Mummies
Dead-Pan
Going Through the Motions
Matchbox Race
Pass the Orange
Postman's Knock
Winking
Feeding the Baby
Dumb Crambo
Zoo Quest
Sardines
The Picture Frame Game
Newspaper Fancy Dress
Taste
Find the Leader
Kim's Game
Up Jenkins
Murder in the Dark
Charades
Drama School

Yes and No

No. of players: Any number
Equipment: Five coins for each player
Complexity: ★★

This is an excellent game for getting people to talk to one another at parties. Each player is given five coins (or if that proves to be too costly, they may be given five matches). The players have to pair off and engage each other in conversation. The aim is to trick the other player into using the words 'Yes' or 'No'. The first player of the pair to say 'Yes' or 'No' is presented with a penny by the other player. The two players then split up and move on to new partners. The first player to get rid of his five coins is the winner.

Odd or Even

No. of players: Any number
Equipment: Ten coins (or matchsticks) for each player
Complexity: ★

This game bears some resemblance to *Yes and No* but places fewer demands on the conversational abilities of the players.

Each player is given ten coins. Putting any number of them in one hand, he holds out his clenched fist to any other player whom he might choose as an opponent and demands 'Odd or even?' The opponent, if he guesses wrongly, receives a coin – if he guesses correctly, he hands over a coin. The two players then reverse roles, the opponent going through the same rigmarole with some of his coins. The two players then split up and seek new opponents.

The first player to succeed in getting rid of all his coins is the winner. The player who finishes with most coins may be allowed to keep them to compensate for his terrible luck.

Shopping List

No. of players: Any large number
Equipment: None
Complexity: ✫

One of the players is the shopper. The other players, in teams of four to six, represent rival department stores. The shopper calls out items from his shopping list, which may be prepared beforehand or may be made up on the spur of the moment. The items on the list should be objects which some, at least, of the players might reasonably be expected to have about their persons: a blue comb, a safety pin, a bus ticket, a pair of braces, a theatre or cinema ticket, a key-ring with five keys on it, a matchbox containing twenty-three matches, an eyebrow pencil, a pair of socks etc. A point is awarded to the first 'store' to supply the shopper with each item, and the store with most points at the end of the game is the winner.

Pan Tapping

No of players: Any number
Equipment: A saucepan and a spoon
Complexity: ✫

One player is sent out of the room while the others decide on some task they want him to perform when he returns. The task may be anything – switching on the radio, perhaps, or sitting on a particular chair, or tearing up a newspaper, or kissing the earlobe of one of the female players.

The outsider is summoned back into the room and he is guided towards the task he has to perform by one of the other players equipped with the saucepan and spoon. This player taps the pan with the spoon, faster and louder as the outsider approaches the object he has to touch – the radio, chair, newspaper, earlobe or whatever – and slower and softer as he moves away from it. In this manner the pan-tapper guides the outsider towards the appointed object and helps him to realise what action he has to perform with it.

When the required task has been performed it becomes the pan-tapper's turn to go out of the room while a new task is chosen for him to perform.

Apple Ducking

No. of players: Any number
Equipment: Apples and a bowl of water
Complexity: ☆

This game is a traditional favourite for Hallowe'en, but it can provide fun at any time of the year.

Fill a large bowl with water and float in it half a dozen apples. Place it on the floor and surround it with towels or newspaper in case of splashes. Each player must then kneel by the bowl, with his hands behind his back, and extract an apple from the water, using only his mouth and teeth.

The more sedate version of this game involves one player ducking at a time with, say, a two-minute time limit. The more rumbustious version is in the form of a race, with several or all of the players ducking for apples at the same time, the first player to lift an apple from the water being the winner. When playing this version, the fun (which may embrace bumped heads and spilled water) may be enhanced by using apples which have been coated liberally with honey or syrup.

A closely related game is *Bob Apple*, in which one apple for each player is suspended on a string. Each player is then required to eat his apple down to the core without using his hands. The first player to succeed in this is the winner.

Execution

No of players: 4, 5 or 6
Equipment: A length of string
Complexity: ☆

This gruesome little game originated in Britain in the days before the abolition of capital punishment, when convicted murderers were still sent to the scaffold.

One player is chosen to be the executioner. The other players sit or stand in a circle with the tips of their raised forefingers pressed together in the centre of the circle. The executioner, standing outside the circle, slips a running noose over the fingers and holds the ends of the string. He cries 'Death!' and jerks up the string. The players, if their reflexes are quick enough, whip their fingers away. Any player whose finger is caught in the noose is suspended from the game and hangs about while the others continue playing.

Moriarty

No. of players: 2 (plus audience)
Equipment: Two blindfolds and two rolled-up newspapers
Complexity: ☆

As Sherlock Holmes might have said, this game is elementary. The two players are blindfolded and lie flat on the floor, face down, with their heads about a foot apart. Each player grasps the other's left wrist with his left hand and holds a rolled-up newspaper in his right hand. One player calls out 'Are you there, Moriarty?' The other player replies 'Yes' (or words to that effect) and promptly rolls out of the way while the inquirer attempts to smack him on the head with a single well-aimed blow from his rolled-up newspaper. Each player has an equal number of turns to be the assailant, and the player who scores the greater number of direct hits is the winner.

The better Sunday newspapers (complete with supplements and colour magazines) are to be preferred for this game as their prose is weightier than that of the popular tabloids. Real devotees of the game, of course, use bound volumes of *Strand Magazine*.

Mummies

No. of players: 4 or more
Equipment: A roll of toilet paper for each couple
Complexity: ☆

The players pair off into mixed couples, and the female member of each couple is given a roll of toilet paper. A three-minute time limit is set, within which each female has to use the toilet paper to swathe her male partner from head to foot so that he resembles an Egyptian mummy. The couple who are judged to have made the best mummy are the winners.

Dead-Pan

No. of players: Any number
Equipment: None
Complexity: ☆

The players sit or stand in a circle, and one of them is chosen to be the leader. The leader nudges the player on his left, who nudges the player on *his* left, who nudges the player on *his* left, and so on round the circle back to the leader. The leader now tweaks the ear of the player on his left, who tweaks the ear of the player on *his* left, and so on round the circle once more. For the third and subsequent rounds the leader shakes his neighbour's hand, or tickles him under the chin, or blows in his ear, or pulls his nose, or whatever turns him on, and the other players do the same around the circle.

The idea is that the players should perform all these actions without displaying any sign of amusement. A player drops out of the game if he laughs or smiles. The last player left in is the winner.

Going Through the Motions

No. of players: Any number
Equipment: None
Complexity: ☆

The players form a circle. The first player performs any action he chooses – tapping his foot, twitching his nose, winking, bobbing up and down, or whatever. The second player must copy the action of the first player and at the same time perform an additional action of his choice. The third player must copy the actions of the second player and at the same time perform some other action. And so on round the circle, each player copying the actions of the previous player and adding another simultaneous action. Any player who fails to do so or who falls over, suffering from exhaustion, is out of the game. The last player left winking, nodding, bobbing and jerking is the winner.

Matchbox Race

No. of players: 8 or more
Equipment: Two matchboxes
Complexity: ☆

The players divide into two teams, each team forming a straight line, and the player at the head of each line is given a matchbox cover. On the word of command, the leader of each team pushes the matchbox cover over his nose and has to transfer it from his own nose to the nose of the next player in the line. Neither player may touch the matchbox cover with his hands. The second player transfers the matchbox cover in the same manner to the nose of the third player, and so on to the end of the line. If any player touches the matchbox cover with his hands or lets it drop on the floor, it must be returned to the leader of the team, who puts it on his nose and starts all over again. The first team to transfer the matchbox cover successfully to the end of the line wins the game.

Pass the Orange

No. of players: 8 or more
Equipment: Two oranges
Complexity: ✩

The players are divided into two teams, and the members of each team stand in a straight line. The player at the head of each line is given an orange, which he tucks under his chin. On the word 'Go!' he turns to the next player in the line and attempts to transfer the orange to the next player's chin. The second player then passes the orange to the third player, and so on down the line. At no time may the orange be touched by hand, and if it falls to the ground it must be returned to the player at the head of the line, who starts all over again. The first team to succeed in passing the orange down the line wins.

It has been found that when the lines are arranged so that males alternate with females this game usually lasts much longer. For some reason, it appears that the game is so much fun this way that players will sometimes prolong it quite unnecessarily.

Postman's Knock

No. of players: 8 or more
Equipment: None
Complexity: ✩

Postman's Knock, for some strange reason, is usually considered to be a childish game, and this source of innocent pleasure is quite unjustly neglected. Medical evidence shows that frequent applications of *Postman's Knock* makes people healthier and happier.

A male player leaves the room while all the other players are given numbers – odd numbers for the men, even numbers for the women. The outsider knocks, rat-a-tat, on the door, and the assembled players call out 'Who's there?' 'It's the postman,' replies the outsider, 'and I have something for Number 6.' (or Number 2 or Number 14 or any other even number). Out goes Number 6 to join the postman who gives her a long, lingering kiss. She remains outside to be the next postwoman while the former postman returns to the assembled players. When the players have chosen new numbers, she knocks on the door and announces that she has something for Number 9 (or any other odd number). The lucky fellow goes out to claim his kiss, and then has a turn at being the postman. And so the game continues until every player has been thoroughly kissed.

Winking

No. of players: 15 or more
Equipment: Chairs for half the players
Complexity: ☆

A circle of chairs is formed, facing inwards. A woman sits in each chair, except for one chair which is left empty. Behind each chair, including the empty one, stands a man with his hands resting on the back of the chair, but not actually touching the woman sitting there.

The man standing behind the empty chair has to wink at one of the women. The women who is winked at must immediately attempt to leave her chair and dash to the empty one, while the man standing behind *her* chair attempts to restrain her by placing his hands on her shoulders. If he succeeds in putting his hands on her shoulders before she escapes, she must stay where she is and wait for another wink, he replaces his hands on the back of the chair, and the man standing behind the empty chair has to choose another woman to wink at. If the woman who is winked at does manage to get away to the empty chair, it becomes the turn of the man who let her escape to entice some other woman to his now empty chair.

After a while, when all the women have received their fair share of winks, the players change over – the men sit in the chairs and the women stand behind them and do the winking.

Feeding the Baby

No. of players: 6 or more
Equipment: A baby's bottle and a bib for each couple
Complexity: ✫

The women sit at one end of the room, each woman holding a bib and a half-filled baby's bottle. The men stand opposite their partners at the other end of the room. When the word of command is given each man dashes to his partner and sits on her knee. She fastens the bib around his neck, and feeds him from the bottle as quickly as possible. He may cling to her if he wishes (and if she permits) but he may not touch the bottle with his hands. As soon as the bottle is emptied, she removes his bib and the couple dash back to the other end of the room where the men started. The first couple to finish win the game.

The contents of the bottles – milk, gin, lemonade, champagne, or whatever – depend, of course on the type of party.

Dumb Crambo

No. of players: Any number
Equipment: None
Complexity: ✫

The players divide into teams. Team A goes out of the room while the members of team B confer among themselves to choose a word. When team A returns, team B announce a word that rhymes with the word they have chosen. Team B then are allowed three guesses in which to discover the word chosen by team A. The only restriction is that they are not allowed to speak – they must present their guesses in mime. Any player who speaks loses the game for his team. Incorrect guesses are greeted with boos and hisses. A correct guess is rewarded with applause and a point for the successful team.

The teams alternate roles, and the team with the most points when no one wants to play any longer is the winner.

Zoo Quest

No. of players: 6 or more
Equipment: A box of chocolates
Complexity: ☆

The players are split into teams, with three, four or five players in each
team. One member of each team is chosen to be the leader and the other
players assume the identities of various animals. They should be
discouraged from being obvious animals like dogs, cats and cows —
instead they should be urged (or coerced) into being, for example, a
coyote, a rhinoceros, a hyena, a gorilla, a three-toed sloth and so forth.
    The chocolates are scattered in various locations about the house.
The team members then go off in search of the chocolates, leaving their
leaders to have a few moments rest. When a player finds a chocolate he
makes a noise appropriate to the animal he is impersonating, and the
leader, on hearing one of his animals, goes and collects the chocolate.
    After ten minutes, the team whose leader has collected the most
chocolates is the winning team. Greedy players who eat the chocolates
they find instead of calling their leader deserve to lose.

Sardines

No. of players: 6 or more
Equipment: None
Complexity: ☆

Sardines is best played in a large house with lots of possible
hiding-places. All the players assemble in one room. The first player
leaves the room and hides himself away somewhere in the house. The
remaining players follow after, one at a time, at one-minute intervals.
The second player has to find the first player's hiding-place and join him
there. The third player has to find the first two and join them. The fourth
player . . . and so on. The game ends when all the players are packed
together in the larder or under the bed or wherever the hiding-place
happens to be.

The Picture Frame Game

No. of players: Any number
Equipment: An empty picture frame
Complexity: ☆

This is a simple, silly game which nevertheless calls for great self-control. Each player in turn holds up in front of his face the empty picture frame, through which he regards the other players. For sixty seconds he has to keep his face absolutely immobile (apart from the occasional blink) while the other players cavort and caper and grimace and call out ribald remarks. Any player who lasts out the full minute as a picture of still life should receive a suitable reward.

Newspaper Fancy Dress

No. of players: Any number
Equipment: A newspaper for each player, and a supply of pins
Complexity: ☆☆

Each player is given a newspaper and some pins, from which he has to make himself a fancy-dress costume. The players have ten minutes in which to do this. When the ten minutes have elapsed, the players parade around the room, and the winner is the player who is judged to have made the cleverest, most amusing or most original costume.

Taste

No. of players: Any number
Equipment: Various (see text)
Complexity: ★★

Before the game begins a number of cups or glasses are set out and filled with an assortment of beverages – water, cold tea, lemonade, ginger ale, tonic water, beer, vinegar etc. The players are led in one at a time and blindfolded. Then (having been assured that they will come to no harm) they are given a sip of each liquid, which they then have to identify. The player who identifies correctly the greatest number is the winner.

Find the Leader

No. of players: 6 or more
Equipment: None
Complexity: ★★

This game, while it may appear to be silly (and there's no harm in that), can actually be quite a challenging test of observation.

One player is sent out of the room, and the other players select a leader. The leader performs some repetitive action, such as rubbing his nose (or scratching his head, or tapping his foot, or whatever) which the other players all copy. The outsider is summoned back into the room, where he finds all the players busily rubbing or tapping or scratching. Suddenly the leader switches to some different action and the other players immediately follow his lead. The leader initiates different actions at frequent intervals. The outsider, by observing closely all the players, has to determine which of them is the leader.

Each player takes a turn at being the outsider.

Kim's Game

No. of players: Any number
Equipment: a collection of miscellaneous objects; paper and
a pencil for each player
Complexity: ✫✫

Kim's Game is a fine test of observation and memory which, for that reason, was a favourite game of Baden Powell, the founder of the Scout movement. It is also a lot of fun.

Before the party guests arrive or while the players are in another room, a collection of twenty or thirty objects – as varied as possible – is assembled on a tray or on a table and is covered with a cloth. The players are gathered round, the cloth is removed for thirty seconds and is then replaced. Each player is given a pencil and paper and has to list as many objects as he can remember. A player scores one point for every object he remembers, but a point is deducted for any object listed that was not actually there. The player who scores most points is the winner.

Up Jenkins

No. of players: 6, 8 or 10
Equipment: A coin (or ring or thimble or other small object)
Complexity: ✫✫

Up Jenkins is a light-hearted game of observation and deduction which offers plenty of scope for bluffing and general merriment.

The players are divided into two equal teams, seated on opposite sides of a table. If the table is small and the players are squashed together this only adds to the fun. The members of one team pass the coin from hand to hand below the table. When the leader of the opposing team calls 'Up Jenkins', the players on the team with the coin raise their hands, with fists clenched, well above the table. One fist, of course, will be concealing the coin. The leader of the opposing team then calls 'Down Jenkins' and the raised hands must be slapped down on the table with palms flat.

The opposing team now have to guess which hand the coin is under. The leader confers with his team-mates and then taps the hand that they think conceals the coin. That hand is raised, and if the coin is revealed the guessing team scores a point, otherwise the team with the coin scores a point.

The team then change roles for the next round. The winners are the team with the most points when an agreed number of rounds have been played.

The game may be played so that the guessing team is allowed three guesses to discover the hand concealing the coin, scoring three points if their first guess is correct, two points if their second guess is correct, and one point if their third guess is correct.

Murder in the Dark

No. of players: 8 or more
Equipment: Slips of paper
Complexity: ★★

A number of slips of paper are prepared, one for each player. One slip is marked with a circle, another is marked with a cross, and the rest are blank. The slips are folded and mixed up and each player picks one at random. The player who picks the circle is the detective, and he identifies himself. The player who picks the cross is the murderer and says nothing.

All the lights in the house are turned off, and all the players, apart from the detective, disperse throughout the house. The murderer prowls about until he chances upon a suitable victim in a lonely spot. Creeping up on his victim, the murderer whispers in his ear 'You're dead'. The victim screams frenziedly and falls to the floor as the murderer slinks away. As soon as the scream is heard the other players must remain where they are, while the detective makes his way as quickly as possible to the scene of the crime, switching on all the lights on his way.

The detective inspects the scene of the crime; notes the whereabouts of all the suspects; and then summons everyone into the drawing-room to be questioned in true Agatha Christie fashion. By questioning the suspects as to their movements and their location at the time of the murder, and by looking for inconsistencies in their stories, as well as by watching for signs of guilt in their faces, the detective has to identify the murderer. Each player must answer all questions with the truth and nothing but the truth – except, of course, for the murderer, who can lie as much as he likes until asked the direct question 'Are you the murderer?' when he must break down and confess all. The detective is allowed two guesses at the identity of the murderer.

Charades

No. of players: Any number
Equipment: None
Complexity: ☆☆

Charades is a deservedly popular game in which one team of players has to guess a word of several syllables presented in dramatic form by the other team.

The players are divided into two teams, and the first team goes into another room to choose a suitable word. The chosen word must contain several syllables, each of which may be presented in the form of a dramatic sketch, as must the word as a whole. Only the sound of the syllables is considered, not the spelling, and syllables may be grouped together. For example, the word 'trampoline' may be chosen and split into 'tramp', 'pole' and 'lean'. Or the chosen word may be 'illuminate', split up as 'ill', 'human' and 'ate'.

Having decided on the word and on the sketches they are going to perform, the members of the team return to the other room for their performance. The leader declares the number of syllables, and the players perform their sketches for the edification of the opposing team, acting out first the syllables and then the whole word. They may use speech in their sketches but it is more conventional for the sketches to be presented entirely in mime.

When the opposing team have guessed the word being presented it becomes their turn to leave the room and decide on a charade.

Another popular form of *Charades* involves acting the titles of books, films, TV programmes, songs etc. In this form of the game the titles are usually broken down into individual words rather than syllables. Another variation is *Solo Charades*, in which individual players take it in turn to perform the words or titles they choose.

Drama School

No. of players: 3 to 8
Equipment: None
Complexity: ★★

One player is chosen (or elects himself) to be the judge, and the other players sit or stand in a row facing him. The judge commands them to express various moods or emotions – anger, despair, panic, delight, boredom, pride, fear, enthusiasm, benevolence, lust, incomprehension, smugness, guilt, and so on – and awards a point to the best actor of each mood or emotion. The winner is the player who amasses the most points.

The players may be allowed full scope to use speech, gesture and facial expression or, to make it more difficult, they may be restricted to facial expression only.

2   **WORD GAMES**

I Spy
Spelling Bee
Backward Spelling
Action Spelling
I Love my Love
I Went to Market
A Was an Apple Pie
Traveller's Alphabet
Buzz, Fizz, Buzz-Fizz
Crambo
Initial Answers
Sausages
Word Associations
Proverbs
Last and First
I Packed my Bag
Tennis, Elbow, Foot
Number Associations
Coffee Pot
Taboo
Twenty Questions
Leading Lights
Donkey
Botticelli
What Nonsense!
Stepping Stones

I Spy

No. of players: 2 or more
Equipment: None
Complexity: ☆

One of the players thinks of some object that is visible in the room – a spoon, let us say, for example – and announces to the other players its initial letter, saying 'I spy with my little eye something beginning with S'. The other players then have to guess what the object is:

'Sofa?' 'No'
'Sugar?' 'No'
'Slippers?' 'No'
'Ceiling?' '???'
'Shoelace?' 'No'
etc. etc.

The first player to guess correctly is allowed to 'spy' the next object.

Spelling Bee

No. of players: 3 or more
Equipment: None
Complexity: ☆

One players acts as question-master and calls out a word to each of the other players in turn, who must then give the correct spelling of the word. If the player spells the word correctly he scores one point.

The question-master may call the words from a prepared list or he may make up the list as he goes along. It is, of course, most important that the words used should be matched to the abilities of the players taking part. It would be just as silly to ask a group of six-year-olds to spell words like Parallel, Psychological, Committee and Furlough as it would be to ask an average group of teenagers or adults to spell the words like Door, School, Yellow and Horse.

When a predetermined number of rounds have been played, the player with the most points is the winner.

Variation 1
The game is played as described above, except that a player who fails to spell a word correctly drops out of the game. The winner is the last player left in.

Variation 2
A player who spells a word correctly is given another word to spell. If he spells that correctly he is given another, and so on. He scores a point for each correct spelling and his turn ends only when he fails to spell a word correctly. The player with the most points at the end of the game is the winner.

Variation 3
The players are divided into two teams, sitting opposite each other. The question-master calls out a word to each player in turn, selecting the two teams alternately. A player who spells a word correctly scores a point for his team. If a player fails to spell a word correctly, the same word is offered to his opposite number in the other team who, if he can spell the word correctly, may score a bonus point for his team.

Backward Spelling

No. of players: 3 or more
Equipment: None
Complexity: ✩

This is a form of *Spelling Bee* which is made a little more difficult for the players since the words called out have to be spelled backwards. This game may be played in any of the ways described for *Spelling Bee*.

Action Spelling

No. of players: 3 or more
Equipment: None
Complexity: ☆

Action Spelling is a form of *Spelling Bee* that is played strictly for laughs. It can be organised in any of the ways described for *Spelling Bee* but, usually, words less difficult to spell will be used.

The point of the game is that certain letters must not be spoken by the players when spelling the words – actions must be substituted instead. For example, the rule may be that no vowels may be spelled out – instead of saying 'A' a player must raise his left hand; instead of saying 'E' he must raise his right hand; instead of saying 'I' he must point to his eye; instead of saying 'O' he must point to his mouth; instead of saying 'U' he must point to any other player.

Alternatively, actions may be substituted for other letters – a growl for a 'G', a whistle for an 'S', shading one's eyes for a 'C', a buzz for a 'B', and so on. The game can be made as silly and as complicated as one wants it to be.

I Love my Love

No. of players: 3 or more
Equipment: None
Complexity: ☆

This is a popular game with young children, especially little girls. The players have to complete the sentence 'I love my love because he/she is ————' with adjectives beginning with each letter of the alphabet in turn. The first player has to find an adjective beginning with A, the second with B, the third with C, and so on. Thus:

> Judith: 'I love my love because he is adorable.'
> Roy: 'I love my love because she is beautiful.'
> Josie: 'I love my love because he is charming.' etc.

It is not usually a requirement that the adjectives should be flattering – instead of being adorable, beautiful and charming, my love might be awkward, bald and careless.

Any player unable to think of an adjective beginning with the next letter of the alphabet drops out of the game, and the next player starts again using the letter A. The last player left in is the winner.

A variation of this game is to require each player to complete the longer refrain 'I love my love because he/she is ————. His/her name is ———— and he/she lives in ————', using three words beginning with the same letter, e.g. 'I love my love because she is zealous. Her name is Zoe and she lives in Zanzibar.'

I Went to Market

No. of players: 3 or more
Equipment: None
Complexity: ☆

This game is similar to *I Love My Love*, the difference being that the players have to think of nouns beginning with each letter of the alphabet in turn to complete the sentence 'I went to market and I bought ————.' For example: 'I went to market and I bought apples.' 'I went to market and I bought books.' 'I went to market and I bought cheese'. etc.

A Was an Apple Pie

No. of players: 3 or more
Equipment: None
Complexity: ☆

This game, again, is similar to *I Love My Love*, the players having to supply verbs beginning with each letter of the alphabet in turn. For example, 'A was an apple pie. A ate it', 'B bought it', 'C cut it', 'D delivered it' and so on.

Traveller's Alphabet

No. of players: 3 or more
Equipment: None
Complexity: ☆

Traveller's Alphabet is a slightly more demanding form of alphabet sequence game. The players sit in a circle. Each player in turn asks the player on his left two questions: 'Where are you going?' and 'What will you do there?'. The replies consist of the name of a country and the description of an activity, using verb, adjective and noun, all beginning with the same letter. The first player's replies must beginning with the letter A, the second player's with B, the third player's with C, and so on.

For example, the conversation might go like this:

Mary: 'Where are you going?'
David: 'Australia.'
Mary: 'What will you do there?'
David: 'Assist aged Aborigines.'
David: 'Where are you going?'
Edward: 'Belgium.'
David: 'What will you do there?'
Edward: 'Buy big boots.'
Edward: 'Where are you going?'
Mary: 'China.'
Edward: 'What will you do there?'
Mary: 'Carve cheap chopsticks.' etc. etc.

Any player who fails to reply within a reasonable time limit drops out of the game. The winner is the last player left in.

Buzz, Fizz, Buzz-Fizz

No. of players: 3 or more
Equipment: None
Complexity: ☆

Buzz, Fizz and Buzz-Fizz are three closely-related games, and are very silly. For any of the three games the players sit or stand in a circle and call out numbers, one after the other – the first player calling 'One', the second player 'Two', the third player 'Three' and so on, round and round the circle, as quickly as possible.

If Buzz is being played, then the word 'Buzz' must be substituted for every multiple of 5, and substituted for the digit 5 whenever it occurs in a number. Thus 5, 10 and 15 should all be pronounced 'Buzz' and 50 and 51 should be pronounced 'Buzzty' and 'Buzzty-one'.

Fizz is similar except that 7 is the forbidden number, not 5, and the word 'Fizz' is substituted.

Buzz-Fizz (believe it or not) is a combination of Buzz and Fizz. 57, for example, becomes 'Buzzty Fizz' and 75 becomes 'Fizzty Buzz'.

You may, if you wish, switch from Fizz to Buzz to Buzz-Fizz in the course of a game, just to make it more confusing.

Any player who says a number instead of fizzing (or vice versa) or who fizzes when he should buzz (or verse vica) drops out of the game. The last player left is the winner.

Crambo

No. of players: 2 or more
Equipment: None
Complexity: ☆

Crambo, although it is a very unsophisticated game, has been popular for several centuries. One of the players thinks of a word and then announces to the other players a word that rhymes with the word he has chosen. For example, he might think of the word 'dull' and announce the word 'hull'. The other players are then each allowed three guesses to discover the word thought of by the first player. If a player guesses the word correctly he has the honour of choosing the word for the next round. If none of the other players can guess the word or if they have all fallen asleep then the original player has another turn.

Initial Answers

No. of players: 3 or more
Equipment: None
Complexity: ✫

One of the players is chosen to be the questioner for the first round. He asks any appropriate question, which must be answered by each of the other players in turn. Each player's answer must consist of words beginning with his own initials. For example, to the question 'What kind of food do you like?', Bob Hope might reply 'Boiled ham', Liza Minelli might reply 'Lemon meringue', Frank Sinatra might reply 'French snails', and Zsa Zsa Gabor might decide that she did not want to play such a silly game. A player who fails to give a satisfactory answer within five seconds becomes the questioner for the next round.

Sausages

No. of players: 3 or more
Equipment: None
Complexity: ✫

One of the players is chosen to be the questioner. He may ask any of the other players whatever personal questions he might choose – 'What do you think your legs look like?' – 'What are your shoes made from?' – 'To what do you attribute your beauty and vitality?' Whatever the question, the player being asked must reply 'Sausages!'. The first player who smiles or laughs or giggles or smirks or titters or grins or chortles or simpers or guffaws or sniggers or otherwise betrays any emotion other than deadly seriousness is out, and he takes the next turn at being the questioner.

Instead of using the word 'Sausages', the game may be played with any other word which the particular group of players consider to be inherently mirth-provoking.

Word Associations

No. of players: Any number
Equipment: None
Complexity: ☆

The players sit or stand in a circle. The first player says the first word that comes into his mind. The second player immediately says the first word that comes into *his* mind in response to the first player's word. The third player responds likewise to the second player's word, and so on round and round the circle. If a player hesitates before saying his word he is out. The last player left in is the winner.

This game is sometimes called Psychotherapy, and psychiatrists may charge very high fees for playing it with you.

Proverbs

No. of players: 2 or more
Equipment: None
Complexity: ☆

If more than two are playing, one player leaves the room while the others decide on a proverb. When he returns he has to guess the proverb chosen by the other players. He does this by asking each of them in turn a question, which may be about any subject under the sun. The first answer must contain the first word of the proverb, the second answer must contain the second word, and so on. When all the words of the proverb have been used, the players begin again with the first word.

For example, if the chosen proverb were 'Look before you leap' the dialogue might proceed as follows:

'How old are you?'
'I'm older than I *look* but not as old as I feel.'
'What is your favourite colour?'
'White was my favourite *before* I married, but I'm not so sure now.'
'What time is it?'
'It is time *you* bought yourself a watch.'
'What do you think of the Government?'
'I think that their forward-looking policies are a great *leap* backwards.'
'Where are you going for your holiday next year?'
'I don't know until I've had a chance to *look* through the brochures.'

The questioner is allowed to ask as many questions as he wishes within a time limit of, say, five minutes. An incorrect guess or failure to find the proverb within the time limit means that the questioner must take another turn, otherwise the player who answered the last question becomes the next questioner.

To avoid making the answers too obvious it is necessary to choose proverbs without 'awkward' words. If the chosen proverb were 'A rolling stone gathers no moss' it might be difficult to contrive an answer in which the word 'moss', for example, did not stick out like a sore thumb. This problem, however, may be overcome to some extent by making the answers fairly inconsequential (but not too long-winded, as this rather spoils the fun) and by attempting to include in the answers plenty of red herrings, such as 'cloud', 'lining', 'eggs', 'basket' etc.

Last and First

No. of players: 2 or more
Equipment: None
Complexity: ☆

A category is chosen – Birds, Towns, Rivers, TV Programmes, Marxist Historians, or whatever. The first player calls out any word belonging to the chosen category. The second player calls out another, beginning with the last letter of the first word. The next player calls out another, beginning with the last letter of the previous word, and so on. For example, if the chosen category were Animals, the words called out might be: 'Elephant', 'Tiger', 'Rat', 'Toad', 'Dromedary', 'Yak', etc.

All the words called out must belong to the chosen category and no word may be repeated. If a player fails to think of a word or calls out a word which does not belong to the category or which has already been used then he drops out of the game. The last player left in is the winner.

I Packed My Bag

No. of players: 3 or more
Equipment: None
Complexity: ★★

This game is a test of memory and concentration, in which the players attempt to remember and repeat an increasing list of objects. For example, the first player might say 'I packed my bag with a pair of pyjamas'. The second player might say 'I packed my bag with a pair of pyjamas . . . and a silver snuff-box'. The third player might say 'I packed my bag with a pair of pyjamas, a silver snuff-box . . . and a pocket calculator'. The game continues with each player in turn repeating the list and adding one more item of his own choice. Any player who forgets an item or who gets them in the wrong order drops out of the game. The last player left in the game is the winner.

Tennis, Elbow, Foot

No. of players: 3 or more
Equipment: None
Complexity: ★★

Each player in turn calls out a word which is either directly associated with the word previously called out or which rhymes with it. For example, 'Tennis', 'Elbow', Foot', 'Ball', 'Wall', 'Paper', 'Tiger', 'Stripe', 'Ripe', 'Fruit', 'Apple', 'Core', 'Door', Key', 'Note', 'Boat', and so on. Players are out if they hesitate, if they repeat a word already called out, or if they call out a word which neither relates to the previous word nor rhymes with it. The last player left in is the winner.

Number Associations

No. of players: 3 or more
Equipment: None
Complexity: ☆☆

Each player in turn calls out any number between 1 and 12. Whoever is first among the other players to respond with an appropriate association scores a point. For example, the number 2 might prompt the associations 'Two turtle doves', 'Two lovely black eyes', 'Two-way stretch', 'Tea for Two', 'A Tale of Two Cities', 'Two heads are better than one' etc. The number 7 might prompt 'Seven Pillars of Wisdom', 'Seven seas', 'Seven dwarfs', 'Seven deadly sins', 'The Magnificent Seven' etc. No association may be repeated. The player with the most points when everyone has had enough of the game is the winner.

Coffee Pot

No. of players: 3 to 8
Equipment: None
Complexity: ☆☆

One player thinks of a word which has two meanings (e.g. duck) or a pair of words which have different meanings but which sound the same (e.g. bored and board). He then says aloud a sentence using both meanings but substituting the words 'coffee pot' for both of them – for example 'If you see a low flying coffee pot you'd better coffee pot,' or 'I was on the coffee pot but I quit because I was so coffee pot'.

Each of the other players may then ask one question, and the first player's answer must include one or other of his words, again disguised as 'coffee pot'. If one of the players manages to identify the 'coffee pot' word he scores a point, otherwise the first player scores the point. Each player in turn has a go at being a 'coffee potter', and the player who finishes with most points is the winner.

Taboo

No. of players: 3 or more
Equipment: None
Complexity: ☆☆

One of the players is selected to be the umpire for the first round. The umpire chooses any commonly used word – such as 'yes', 'no', 'and', 'is', 'you', 'the' – and declares that word to be taboo. He then asks questions of each of the other players in turn, and each player must reply immediately with a sensible and relevant sentence. If the player hesitates or uses the forbidden word he is out. The last player to stay in the game is the winner of that round and becomes the umpire for the next round.

In a somewhat more taxing version of this game the umpire declares a certain letter of the alphabet to be taboo and the players must then reply with a sentence that does not contain the forbidden letter.

Twenty Questions

(*Alternative name:* Animal, Vegetable, Mineral)

No. of players: 2 or more
Equipment: None
Complexity: ☆☆

One player thinks of an object and announces to the other players whether it is animal, vegetable or mineral or any combination thereof. The other players, in turn, ask any questions they like, provided that they can be answered by a simple Yes or No, the aim being to narrow down the field and eventually identify the mystery object. Twenty questions are allowed.

If the object has not been identified when twenty questions have been asked, the player who thought of the object in question reveals to the other players what it is. He then selects another object for the other players to identify. If any player correctly identifies the mystery object then that player is given the privilege of selecting the next object.

Leading Lights

No. of players: Any number
Equipment: None
Complexity: ☆☆

The name of a well-known person is proposed. Each player has to think of an appropriate phrase which begins with the same initials as the name in question. For example, Wolfgang Amadeus Mozart might prompt the phrases 'Was Austrian Musician' or 'Wrote Appealing Melodies'; Sigmund Freud might give rise to 'Subconscious Fantasies' or 'Sychic Fenomena' (???) or 'Sex Fiend'; Brigitte Bardot might make players think of 'Beautiful Body' and so forth.

Donkey

No. of players: 2 or more
Equipment: A dictionary (optional)
Complexity: ☆☆

In this game words are built up by each player in turn adding a letter while trying to avoid being the player who completes a word.

The players sit in a circle. The first player thinks of any word of four or more letters and calls out its first letter. The second player then thinks of a word beginning with that letter and calls out the second letter of the word he has thought of. The third player thinks of a word beginning with the two letters already called out and calls out its third letter. And so on, each player trying to keep the chain of letters going without calling out the last letter of a word. The player who completes a word loses a life.

For example, suppose there are three players.

Ann thinks of DANGER and calls out 'D'.
Bob thinks of DIVIDE and calls out 'I'.
Chris thinks of DISTANT and calls out 'S'.
Ann thinks of DISORDER and calls out 'O'.
Bob thinks of DISOWN and calls out 'W'.
Chris now has no option and has to call out 'N', thus completing a word and losing a life.

A player must have a valid word in mind when he adds a letter. He may be challenged by any other player who suspects that the letter called out does not help to form a word. The challenged player must then declare the word he has in mind. If he cannot do so or if his word is not a valid one then he loses a life. If he can declare a valid word then the challenger loses a life. A dictionary may be needed at this point to resolve disputes.

A player may also lose a life if he hesitates for too long before calling out a letter.

When a player has lost three lives he becomes a donkey and drops out of the game. The last player to be left in wins the game.

For a longer game the number of lives may be increased.

Botticelli

No. of players: Any number
Equipment: None
Complexity: ★★

Why this game should be named after a fifteenth-century Florentine painter is a moot point. Perhaps it is so named because people could not agree on the correct pronunciation for 'Breughel'. Whatever its origin, *Botticelli* is a fascinating guessing game, requiring a fairly good standard of general knowledge.

One player thinks of the name of a famous person or fictitious character – one who should be known to the other players – and tells the other players the initial letter of his subject's surname. The other players now have to identify the mystery person, and they do this by asking two types of question – direct questions and indirect questions. Direct questions may be asked only if the first player fails to provide a satisfactory answer to an indirect question.

For example, suppose the first player had thought of Lewis Carroll and had declared the initial letter to be 'C'. The other players might ask indirect questions such as 'Are you a famous scientist?' or 'Are you a film star?' or 'Are you a Dickens character?' The first player might reply to these questions 'No, I am not Marie Curie,' or 'No, I am not Charlie Chaplin', or 'No, I am not David Copperfield'.

If the first player, however, cannot give a satisfactory answer to a question of this type – if, for example, he can't remember the names of any Dickens characters beginning with 'C' – then the questioner may ask a direct question. A direct question should be framed so as to elicit more information about the mystery person – e.g. 'Are you living?' or 'Are you female?' or 'Are you American' – and the first player must answer, truthfully, either Yes or No.

Since truthful answers must be given to direct questions it is important that the first player should choose a character about whom he has some knowledge.

The other players should do their best to ask awkward indirect questions in the hope that the first player will not be able to answer them satisfactorily and will thus give them the opportunity to ask as many direct questions as possible, thus narrowing down the field. But a player may not ask an indirect question for which he himself has not in mind a satisfactory answer. For example, he may not ask 'Are you a Swedish film star?' unless he knows the name of a Swedish film star beginning with the given initial letter.

The mystery person may finally be revealed either by means of an indirect question which is so specific that the first player must identify himself – 'Are you an Oxford don who wrote about a Mad Hatter's tea party?' – or by means of a direct question – 'Are you Lewis Carroll?' The player who asks the question that unmasks the mystery person is the winner of that round, and he chooses a character for the next round.

What Nonsense!

No. of players: 3 or more
Equipment: Slips of paper and a pencil
Complexity: ★★

This game requires each player to talk a lot of nonsense about a particular topic for two minutes.

A list of topics is devised – as many topics as there are players – and each topic is written on a slip of paper which is then folded. The topics may be fairly straightforward, like these examples:

1   New uses for old toothpaste tubes.
2   Are chocolate sweets a health hazard?
3   Teaching goldfish to talk.
4   Who *did* kill Cock Robin?
5   Was Hiawatha really a Martian?
6   Why is a raven like a writing-desk?

Or they may be just a little more rarefied, like these examples:

7   Is it Wednesday in Bolivia?
8   The answer that cannot be questioned.
9   If not, why not?
10   The functionalism of inverse dichotomy.

Each player in turn chooses a slip at random and then has to speak for two minutes on the topic he has chosen. The player who attains the highest peaks of lunacy is the winner.

Stepping Stones

No. of players: 2 to 8
Equipment: None
Complexity: ★★★

Stepping Stones is a mentally stimulating game of word associations, which may be played on any level from the banal to the esoteric. Each player in turn is given five themes by the other players. For example, a player may be told to get from 'Music' to 'Astronomy' via 'Cookery', 'Finance' and 'Cars'. He may use up to nine statements or phrases as stepping stones and must touch on each of the themes in the order given. The other players, acting collectively as umpires, must satisfy themselves that all the themes have been touched upon, that the sequence of associations is valid, and that any puns, jokes, allusions and the like are not too far-fetched.

Here are two ways in which the example quoted might work out:

1   Dame Nellie Melba was an opera singer. (*Music*)
2   Peach Melba was named in her honour. (*Cookery*)
3   Every peach contains a stone.
4   A stone is fourteen pounds.
5   Pounds are Sterling. (*Finance*)
6   Stirling Moss was a British racing driver. (*Cars*)
7   Moss, so they say, is not gathered by rolling stones.
8   The Rolling Stones are rock stars.
9   Stars, in fact, are formed from gas not from rock. (*Astronomy*)

1   Musicians usually begin by learning scales. (*Music*)
2   Scales are found on fish.
3   Salmon is the fish most often served with salads. (*Cookery*)
4   Salmon may be caught from river banks.
5   Banks are financial institutions. (*Finance*)
6   Bank managers usually play golf.
7   The Golf is an imported car, unlike the Mini. (*Cars*)
8   Mini-skirts should only be worn by women with heavenly bodies.
9   Stars and planets are heavenly bodies. (*Astronomy*)

3 PAPER AND PENCIL GAMES

Noughts and Crosses
Hangman
The Worm
Boxes
Sprouts
Battleships
Salvo
Aggression
Wordpower
Bulls and Cows
Categories
Guggenheim
Wordbuilder
Combinations
Anagrams
Scaffold
Alpha
Arena
Vowels
Stairway
Acrostics
Advertisements
Crossword
Crosswords
Consequences
Picture Consequences
Telegrams
Short Story

Noughts and Crosses

(*Alternative names*: Oxo or Tic-Tac-Toe)

No. of players: 2
Equipment: Paper and two pencils
Complexity: ✩

Noughts and Crosses is a tremendously popular children's game which, for generations of schoolchildren, has been one of the principal means of relieving the tedium of boring lessons. Before play begins a framework is drawn, consisting of two pairs of parallel lines crossing at right angles.

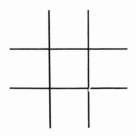

   The players play alternately, the first player drawing a nought, and the second player drawing a cross, in any one of the nine spaces which is vacant. The aim of the first player is to complete a row of three noughts, and the aim of the second player is to complete a row of three crosses, while at the same time each player tries to block his opponent. The winner is the first player to complete a row, horizontally, vertically or diagonally.

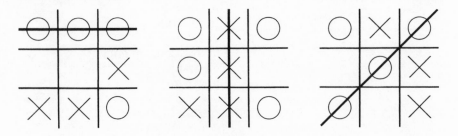

   Once one learns the simple strategy required for this game it is impossible to lose unless one makes an absolutely appalling blunder. Between two experienced players every game will end in a draw, with neither player being able to complete a row.

Hangman

No. of players: 2
Equipment: Paper and two pencils
Complexity: ☆

In this popular game one player thinks of a word, preferably of six or more letters, which the other player has to discover by guessing letters. The first player writes down a series of dashes to indicate the number of letters in the word, thus: – – – – – – – –. The second player then starts guessing the letters in the word, calling out one letter at a time. If the letter occurs in the word the first player writes that letter above the appropriate dash (or dashes) wherever the letter occurs.

For each letter called out which does not occur in the word the first player draws a part of the Hangman picture, in the order shown here:

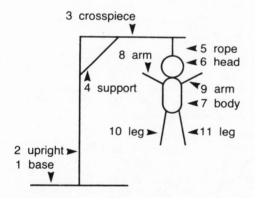

The incorrectly guessed letters are also recorded underneath the dashes so that the second player can see which letters he has already tried.

The second player wins if he correctly guesses all the letters in the word before the picture is completed. He then chooses the word in the next game for the other player to guess.

If the picture is completed before the second player has identified all the letters he is 'hanged' and loses, and the first player selects another word for him to guess.

Sometimes the game is played using agreed themes, such as Book Titles or Pop Stars, in which case the name or title to be guessed may consist of more than one word. In this case the first player will draw the dashes to show the number of letters in each word with spaces between the words.

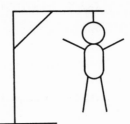

_ **A N G** _ **A N**

E R S I T O U L C D P

The Worm

No. of players: 2
Equipment: Paper and two pencils
Complexity: ☆

To begin, ten rows of ten dots each are marked on a sheet of paper, like this:

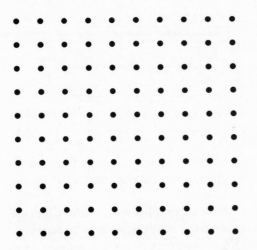

The first player draws a horizontal or vertical line to join any two adjacent dots. Diagonal lines are not allowed. The second player then draws another line, connecting either end of the existing line horizontally or vertically to any adjacent dot. The players then continue playing alternately in this manner, drawing a line from either end of the existing line ('the worm') to an adjacent dot. The objective is to force one's opponent into a position in which he has to draw a line which will join either end of the worm back on to itself, thus losing the game.

For example, in the game illustrated below the player whose turn it is to move is bound to lose since, no matter which end he plays, he has to join the worm back on to itself.

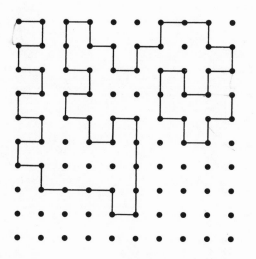

Boxes

No. of players: 2
Equipment: Paper and two pencils
Complexity: ★★

To begin, ten rows of ten dots are marked on a sheet of paper, as shown for the previous game. The players take it in turn to draw a straight line connecting any two dots which are next to each other, either horizontally or vertically. Diagonal lines are not allowed. The objective is to complete as many 'boxes' as possible. A box is completed by drawing the fourth side of a square when the other three sides have already been drawn. Therefore, as a matter of strategy, a player generally tries to avoid drawing the third side of any square as this would give his opponent a chance to complete a box.

Whenever a player completes a box he writes his initial inside it, and he has to draw another line. Thus a player's turn does not end until he draws a line which does not complete a box.

The game ends when all the boxes have been completed. The player who has completed the highest number of boxes is the winner.

In the game illustrated here (in which neither player has played very skilfully!) the player who has the next turn will be able to complete three boxes in the lower right-hand corner.

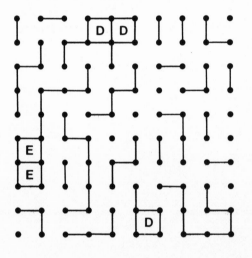

The game may begin with fewer dots if a quick game is required or with more dots if a longer game is wanted.

Another version of the game is played so that the winner is the player who completes fewer boxes than his opponent. In this version players try to avoid having to draw the fourth side of a box.

Sprouts

No. of players: 2
Equipment: Paper and two pencils
Complexity: ☆☆

This game originated in the early 1960s. Since then it has spread around the world and has become a firm favourite among pencil and paper games. It looks very simple but a lot of concentration is required if one is to play it really well.

To begin, 3, 4 or 5 dots are marked at random on a sheet of paper. Each player in turn draws a line beginning and ending on any of the dots (so a line may join two dots together or may loop round and end on the dot it started from) and then draws a new dot on the line he has just drawn. So, starting with 4 dots, after both players have had one turn the position might look like this:

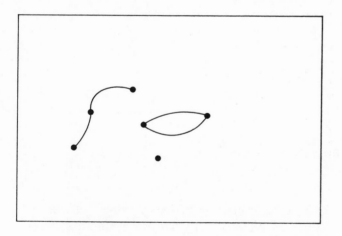

In drawing the lines, two simple rules must be observed:
(a) No line may cross any other line or pass through a dot.
(b) No dot may have more than three lines leading from it.

The players continue playing alternately until no more lines can be drawn, and the player who draws the last line is the winner.

For example, in the position illustrated below, the player with the next turn must win. The only line that can be drawn will connect the top and bottom dots and, even though a new dot will be created on that line, it will be impossible to draw any further lines.

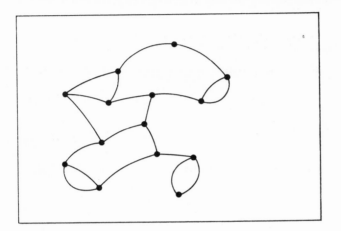

Battleships

No. of players: 2
Equipment: Paper and a pencil for each player
Complexity: ✶✶

It is said that this game was invented by British prisoners-of-war in Germany during the First World War. Whether or not that is so, it is certainly true that this is a very popular game, one in which skill and luck are equally blended.

Before the game begins each player marks out on his sheet of paper two identical playing areas, each area consisting of a large square divided into 100 smaller squares, ten squares across by ten squares down. This preparation may be made less of a chore if one uses printed graph paper with squares of a suitable size. Each playing area should have the letters A to J across the top and the numbers 1 to 10 down one side, so that each square may be identified by its letter and number. Thus the squares in the top row are A1, B1, C1 and so on; the squares in the bottom row are A10, B10, C10 etc. One area is marked Home Fleet and the other area Enemy Fleet.

Each player now places his fleet in the Home Fleet area. From this point until the end of the game each player must take care that his sheet cannot be seen by the other player.

A fleet consists of the following ships:

1 battleship   (4 squares)
2 cruisers   (3 squares each)
3 destroyers   (2 squares each)
4 submarines   (1 square each)

A player may place his ships where he likes in the Home Fleet area, subject to the following rules:

(a) The squares forming each ship must be in a straight line, across or down.

(b) There must be at least one empty square between ships – in other words, no two ships may touch, even at a corner.

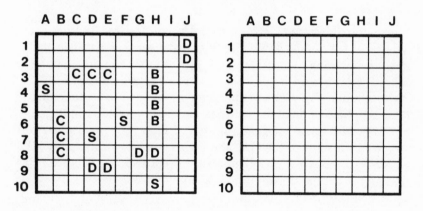

Home Fleet   **Enemy Fleet**

When both players have drawn their fleets then battle can commence. The objective, of course, is to sink the enemy fleet. To sink each ship all the squares forming the ship must be hit.

Each player in turn fires a shot at the Enemy Fleet by naming out loud a square, for example A7 or D3. The opponent then examines his Home Fleet area to see whether that square is occupied by a ship. He must declare whether the shot was a hit or a miss, and if it was a hit he must identify the type of ship. The player firing the shot records a miss by marking the appropriate square in the Enemy Fleet area with a dot, or records a hit by marking the square with a letter identifying the type of ship.

The players continue firing alternately until one of the players wins the game by completely destroying the enemy fleet.

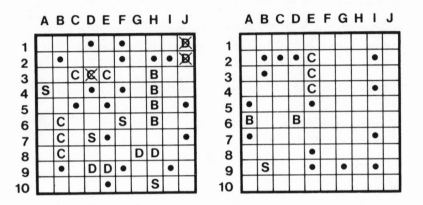

Home Fleet   **Enemy Fleet**

In the game illustrated it is clear that shots on squares B6 and C6 are required to sink the enemy battleship. It is also clear that, because of the rules as to the placing of ships, squares such as D5, F2 and C9 must be unoccupied, so it would be pointless to waste shots on them.

There are many versions of the game of battleships – the version described here being one of the simplest. In other versions of the game the size of the playing area or the number of each type of ship may be different from those described. In some versions, too, ships may be placed diagonally as well as horizontally or vertically, and there may be no restriction on ships occupying adjacent squares.

Salvo

No. of players: 2
Equipment: Paper and pencil for each player
Complexity: ✮✮✮

This game is similar to *Battleships* but with one difference which makes *Salvo* a considerably more skilful game. The difference is that instead of firing one shot in his turn a player fires a 'salvo' of three shots. The opponent then declares whether any of the shots were direct hits and what types of ship were hit by the salvo, but not the results of any individual shot. For example, the first player may call out 'C7, D12 and H2' and the second player may reply 'Two hits, one on a submarine and one on a battleship'.

The fact that a player does not know exactly which of his shots were hits makes this a more complex game than *Battleships*.

Aggression

No. of players: 2
Equipment: Paper and two pencils
Complexity: ✮✮✮

Aggression is a pencil-and-paper wargame in which the players attack and conquer each other's countries. The objective is to reduce as far as possible the number of countries occupied by the opponent's armies while trying to retain as many as possible of the countries occupied by one's own armies. Players can cast themselves in the role of Napoleon versus Wellington, or Montgomery versus Rommel, or America versus Russia – or even, if they prefer, Julius Caesar with his legions versus Genghis Khan with his Tartar hordes!

It is also a good example of a simple-but-complex game, in that it can easily be learned and played at a basic level by children or it can be played by professors of mathematics with considerable in-depth analysis of strategy and tactics.

The first stage of the game is the drawing of the battle area, which is a map of a number of imaginary countries with common boundaries. Any number of countries may be drawn, but twenty is the usual number. They may be any size and shape, but should not be too small. The players take it in turn when drawing the map, each adding one country in his turn. The countries are then marked with letters for identification.

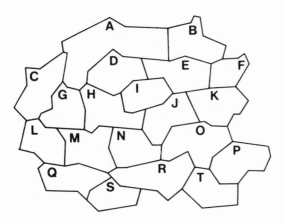

The second stage of the game is to occupy the countries with armies. Each player has 100 armies. The players take it in turn to allocate any number of their armies to an unoccupied country, writing the number of armies in the appropriate area. For example the first player may decide to occupy country D with 20 of his armies, then the second player may decide to occupy J with 22 armies, then the first player may put 3 armies in A, and so on. Preferably, pencils of two different colours should be used to distinguish one player's armies from those of his opponent; alternatively, one player may underline his numbers.

It is for each player to decide whether he occupies a few countries with large numbers of armies or whether he places a few armies in each of a large number of countries.

This stage of the game finishes when both players have allocated all their armies or when all the countries have been occupied.

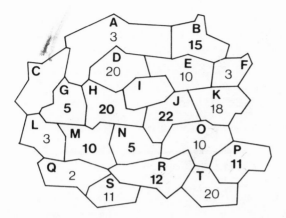

The third and final stage of the game is the aggressive part. Each player in turn uses the armies in one or more of the countries occupied by him to conquer an adjacent country occupied by his opponent, thus wiping out the opponent's armies stationed in that country. Adjacent countries are those with a common boundary. For example, in the game illustrated here, A, E and F are adjacent to B, and E, F, J and O are all adjacent to K.

A player may conquer one of his opponent's countries only if he has more armies in adjacent countries than the opponent has in the country being attacked. The number of armies in the conquered country is crossed out, playing no further part in the game. The conquering armies, however, remain intact.

It should be noted that conquering a country does not increase the number of countries that a player occupies – it simply decreases the number of countries occupied by the opponent. It should also be noted that countries not occupied by either player take no part in this stage of the game except as 'neutral zones'.

The game ends when neither player can conquer any more of his opponent's countries. The player left occupying the highest number of countries is the winner.

The game that we have illustrated might proceed in this way:

Player 1	Player 2
A, E, F conquer B	P, R conquer T
A, D conquer H	J conquers K
O conquers N	R conquers S
A, L conquer G	J conquers O
(Player 1 passes	J conquers E
as he cannot conquer	M conquers L
any more countries)	M conquers Q

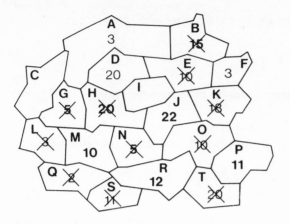

The second player wins, since he has four countries left while the first player is left with only three.

Wordpower

No. of players: 2
Equipment: Paper and a pencil
Complexity: ✭✭✭

The first player thinks of a 5-letter word which has to be guessed by the second player.

Guessing the mystery word involves logical deduction and a process of elimination. The second player proposes any 5-letter word and the first player indicates how close this word is to the mystery word by awarding points – one point for each letter in the proposed word that corresponds with a letter in the mystery word. Note that the second player is not told which letters are correct, only how many. The second player carries on making guesses until he has enough information to identify the mystery word. The paper and pencil are needed for the second player to record his guesses, the points they scored, and the letters that can be eliminated.

The players then change roles for the second round, and the first player has to guess a 5-letter word thought of by the second player. The winner of the game is the player who identifies the mystery word in the fewer number of guesses.

Here is a sample round, showing the sort of reasoning that is required:

1 **DANCE** 1 point
2 **SANDY** 2 points
3 **HANDY** 1 point   (There must be an **S** and no **H**)
4 **SOUND** 1 point   (That eliminates **O, U, N, D**—from guess 2 there must be an **A** or **Y**)
5 **SUNNY** 1 point   (That eliminates **Y**. The word contains **S, A** — from guess 1, that eliminates **C, E**)
6 **FAILS** 2 points   (That eliminates **F, I, L**)
7 **STRAP** 4 points   (The word contains two of the letters from **T, R, P**)
8 **GRASP** 3 points   (So the word contains **T** and no **G** – we now have **S, A, T** plus either **R** or **P** and one other or a repeated letter)
9 **STAMP** 3 points   (So it's **S, T, A, R** and another – no **M** or **P**)
10 **STRAW** That's it!

A̶B̶C̶D̶E̶F̶G̶H̶I̶JKL̶M̶N̶O̶PQRST̶U̶VWXY̶Z

Bulls and Cows

No. of players: 2
Equipment: Paper and a pencil
Complexity: ✩✩✩

Bulls and Cows is another game of logical deduction that is similar to *Wordpower* except that numbers not words are to be guessed and the scoring of guesses is rather different.

The first player thinks of a 4-digit number (e.g. 4711 or 9362). The second player guesses by proposing any 4-digit number. The first player tells him how close his guess is by saying how many 'bulls' and 'cows' he has scored. A bull means that the guess contains a correct digit in the correct position; a cow means that the guess contains a correct digit but that it is in the wrong position. The second player continues guessing until he has enough information to identify the mystery number. For example, if the number thought of by the first player was 9362 then the guesses and responses might proceed like this:

'1234'	'2 cows'
'2468'	'1 bull, 1 cow'
'1580'	'Nothing'
'2346'	'1 bull, 2 cows'
'4367'	'2 bulls'
'9362'	'4 bulls. That's it!'

The paper and pencil will be needed by the second player to record his guesses and their scores, and possibly to work out which digits can be eliminated and what possibilities remain.

When the mystery number has been guessed, the players change roles and the first player has to guess the number thought of by the second player. The player who requires the fewer number of guesses to identify the mystery number is the winner.

Categories

No. of players: 2 or more
Equipment: Paper and a pencil for each player
Complexity: ✭✩

The players decide on a list of categories (preferably twelve or more). The fairest way is for each player to propose an equal number of categories. These may be simple and straightforward (e.g. Animals, Countries, TV Programmes, Indoor Games) or more specialised (e.g. Peruvian Footballers, Hydrocarbons, People And Places Named In Proust's *A La Recherche Du Temps Perdu*) depending on the composition of the group that is playing.

Each player writes down the list of categories on his sheet of paper, and then a letter of the alphabet is chosen at random. A time limit of, say, ten or fifteen minutes is agreed. The players then have to write down as many words as they can beginning with the chosen letter for each of the categories.

When the time is up each player in turn reads out his list of words. A word which has not been thought of by any other player scores two points. A word which one or more other players have also listed scores one point. The player with the most points is the winner.

For subsequent rounds a new initial letter is chosen. The same categories may be used again or a new list of categories may be selected.

Guggenheim

No. of players: 2 or more
Equipment: Paper and a pencil for each player
Complexity: ✫✫

Guggenheim is basically a variation of the previous game, *Categories*. A list of categories is chosen and each player writes the list down the left-hand margin of his sheet of paper. A keyword of five or more letters is then chosen and each player writes the keyword, spaced out, along the top of his sheet of paper. A time limit of ten or fifteen minutes is agreed, and each player must then write down one word beginning with each letter of the keyword for each category. For example, with a keyword of **MAYBE** a completed list might look something like this:

	M	**A**	**Y**	**B**	**E**
Colours	Mauve	Amber	Yellow	Bistre	Ebony
Items of clothing	Mitten	Apron	Yashmak	Blouse	?
Birds	Mallard	Albatross	Yellow-hammer	Bantam	Egret
Indoor Games	Muggins	Aggression	Yacht	Back-gammon	Euchre
Countries	Malaysia	Andorra	Yemen	Burundi	Ethiopia
Poets	Milton	Arnold	Yeats	Burns	Eliot

Wordbuilder

No. of players: 2 or more
Equipment: Paper and a pencil for each player
Complexity: ✫✫

The players are all given the same starter word, which should be a moderately long word such as HIPPOPOTAMUS or CONTRABAND.

Each player then has to write down a list of words using the letters contained in the starter word. A time limit of ten minutes is set, and the player who lists the most words within this time limit is the winner.

The following rules are usually applied:

(a)   Each word must contain at least four letters.
(b)   Proper nouns (names of people, places etc.) are not allowed.
(c)   Foreign words, abbreviations and plurals are not allowed.
(d)   A letter may be used in any word no more than the number of times it occurs in the starter word.

It might be a good idea to have a dictionary available to check disputed words.

As an example the following list shows some of the words that might be made from CONTRABAND:

Band	Crab	Cord	Carton	Brand
Bard	Drab	Cobra	Brat	Bacon
Dart	Drat	Cart	Adorn	Road
Baron	Acorn	Card	Abandon	Broad
Barn	Corn	Cant	Trod	Toad

Combinations

No. of players: 2 or more
Equipment: Paper and a pencil for each player
Complexity: ★★

A list of ten or more 2-letter or 3-letter combinations which could occur within words is prepared. Such a list might contain letter combinations such as the following:

–BL–	–RF–	–IX–	–GTH–	–MON–
–QU–	–MN–	–SU–	–BUL–	–TOG–

Each of the players writes down the list on his sheet of paper. A time limit of five minutes is set, in which each player has to find as long a word as possible containing each of the letter combinations. The scoring is one point per letter for each word, and the player with the highest total score is the winner.

For example, using the combinations shown above, a player might achieve this result:

Troublesome	=	11
Perfection	=	10
Sixteenth	=	9
Strengthen	=	10
Commonwealth	=	12
Prerequisite	=	12
Condemned	=	9
Persuasively	=	12
Ebullience	=	10
Photographic	=	12
Total score	=	**107**

Anagrams

No. of players: 2 or more (plus a question-master)
Equipment: Paper and a pencil for each player
Complexity: ☆☆

The question-master chooses a category such as Countries, Birds, Garden Flowers or Rivers, and prepares a list of words belonging to that category. He then prepares another list of the same words but with the letters of each word jumbled up. The list of jumbled words is placed in a position where all the players can see it, or alternatively each player is given his own copy. A time limit of five or ten minutes is set, in which each player has to discover the original words by unscrambling the jumbled versions. The winner is the first player to unscramble all the words correctly or the player with the most correct words when the time limit has expired

For example:

Jumbled Countries

1	Neaky	5	Nomoac	9	Regalia
2	Rumba	6	Bedraum	10	Agalamute
3	Courade	7	Waliam	11	Englander
4	Wednes	8	Presagion	12	Netsetinchile

Solution

1	Kenya	5	Monaco	9	Algeria
2	Burma	6	Bermuda	10	Guatemala
3	Ecuador	7	Malawi	11	Greenland
4	Sweden	8	Singapore	12	Liechtenstein

Scaffold

No. of players: 2 or more
Equipment: Paper and a pencil for each player
Complexity: ☆☆

The players are all given the same three letters – R, D, T, for example – and they have ten minutes in which to form a list of words which contain those three letters in the order given. Such a list might contain the following words if R, D, T were the letters given:

CORDITE	**PRODUCT**
CORDIALITY	**CREDIT**
RADIOLOGIST	**ARIDITY**
RADIATOR	**GRADUATE**
PREDATOR	**INTRODUCTION**

Players score one point for each word listed, and the player with the highest score is the winner.

The three letters should be chosen carefully so that it is possible to find a good number of words which use them. Thus L, M, E or R, F, N or M, I, T, for example, would be satisfactory, but Z, Q, N or W, X, F could just possibly result in scores of zero all round (unless you are playing with a group of Serbian lexicographers).

Alpha

No. of players: 2 or more
Equipment: Paper and a pencil for each player
Complexity: ✩✩

This is a word-listing game in which the players have a time limit of ten minutes in which to list words beginning and ending with the same letter of the alphabet. There are two different versions of the game.

In the first version the players simply have to list as many words as they can that end with the same letter with which they begin. The winner is the player who produces the longest list of such words.

In the second version, which is a more demanding test of vocabulary, each player first writes the letter of the alphabet down the left-hand margin of his sheet of paper. Then for each letter he has to find the longest possible word which begins and ends with that letter. When the time limit has expired, the players score one point for each letter of each word they have listed and the player with the highest total score is the winner. One player's completed list might look something like this:

A	AMNESIA	=	7	**N**	NATIONAL- ISATION	=	15
B	BEDAUB	=	6	**O**	OVERDO	=	6
C	CYCLONIC	=	8	**P**	PARTNERSHIP	=	11
D	DEDICATED	=	9	**Q**			
E	EVERYONE	=	8	**R**	REGULATOR	=	9
F	FLUFF	=	5	**S**	SUCCINCTNESS	=	12
G	GRADUATING	=	10	**T**	TOURNAMENT	=	9
H	HUNCH	=	5	**U**			
I				**V**			
J				**W**	WINDOW	=	6
K	KAYAK	=	5	**X**			
L	LONGITUDINAL	=	12	**Y**	YELLOWY	=	7
M	METAMORPHISM	=	12	**Z**			

Arena

No. of players: 2 or more
Equipment: Paper and a pencil for each player
Complexity: ★★

The players have ten minutes in which to form as long a list as possible of 5-letter words which have a vowel as the first letter, a consonant as the second, a vowel as the third, a consonant as the fourth, and a vowel as the last letter. Such a list might include words such as these:

ARENA	OPERA	UNITE
AROMA	ABODE	AMUSE
ELOPE	AWAKE	OKAPI
EVADE	IMAGE	AGATE

The player who produces the longest list will be the winner.

Vowels

No. of players: 2 or more
Equipment: Paper and a pencil for each player
Complexity: ★★

This is another word-listing game which is a good test of vocabulary. A particular vowel is chosen, and the players have ten minutes in which to produce a list of words which must conform to the following simple rules:

(a)   Each word must contain at least five letters.
(b)   Each word must contain the chosen vowel twice or more, and must contain no other vowel.
(c)   Proper nouns, foreign words and hyphenated words are not allowed.

Here are typical words which might be listed for each chosen vowel:

A CATAMARAN, KAYAK, BALLAD, ANAGRAM, SALAD, BANTAM . . .

E REBEL, PRECEDE, REDEEMER, REFEREE, BEETLE, FEEBLE . . .

I MINIM, CIVIL, PIPPIN, RIPPING, ILLICIT, IMPLICIT . . .

O ROBOT, MORON, COMMON, DOCTOR, CORDON, MONSOON . . .

U SUBURB, HUMDRUM, UPTURN, SUNBURN, RUMPUS, SUCCUBUS . . .

Players score one point for each time the chosen vowel occurs in each of their words. The player with the highest total score is the winner.

Stairway

No. of players: 2 or more
Equipment: Paper and a pencil for each player
Complexity: ★★

A letter of the alphabet is called out and the players have ten minutes in which to form a 'Stairway' of words beginning with that letter. The stairway consists of a 2-letter word, then a 3-letter word, then a 4-letter word, and so on. Here is an example for the letter M:

M
ME
MAN
MINT
MELON
MEADOW
MISSION
MATERNAL
MORTALITY
MISFORTUNE
MAGNIFICENT
MATHEMATICAL
MISCELLANEOUS
MULTIPLICATION
MISAPPREHENSION

The winner is the player who forms the longest stairway.

Acrostics

No. of players: 2 or more
Equipment: Paper and a pencil for each player
Complexity: ☆☆

A word of six or seven letters is chosen, and each player writes the word down in a column on the left side of his sheet of paper. He then writes the same word in another column to the right of the first one, but this time with the letters in reverse order. Let us say the chosen word is CARAMEL, then each player's sheet of paper should look something like this:

```
C          L
A          E
R          M
A          A
M          R
E          A
L          C
```

The players are then given five minutes in which they have to write the longest word they can think of, beginning and ending with each pair of letters provided by the two columns.

The players score one point per letter for each of their words, and the player with the highest total score is the winner.

C hape	L = 6		C ontractua	L = 11
A pple	E = 5		A dministrativ	E = 14
R hyth	M = 6		R egionalis	M = 11
A lgebr	A = 7		A spidistr	A = 10
M othe	R = 6		M usketee	R = 9
E xtr	A = 5		E uthanasi	A = 10
L ogi	C = 5		L inguisti	C = 10
	40			**75**

Advertisements

No. of players: 3 or more
Equipment: Old magazines; paper and a pencil
for each player
Complexity: ☆☆

This game is a test of observation (and of the power of advertising). It relies on the fact that much magazine and newspaper advertising places less emphasis on pictures of the product than on 'images' – sun-drenched beaches, pretty girls, laughing family groups, cartoon characters etc.

Some preparation is required beforehand. You need to sort through a number of old magazines and newspapers, cutting out suitable pictures from advertisements for well-known products. The advertisements should be neither too familiar nor too obscure. You may need to cut out of the pictures the name of the product or any other tell-tale indications. Any number of pictures between twelve and twenty should be sufficient. The pictures must be numbered, and may either be pasted on to a board or simply laid out on a table where all the players can see them.

Each of the players is given a pencil and paper, and they have ten minutes in which to write down the names of the products being advertised. The player with the highest number of correct answers is the winner.

Crossword

No. of players: 2
Equipment: Paper and two pencils
Complexity: ☆☆

Before the game begins a square grid is drawn, with nine squares across and nine squares down. A larger grid may be drawn if a longer game is required. The first player writes a word anywhere in the grid, either across or down, and scores one point for each letter in the word. The players then play alternately, each player forming another word which must interlock with one or more of the previously entered letters in crossword fashion, and scoring one point for each new letter written. For example, if a player writes in the word CROSSWORD, linking with the C and W of previously completed words, he would score 7 points – he cannot claim for the C and W. Proper nouns, abbreviations and foreign words are not allowed.

Play continues until neither player can find further letters that can be inserted to form new words. The player with the highest score is the winner.

D	I	S	C	U	S	S		P
I			H		T			O
S	T	R	E	N	U	O	U	S
T			C		M			T
U	S		K		B	O	O	M
R	O	O	M		L			A
B			A		I		A	N
E		S	T	O	N	E	D	
D	O		E		G		O	X

Mary	Michael
9	8
8	8
6	4
2	4
2	2
1	1
1	
29	27

Crosswords

No. of players: 2 or more
Equipment: Paper and a pencil for each player
Complexity: ★☆

Although this and the previous game have similar names they are in fact quite different. (An interesting, though irrelevant, point to note is that the completed grid in the previous game resembles the type of crossword that is popular in Britain, whereas the completed grid in this game resembles the type of crossword that is more popular in France.)

Before the game begins each player draws on his sheet of paper a grid with five squares across and five squares down. If a longer game is required or if there are more than five players a larger grid may be used. Each player in turn then calls out any letter of his choice. All the players must then enter that letter in their own grids, in any position they choose. Once a letter has been entered it may not be moved. The aim is to form words either across or down.

The game ends when all the squares have been filled. The scores are then worked out according to the number of letters in the words each player has formed. One point is scored for each letter contained in a valid word – one-letter words, proper nouns, foreign words and abbreviations do not count. A letter may not be shared by two or more words in the same row or column. (Thus if a player has a row that reads **CONET** the most he can score is 4 points for **CONE** – he cannot also score points for **ON, ONE** or **NET**.) One bonus point is scored for each word that completely fills a row or column.

The player with the highest total score is the winner.

Player 1   Player 2

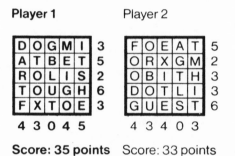

Score: **35 points**   Score: 33 points

Consequences

No. of players: Any large number
Equipment: Paper and a pencil for each player
Complexity: ☆

Consequences is a party game which is very popular with children (particularly grown-up children). It can be marvellously silly, and is played purely for amusement – there are no winners or losers.

Each player is provided with a pencil and a sheet of paper. The idea is to write little stories to which each player contributes a part without knowing what any of the other players has written. This random composition can produce ludicrous results.

For each part of the story the players are told what sort of information is required, e.g. a female character, a male character, where they met, and so on. After writing each part of the story the player folds over the sheet to conceal what he has written and passes the folded sheet to the next player on his left. At the same time he will receive from the player on his right a different folded sheet, on which he will write the next part of the story. This process is repeated until each player has written all the required parts of the story, all on different sheets of paper. The papers are then unfolded and the results read out.

The parts that make up the story may vary, but the traditional Consequences story goes something like this:

1	A female character	e.g. Little Bo-Peep
2	Met a male character	e.g. Met Mao Tse-Tung
3	Where they met	e.g. Behind the Bicycle Shed
4	What he did	e.g. He Pinched Her Bottom
5	What she did	e.g. She Smoked A Big Cigar
6	What he said	e.g. He said 'The End Of The World Is Nigh'
7	What she said	e.g. She said 'We Are Not Amused'
8	What the consequence was	e.g. The Consequence Was a Rise In World Oil Prices
9	And what the world said	e.g. And the World said 'All's Fair in Love and War'

Picture Consequences

No. of players: 3 or more
Equipment: Paper and a pencil for each player
Complexity: ☆

This is another popular party game, for children or for sophisticated adults. Each player is given a pencil and a sheet of paper which has two lines drawn across it to divide the paper into three equal sections. The lines are not absolutely necessary but they do make the game easier for young children (or for the sophisticated adults who may have imbibed too much of the party spirit).

In the top section of the paper the player draws a head – which may be the head of a person, a bird, an animal or whatever he chooses. The neck should be drawn to go just over the line into the middle section. He then folds the top of the paper down to the first line to conceal what he has drawn, and passes the sheet of paper to the next player on his left.

Using the sheet of paper passed to him by his neighbour he draws a body and legs – again either human or otherwise – in the centre section, joining it on to the neck drawn by his neighbour. The legs should be drawn to go just over the line into the lower section. Again the sheet of paper is folded to conceal what has been drawn and is passed on.

Using the next sheet of paper passed to him, he then draws some feet – once more either human or otherwise – in the lower section, to join on to the legs already drawn.

Each player will have contributed parts to three different drawings. It is important that at each stage no player lets any of the other players see what he is drawing. When the pictures are all completed the players unfold the sheets of paper to see what has been drawn, and then laugh themselves silly.

Telegrams

No. of players: 3 or more
Equipment: Paper and a pencil for each player
Complexity: ★★

Each player in turn calls out a letter of the alphabet at random, and all the players write down the letters as they are called out. A list of about 15 letters should be formed in this way. The players then have five minutes in which each of them has to compose a telegram, the words of which must begin with the listed letters in the order given. Stops (full stops) may be inserted where required and the last word of the telegram may, if the player so desires, be the name of the imaginary sender.

For example, if the letters called out were H,A,I,B,B,A,U,T,L,D,H,S,A,O,C one player might write:

> **HAVE ARRIVED IN BLACKPOOL BUT AM UNABLE**
> **TO LOCATE DECKCHAIRS HENCE SAND ALL OVER**
> **CYNTHIA**

whereas another player might write:

> **HURRY AND IMMEDIATELY BRING BACK ALL UNUSED**
> **TEA LEAVES STOP DADDY HATES SUPPING ALE OR COCOA**

When the five minutes are up each player reads out his telegram, and the winner is the player whose telegram is judged to be the most sensible, the cleverest, the wittiest or the silliest.

Short Story

No. of players: 2 or more
Equipment: Paper and a pencil for each player
Complexity: ★★

A time limit of five or ten minutes is set. Within that time limit each player has to compose a short story. The only restriction is that no word used may contain more than three letters. When the time limit has expired all the stories are read out. The player whose composition is judged to be the cleverest or most amusing is the winner.

Here is an example of the sort of story that could be produced:'A man had a pig in a sty. It ate all he fed it. But one day the pig bit the man. By gum, was the man mad! Now the pig is ham in a can.'

CARD GAMES

Whist
Solo Whist
Bridge
Hearts
Black Maria
Slobberhannes
Polignac
Nap
Ecarte
Four-handed Euchre
Three-handed Euchre
Two-handed Euchre
Call-ace Euchre
Rummy
Gin Rummy
Cribbage
Bézique
Cassino
Pontoon
Poker
Draw Poker
Spit in the Ocean
Five Card Stud
Six Card Stud
Seven Card Stud
Brag

Whist

No. of players: 4
Equipment: Standard pack of 52 cards
Complexity: ☆☆☆

Whist, the fore-runner of *Bridge*, is a four-handed partnership game in which points are scored for tricks and honours. The cards rank from ace high to 2 low.

Partners sit opposite each other. The pack is cut to decide first deal, and thereafter each player deals in turn. Thirteen face-down cards are dealt, one at a time, to each player, except that the last card (the dealer's) is dealt face up to establish the trump suit.

Each player picks up the cards dealt to him and arranges them into suits. The player to the left of the dealer leads to the first trick. The other players in turn must follow suit if they can, otherwise they may play a trump or discard a card of another suit as they wish. The trick is won by the highest ranking card of the suit that was led or by the highest trump if any were played. The winner of each trick leads to the next. And so on until all the tricks have been played.

A game is won by the first side to score 5 points. The side winning the majority of tricks (i.e. seven or more) scores 1 point for each trick won in excess of six. Points are also scored for honours – the ace, king, queen and jack of trumps. A side dealt all four honours scores 4 points; or 3 points if dealt any three of them. However, points for honours cannot be scored by a side already holding 4 points towards game at the beginning of the deal. Nor can a side score honours points if the opposing side has already scored sufficient points from tricks to give them the game.

If a player revokes (i.e. fails to follow suit when he could have done so) the penalty is 3 points, which his opponents may either add to their own score or deduct from the score of the revoking side.

A rubber is the best of three games, and the value of a rubber is determined by game points (not to be confused with points from tricks and honours). The side winning a game scores 1 game point if the opposing side has 3 or 4 points, 2 game points if the opposing side has 1 or 2 points, or 3 game points if the opposing side has not scored at all in this game. In addition, the winners of a rubber get 2 extra game points. The value of the rubber is the difference between the game points scored by the winners and the losers, and thus may range from 1 to 8 game points.

Solo Whist

No. of players: 4
Equipment: Standard pack of 52 cards
Complexity: ☆☆☆☆

Solo Whist is a gambling game for four players, each playing for himself though temporary partnerships are possible, and is one of the most popular card games. It is considered by many to be the equal of *Bridge* in terms of skill and complexity and to be superior in terms of enjoyment. Whereas thousands of books have been written about all aspects of *Bridge*, very little has been written about *Solo Whist* – and some players claim this as an advantage, pointing out that *Solo Whist* remains flexible while *Bridge* has become over-systematised.

The cards rank from ace high to 2 low, as normal. The players cut for first deal and the player with the lowest card deals. The cards are dealt three at a time, face downwards, for four rounds and the last four cards are then dealt singly. The last card – the dealer's – is dealt face up to indicate the trump suit.

When all the players have picked up and examined their cards the bidding commences. A bid is a declaration by a player that he will attempt to win a certain number of tricks. Each player in turn, beginning with the player to the left of the dealer, may either pass or make a higher bid than any previous bid. A player whose bid is overcalled by another player may subsequently make an even higher bid, but a player who has passed once is not allowed to make a subsequent bid. A player whose bid is followed by three subsequent passes then has to win the declared number of tricks. If he is successful the other players pay him, otherwise he has to pay them – the stakes depending on the value of the bid.

The bids, in ascending order, are as follows:

(a) **Proposal and Acceptance (Prop and Cop)**
A player calling 'I propose' (or more commonly 'Prop') declares that in partnership with any other player who accepts he will win at least eight tricks with the trump suit indicated by the deal. Unless there has been an intervening higher bid, any subsequent player may become the partner by calling 'I accept' (or more commonly 'Cop'). These two players play in partnership if there is no subsequent higher bid.

(b) **Solo**

A bid to win at least five tricks playing alone against the other three players, with the trump suit indicated by the deal.

(c) **Misère**

A bid to lose every trick, playing with no trump suit.

(d) **Abundance**

A bid to win at least nine tricks, with the trump suit to be declared by the bidder himself. The trump suit is not named at the time of the bid. In some schools the player, if this is the highest bid, declares the trump suit after the other players have passed and before the first trick is played. In other schools the first trick is played with the trump suit indicated by the deal, and the Abundance bidder's choice of trump only takes effect for the second and subsequent tricks.

(e) **Royal Abundance**

A bid to win at least nine tricks, with the trump suit indicated by the deal.

(f) **Misère Ouverte (or Spread)**

A bid to lose every trick, playing with no trump suit, and with the bidder's cards exposed face upwards on the table after the first trick.

(g) **Abundance Declared**

A bid to win all thirteen tricks, playing with no trump suit, but with the bidder having the privilege of leading to the first trick.

If all the players pass without making a bid the hands are thrown in and the deal passes to the next player. If a player makes a Prop bid and the other players all pass he may, if he wishes, make a higher bid — otherwise the hands are thrown in. The one exception to the rule that a player may not bid after having passed is that the player to the left of the dealer (but no other player) may, after passing initially, accept a Prop bid from another player.

The normal rules of trick-taking apply (as in Whist), with the lead to the first trick being made by the player to the left of the dealer (except in the case of an Abundance Declared bid) and the winner of each trick leading to the next.

Each deal counts as a separate game. Stakes are paid individually by the other players to the highest bidder if he succeeds in winning the requisite number of tricks; otherwise, he pays each of them individually. The actual stakes, of course, are a matter of agreement by the players but the relative values of the bids are normally as follows:

Prop and Cop	2 units (1 for each partner)
Solo	2 units
Misère	3 units
Abundance	4 units
Royal Abundance	4 units
Misère Ouverte	6 units
Abundance Declared	8 units

The usual practice is for the stakes to depend solely on whether or not the bid is successful, but some players also include bonuses overtricks and penalties for overtricks (often ¼ or ½ unit per trick).

Bridge

No. of players: 4
Equipment: Standard pack of 52 cards
Complexity: ★★★☆

The game we call *Bridge* (or to give it its full, formal name, *Contract Bridge*) evolved from *Whist* over a number of years. The game of *Biritch* or *Russian Whist*, introduced in about 1880, was a version of *Whist* in which the dealer could nominate the trump suit. *Bridge-Whist*, introduced in 1896, gave the dealer the option of letting his partner nominate the trump suit. *Auction Bridge*, introduced in 1904, had many of the features of the current game but had a much less refined scoring system. *Contract Bridge* was given its present form in 1925 by an American millionaire Harold S. Vanderbilt, and was given its present pre-eminence among card games by the indefatigable promotional activities of Ely Culbertson, who also introduced the first standard bidding system.

Bridge has the pre-eminence among card games that *Chess* has among board games. It is a complex game, and it is said that to learn how to play *Bridge* requires a minimum of six months' study and practice. But there are thousands of dedicated players to claim that the satisfaction to be derived from the game justifies this effort.

Bridge is a partnership game for four players. Partners sit opposite each other, and are usually referred to as North-South and East-West.

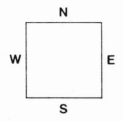

The cards rank from ace high to 2 low. For the purposes of bidding (though not in play) the suits are also ranked in the order: spades (highest), hearts, diamonds, clubs (lowest). Spades and hearts are referred to as major suits, diamonds and clubs as minor suits.

At the beginning of the game there is a draw for partners and first deal. The pack is spread out face down and each player draws a card. The players drawing the two highest cards are partners against the other two, and the player drawing the highest card has first deal.

The normal etiquette observed when dealing is for the player to the left of the dealer to shuffle the pack and for the player to the right of the dealer to cut the pack. The cards are then dealt out, one at a time and face down, to give each player 13 cards.

The game consists of two parts – the bidding (or auction) and the play. The play consists of 13 tricks, and in the bidding each side tries to estimate the number of tricks they think they can win with their combined hands. A bid is a declaration by one side that they will attempt to win a certain number of tricks with a certain nominated trump suit. The highest bid becomes the contract. In the subsequent play the side making the highest bid will attempt to fulfil this contract winning at least the declared number of tricks, while the opposing side will try to stop them.

The bidding begins when every player has had an opportunity to study the cards in his hand. Beginning with the dealer, each player in turn may pass, bid, double or redouble.

To pass a player says 'No bid'. This does not prevent him from making a subsequent bid when his turn comes round again in the bidding.

A bid is a declaration that a player's side will win a certain number of tricks with a nominated trump suit (or with no trumps). Since there are 13 tricks to be taken, the side winning the majority of tricks must win

7 or more. The first 6 tricks won are known as 'the book' and tricks won in excess of 6 are known as 'odd tricks'. Bids are made in terms of odd tricks. Thus, for example, a bid of One Club is a bid to win 7 tricks with clubs as the trump suit, and Two No Trumps is a bid to win 8 tricks with no trump suit.

Each bid must be higher than the previous one. That is, it must be for a higher number of tricks or for the same number of tricks but with a higher ranking suit as trumps. A No Trump bid ranks above a bid in any suit. Thus the possible bids in ascending order are: One Club, One Diamond, One Heart, One Spade, One No Trump, Two Clubs, Two Diamonds, Two Hearts, Two Spades, Two No Trumps, and so on.

Instead of making a bid a player may make a call of 'Double' or 'Redouble'. A call of 'Double', which can only be made after an opponent's bid, signifies that a player is confident of being able to prevent the opposing side from winning the number of tricks bid. A call of 'Redouble', which can only be made if the previous call was a 'Double' from an opponent, signifies that a player is confident that his partner's last bid which has been doubled *can* be successful. Doubling or redoubling doubles or quadruples the points or penalties for success or failure if the bid becomes the contract. A bid that has been doubled or redoubled can be overcalled by a higher bid in the normal way – e.g. the bidding might proceed: Two Clubs, Double, Redouble, Two Hearts – and the double or redouble is thus cancelled.

The contract is established when the last and highest bid (whether undoubled, doubled or redoubled) has been followed by three consecutive Passes. The player on the contracting side who first nominated the trump suit of the contract is the 'declarer', and he will play both his own and his partner's hand.

The opening lead is made by the player to the left of the declarer. As soon as the opening lead has been made, declarer's partner lays all his cards face upwards on the table, with each suit in a separate column of overlapping cards in order of rank. Declarer's partner takes no further part in the play. His hand – known as the 'dummy' – is played for him by the declarer.

The cards are played to each trick in clockwise order, and normal rules of trick-taking apply. A player must follow suit if he can, otherwise he may play a trump or discard a card of any other suit as he pleases. A trick is won by the highest ranking card of the suit that was led, or by the highest ranking trump if any were played. The winner of each trick leads to the next. If the declarer wins a trick from his own hand he must lead to the next trick from his own hand; if he wins a hand from the dummy he must lead to the next trick from the dummy. All the tricks won by one side must be kept in one place and arranged to show clearly the number of tricks won so far.

Scoring is done on a sheet divided into two columns. It is customary for both sides to keep score – to provide a double check – and to record their own score in one column headed WE and their opponents' score in the other column, headed THEY. A horizontal line divides the columns into an upper half and a lower half, and points may be scored 'above the line' or 'below the line'. Only points scored below the line count towards game.

A game is won by the first side to reach or exceed 100 points below the line. A rubber is won by the first side to win two games. A side with one game won is said to be 'vulnerable'.

Details of the scoring are shown in the accompanying table. Trick points can only be scored by the declarer's side, if the contract succeeds. Only the odd tricks contracted for can be scored below the line. Overtricks – those won in excess of the contract – are scored above the line.

A successful contract to win 12 tricks is called a Little Slam. A successful contract to win all 13 tricks is called a Grand Slam. There are bonus points for winning a Slam, and for winning a doubled or redoubled contract. These bonus points are scored above the line.

If the declarer 'goes down' (i.e. if the contract does not succeed) the opposing side score points above the line for each 'undertrick' (i.e. each trick by which declarer falls short of the contract).

Regardless of whether the contract fails or succeeds, either side may score points above the line for 'honours'. Honours are the five highest-ranking cards in the trump suit – A to 10 – or, in a No Trumps contract, the four aces. Points are scored for having been dealt honours in one's hand, and thus represent a pure chance element.

When a game is won, a line is drawn below the trick scores for both sides. Trick points for the next game, starting again from zero, are scored below this line. At the end of a rubber the winning side scores a bonus above the line of 700 points if the opposing side has not won a game, or 500 points if the opposing side *has* won a game. All the points above and below the line are then totalled for each side. The difference between the two scores represents the value of the rubber.

Bridge Scoring Table

Contract succeeds: Points scored below the line for each odd trick bid and won

	Undoubled	Doubled	Redoubled
In minor suit (clubs or diamonds)	20	40	80
In major suit (hearts or spades)	30	60	120
No trumps – first odd trick	40	80	160
No trumps – subsequent tricks	30	60	120

Contract succeeds: Points scored above the line by Declarer

	Not Vulnerable	Vulnerable
Per overtrick, if undoubled	(Trick value-as above)	
Per overtrick, if doubled	100	200
Per overtrick, if redoubled	200	400
Bonus for doubled or redoubled contract	50	50
Little Slam	500	750
Grand Slam	1000	1500

Contract fails: Points scored above the line by Defenders

	Not Vulnerable	Vulnerable
If undoubled, for each undertrick	50	100
If doubled, for 1st undertrick	100	200
If doubled, for subsequent undertricks	200	300
If redoubled, for 1st undertrick	200	400
If redoubled, for subsequent undertricks	400	600

Honours: Points scored above the line

For all 5 trump honours in one hand	150
For any 4 trump honours in one hand	100
For 4 aces in one hand in No Trump contract	150

Rubber and Game Points

For winning rubber, if opponents have won no game	700
For winning rubber, if opponents have won one game	500
Unfinished rubber: for having won one game	300
Unfinished rubber: for having part score in unfinished game	50

Hearts

No. of players: 3 to 7
Equipment: Standard pack of 52 cards
Complexity: ✰✰✰

Hearts is one of a number of games in which the aim is to avoid winning tricks that contain certain penalty cards. The penalty cards in *Hearts* (as one might reasonably anticipate) are hearts, each of which counts one point. Thus there are 13 penalty points to be distributed among the players.

Before the game begins it may be necessary to remove some cards from the pack, according to the number of players, so that the pack may be dealt out fully with each player receiving an equal number of cards. With three players the 2 of clubs is removed; with five players the 2 of clubs and 2 of diamonds are removed; with six players all the 2s are removed; with seven players the 2 of clubs, 2 of diamonds and 2 of spades are removed.

The cards are cut to select the dealer, and the dealer deals out the cards, one at a time and face down.

The player to the left of the dealer leads to the first trick, and thereafter the winner of each trick leads to the next. Players must follow suit if they can, otherwise they may play any card. There are no trumps and a trick is always won by the highest card of the suit that was led.

At the end of the hand each player counts the number of hearts in the tricks he has won and scores that number of penalty points. The winner is the player with the lowest number of points after an agreed number of hands, or the player with the lowest number of points when any player's score reaches a set number such as 50.

An alternative method, when the game is played for stakes, is for each hand to be considered a separate game. Each player pays into a pool one unit for each heart he has taken and the pool is shared by any players with no hearts. If all the players have taken one or more hearts the pool is carried forward to the next game.

Black Maria

No. of players: 3 to 7
Equipment: Standard pack of 52 cards
Complexity: ✰✰✰

Black Maria is similar to *Hearts*, except for the following differences:

(a)   The queen of spades ('Black Maria') is an extra penalty card which counts a hefty 13 penalty points.
(b)   After the deal, but before the first lead, there is an exchange of cards. Each player, after examining the cards in his hand, passes any three cards face down to the player on his right. A player may not look at the cards he has received until he has passed on the cards he has discarded from his own hand.

Slobberhannes

No. of players: 3 to 6
Equipment: Short pack of 32 cards
Complexity: ✰✰

Slobberhannes is played with a pack from which all cards below seven have been removed. If there are three, five of six players the two black 7s are also removed. Cards rank from ace high to 7 low. The objective is to avoid taking the first trick, the last trick, and the trick containing the queen of clubs.

The cards are dealt out one at a time and face down so that each player receives an equal number of cards and there are none left over. The player to the left of the dealer leads to the first trick. A player must follow suit if he can, otherwise he may play any card of his choice. There are no trumps and a trick is won by the highest card of the suit that was led. The winner of each trick leads to the next.

A player taking the first trick, the last trick or a trick containing the queen of clubs is penalised one point. A player unfortunate enough to win all three of these tricks scores an extra penalty point, making four in all.

Polignac

No. of players: 3 to 6
Equipment: Short pack of 32 cards
Complexity: ★★

Polignac is similar to *Slobberhannes* except that the penalties are for taking tricks containing jacks – two penalty points for the jack of spades and one penalty point for each of the other jacks.

Nap

No. of players: 2 to 6 (best with 4 or 5)
Equipment: Standard pack of 52 cards
Complexity: ★★★

Each player is dealt five face-down cards, one at a time. There is then a round of bidding, in which the player who bids to take the highest number of tricks chooses trumps and has to make the number of tricks he has bid in order to win. The bidding begins with the player to the left of the dealer and ends with the dealer, each player having only one opportunity to bid. A player may pass or make a bid higher than any previous bids.

Nap is usually played for stakes. The possible bids, in ascending order, and their stake value if won or lost are as follows:

One	(bid to win one trick)	1 unit
Two	(bid to win two tricks)	2 units
Three	(bid to win three tricks)	3 units
Misery	(bid to win no tricks, with no trumps)	3 units
Four	(bid to win four tricks)	4 units
Nap	(bid to win five tricks)	10 units if won, 5 if lost
Wellington	(bid to win five tricks)	20 units if won, 10 if lost

Wellington may only be bid to overcall a previous bid of Nap and is a declaration to win all five tricks at double stakes.

The player making the highest bid leads to the first trick and, except when the bid is Misery, the card that is led determines the trump suit. Normal rules of trick-taking apply, as in *Whist*.

If the bidder wins his contract each of the other players pays him the appropriate stake. If he fails to win his contract he pays each of the other players the appropriate stake. Stakes are paid only according to the number of tricks that were bid. No account is taken of any excess tricks or of the number of tricks by which a bidder fails to make his contract.

Ecarte

No. of players: 2
Equipment: Short pack of 32 cards
Complexity: ★★☆

Ecarte is an old game of French origin, which is derived from the even older French game of *Triomphe*. It is played with a 32-card pack – a standard pack from which all cards below 7 have been removed. The cards in descending order of rank are K, Q, J, A, 10, 9, 8, 7 – note the unusual position of the ace. The objective of the game is to score points by winning tricks.

Each player deals in turn, and five cards are dealt face down to each player. The cards are dealt either as a batch of two followed by a batch of three or vice versa (but whichever method is chosen should be applied throughout the game). The remainder of the pack is placed face down to form a stock, and the top card of the stock is turned over and placed face up alongside the stock to establish the trump suit. If this card happens to be a king the dealer scores 1 point.

The non-dealer always leads to the first trick but before doing this he may propose an exchange of cards. To do this he says 'cards' and the dealer may either accept or refuse. If the dealer accepts, the non-dealer discards any number of cards (from one to five) face down and draws an equal number from the top of the stock; the dealer then does likewise. The non-dealer may then, if he wishes, propose another exchange of cards and again the dealer may accept or refuse. This continues until the non-dealer chooses to lead, or until the dealer refuses a proposal or until the stock is exhausted.

The non-dealer leads to the first trick, and thereafter the winner of each trick leads to the next. The second player to a trick must follow suit if he can; if he cannot follow suit he must play a trump if he has one; he must also win the trick if he can do so.

The scoring is as follows:

(a) If any cards were exchanged, the winner of the hand scores 1 point for winning 3 or 4 tricks or 2 points if he wins all 5 tricks.

(b) If the non-dealer loses after failing to propose or if the dealer loses after refusing the first proposal then the winner scores 2 points regardless of the number of tricks won.

(c) A player holding the king of trumps scores 1 point if he declares it immediately before playing to the first trick.

The game is won by the first player to score 5 points.

Four-Handed Euchre

No. of players: 4
Equipment: Short pack of 32 cards
Complexity: ★★☆

Euchre, like *Ecarte*, is a descendant of the old game of *Triomphe*. It originated in the United States and remains most popular in the north-eastern United States and Canada.

There are several variations of *Euchre*, for any number from two to seven players. The most popular version is the four-handed partnership game described here.

From a standard 52-card pack all cards below 7 are removed to leave a 32-card pack. The highest trump is the jack, called the 'right bower'. The other jack of the same colour as the trump suit, called 'left bower', is also regarded as a trump and ranks second. For example, if hearts are trumps the jack of hearts is right bower and the jack of diamonds is left bower. Thus in the trump suit there are nine cards, ranking right bower, left bower, A, K, Q, 10, 9, 8, 7; in the other suit of the same colour as trumps there are seven cards, ranking A, K, Q, 10, 9, 8, 7; and in each of the remaining suits there are eight cards, ranking A, K, Q, J, 10, 9, 8, 7.

Partners sit opposite each other. Players draw to decide first deal, and thereafter the deal passes to the left.

Each player is dealt five cards, in batches of two and then three (or three and then two). The next card is turned face up to propose the trump suit — but this only becomes the trump suit if accepted by one of the players. Beginning with the player to the left of the dealer each player may either pass or accept the trump suit. To pass, a player says 'Pass'. To accept, an opponent of the dealer says 'I order it up', the dealer's partner says 'I assist' or the dealer says 'I call it up'. Once one player has accepted, the dealer has the option to taking the turned-up card into his hand and discarding any other card or of retaining his existing hand. Play then begins.

If all four players pass, the turned-up card is turned face down. There is then a second round in which each player in turn may either pass or nominate a trump suit of his own choice. Once one player has nominated a trump suit play may begin. If all four players pass, the hands are thrown in and the next player deals.

The player who decides the trump suit, whether by accepting or nominating, becomes the 'maker'. He has the option of playing the hand without his partner (to aim for a higher score), in which case he says 'I play alone'. His partner then lays his cards face down on the table and remains out of the game (although he still shares in the stakes).

If the maker is playing alone, the opening lead is made by the player to his left. Otherwise, the opening lead is made by the player to the left of the dealer. The usual rules of trick-taking apply, as in *Whist*.

Points are scored by the partnership winning three or more tricks. Winning three or four tricks is called 'the point'; winning all five tricks is called 'the march'. If the maker and his partner win less than three tricks they are said to be 'euchred'. The maker and his partner score 1 for the point and 2 for the march, but a maker playing alone scores 4 for the march. If they are euchred, the opponents score 2.

The first partnership to score a previously agreed number of points (usually 5, 7 or 10) wins the game.

Three-Handed Euchre

No. of players: 3
Equipment: Short pack of 32 cards
Complexity: ☆☆☆

In this version of the game the maker always plays alone and the other two players form a temporary partnership against him. The maker scores 1 for the point and 3 for the march; his opponents score 2 points if he is euchred. Otherwise, the rules of the four-handed game apply.

Two-Handed Euchre

No. of players: 2
Equipment: Short pack of 32 cards
Complexity: ☆☆☆

This is similar to the four-handed game except that (of course!) there are no partnerships and the maker always plays alone. Scoring is 1 for the point, 2 for the march and 2 for euchre. The game may also be played with a 24-card pack (that is, with all cards below 9 removed).

Call-Ace Euchre

No. of players: 4, 5 or 6
Equipment: Short pack of 32 cards
Complexity: ☆☆☆

Trumps are chosen in any of the ways described for the four-handed game. The maker may then opt to play alone, or he may select a partner by naming any suit. The player holding the highest card of that suit in play becomes the maker's partner.

Thus, at the start of play the maker does not know the identity of his partner. Nor can any of the other players be sure whether or not he is the maker's partner – unless he happens to hold the ace of the nominated suit. Even then he does not announce the fact. The identity of the maker's partner only becomes revealed as the cards are played. It may indeed turn out to be the case that the maker is playing alone, if he himself holds the highest card of the nominated suit.

Scoring is as in the four-handed game, except that each player individually scores for point, march or euchre.

Rummy

No. of players: 2 to 6
Equipment: Standard pack of 52 cards
Complexity: ✩✩✩

Rummy is one of the most popular card games – and like almost all popular card games it has given rise to a host of variations. The standard version is described here.

The objective of the game is to be the first player to 'go out' (i.e. get rid of all the cards in one's hand) by 'melding'. Melding consists of forming groups or sequences of cards. A group is three or more cards of the same rank (e.g. three kings). A sequence is three or more cards of the same suit in sequence (e.g. 5, 6, 7 of clubs). Normally the ace ranks low, so A, 2, 3 is a sequence, but Q, K, A is not. A secondary objective is to reduce as far as possible the total face value of the unmelded cards left in one's hand.

The dealer is chosen in the customary way, by cutting or drawing. The players are dealt their cards one at a time and face down. The number of cards each player receives depends upon the number of players in the game – ten cards each for two players; seven cards each for three or four players; six cards each for five or six players. After the deal the remainder of the pack is placed face down in the centre of the table to form the stock, and the top card of the stock is turned face up beside it to form the first card of the discard pile.

Each player in turn draws either the top card of the stock or the top card of the discard pile, and adds it to his hand. He may then, if he so desires, place any melds he has been able to form on the table in front of him. He may also 'lay off' any individual cards that extend existing melds on the table – he may add cards on his opponents' melds as well as on his own. Finally he discards one card, placing it face up on top of the discard pile.

A player goes out, and thereby wins the hand, when he plays the last card from his hand, whether as part of a meld, a lay off or a discard. The face value of the cards left in the hands of his opponents is totalled to give his score for the round. For the purposes of scoring, an ace counts as 1 and a court card counts as 10.

A player 'goes rummy' if he goes out by melding his entire hand in one turn without previously having melded or laid off any cards. In this case his score is doubled.

If no player has gone out by the time the stock is exhausted, the discard pile is simply turned over to form a new stock and the game continues as normal.

The first player whose score reaches a predetermined number of points wins the game.

Gin Rummy

No. of players: 2
Equipment: Standard pack of 52 cards
Complexity: ☆☆☆

As in Rummy, the objective of the game is to meld the cards in one's hand into groups or sequences. There are, however, certain important differences in the way the game is played.

The players cut the pack to determine the lead. The player who cuts the higher card may choose to deal first or may require his opponent to do so. Thereafter the deal alternates. Ten cards are dealt, one at a time, to each player. The remainder of the pack is placed face down on the table to form the stock, the top card of the stock being turned over and placed face up alongside it as the first card of the discard pile.

The non-dealer may begin play by taking the face-up card. If he does not want to take it, the dealer may take it. If both players refuse it, the non-dealer draws the top card of the stock. As in Rummy, each player in turn takes the top card from either the stock or the discard pile and discards one card from his hand.

Melds are not laid down on the table in the course of play. Instead a player keeps his melds in his hand and goes out by 'knocking' when his 'deadwood' (that is, the cards in his hand that do not form part of a group or sequence) total ten points or less. A player may knock only when it is his turn. After drawing from the stock or discard pile the usual practice is for the player to knock on the table and then discard face down. The player then lays his hand face up on the table, sorted clearly into melds and deadwood. His opponent similarly lays down his hand, but is then allowed to 'lay off' – that is, to add odd cards from his own hand to melds in the knocker's hand. If, however, the knocker has laid down a 'gin hand' – one with no deadwood – his opponent may not lay off any cards.

If the knocker's deadwood count is lower than that of his opponent he scores the difference. If a player lays down a gin hand he scores the total value of his opponent's deadwood plus a 25 point bonus. However, if a player knocks and his opponent has an equal or lower deadwood count, then the opponent wins the hand, scoring the difference plus a 25 point bonus for 'undercut'. A gin hand cannot be undercut.

The score is kept with pencil and paper. A player's score for a hand is added to his previous score and a line is drawn under it. A game ends when one player's score reaches 100. He then scores a bonus of 100 points for game. If his opponent has failed to win a single hand the winner's total score is doubled for 'shut-out'. Finally, to each player's score is added 25 points (called a 'line bonus' or 'box bonus') for each hand he has won.

Roy	Nigel
24	17
55	39
68	86
87	
	161
115	
100	
100	
315	

Roy wins by 154 points (315 – 161)

The last two cards in the stock may not be drawn. If there are only two cards left in the stock and neither player has knocked, then the hand is a tie and no points are scored. The same dealer deals again for the next hand.

Cribbage

No. of players: 2
Equipment: Standard pack of 52 cards; cribbage board for scoring
Complexity: ✩✩

The game of Cribbage is said to have been invented by Sir John Suckling, the seventeenth-century poet, soldier and courtier. There are three main variations of the game – five-card, six-card and seven-card Cribbage – plus other versions for three or four players. The original five-card game for two players – still the most popular version of the game – is described here.

Cribbage is all about scoring points in the course of play. A cribbage board is therefore really essential for recording each player's score. A game is usually played to 61 points.

The players cut to decide first deal, and thereafter the deal alternates. The generally observed etiquette is that the dealer shuffles the pack and places it in front of his opponent who cuts it. The dealer then deals five cards face down to each player and places the remainder of the pack face down on the table. On the first deal of the game the non-dealer immediately pegs three points – '3 for last' – to offset his opponent's advantage of first deal.

Each player discards two of his five cards face down, to form a 'crib' of four cards. The crib belongs to the dealer and, as will be described shortly, will be used by him later to score points. Therefore the dealer will discard cards which should help to form scoring combinations, whereas the non-dealer will discard cards which he thinks will be least useful to the dealer.

The remainder of the pack is cut once more by the non-dealer and the dealer turns up the top card of the lower half. This card is the 'start' and remains face up during play. If the start is a jack the dealer pegs two points – '2 for his heels'.

The play consists of each player in turn laying one of his three cards face up on the table before him and announcing the cumulative total of the cards played so far. This continues until all six cards have been played or until the total face value of the cards played reaches 31. All court cards count as 10, aces count as 1, and other cards count their pip value.

A player who plays a card to bring the total to exactly 15 scores 2 points. The total of the cards played may not go over 31 – if a player cannot lay down a card without going over this total he says 'Go'. His opponent then continues playing if he can. Whoever plays the last card scores 2 points if he brings the total to exactly 31, otherwise he scores '1 for last'.

Points are also scored in the course of play for pairs and runs. A player laying down a card of the same rank as the card just played by his opponent scores '2 for a pair'. Note that although court cards count as 10 they can only be scored as pairs if they are of the same rank – e.g. two kings but not king and queen. If the first player follows with a third card of the rank he scores 6 for a 'pair royal'. If the second player can then play a fourth card of the same rank – a rare occurrence – he scores 12 for a 'double pair royal'.

A run is a sequence of three or more cards of consecutive rank, which do not have to be of the same suit. Runs count 1 point for each card in the run. The cards do not need to be played in order – for example, if the first player plays a 3 and the second player a 5, the first player might then play a 4 and peg 3 points for a run. The second player could then score 4 points for a run of four by playing either a 2 or a 6.

After the hands have been played in this way we come to the 'show'. Both players gather up their own cards. The non-dealer shows and scores for his hand first. For this purpose the start, though it is not removed, is considered part of his hand, and he scores for all combinations in the four cards.

Two points are scored for each combination of cards totalling fifteen. The same card may be counted several times in different combinations. Thus a hand of 3, 6, 6, 9 would yield 6 points for fifteens (for 6–6–3, for 6–9, and for another 6–9). Points are scored in the same way for pairs and for runs (with scoring similar to that in the play) and for flushes. A player scores 3 points for a flush if the three cards in his hand are of the same suit or 4 points if the start is also of the same suit. Finally he scores '1 for his nob' if his hand contains the jack of the same suit as the start.

The dealer then shows his hand and scores in the same way for any combinations in his three cards together with the start. He then turns over the four cards of his crib. The dealer scores for the crib, again in conjunction with the start, in exactly the same way except that a flush is scored only if all five cards are of the same suit and is worth 5 points.

The Cribbage Board

The Cribbage board is a very convenient device for recording scores in the game of *Cribbage*, where points are scored throughout the course of play. It may also be used for scoring in some domino games such as *Fives and Threes*.

In its traditional form it is an oblong piece of wood, about 10 in by 3 in.

There are two rows of 30 holes (arranged in groups of 5) plus an end hole for each player, and is designed for scoring games to 61 or 121 points.

Normally each player marks his score with two pegs, which are moved up the outer row and down the inner row to the end hole, according to the number of points scored. When a game is played to 121 points the pegs travel round twice before reaching the end hole.

The first score made by a player is marked by placing one peg that number of holes from the start. His next score is marked by placing his second peg that number of holes in front of his first peg. Subsequent scores are marked by moving the rearmost peg the appropriate number of holes in front of the leading peg. This leap-frogging method provides a check on accuracy.

Bézique

No. of players: 2
Equipment: 2 32-card packs (Bézique packs)
Complexity: ★★

Bézique is an excellent card game for two players, being quite easy to learn and not too demanding to play. It is a trick-taking game but the scoring, in the main, is based on declaring combinations of cards from one's hand. Points are scored for taking tricks containing certain point-scoring cards, which are known as 'Brisques', but the principal purpose of taking tricks is to enable one to declare one's combinations – and to prevent one's opponent from doing so.

Bézique is played with two 32-card packs – normal packs from which all cards below seven have been removed. The order in which cards rank for the purpose of taking tricks is: ace, 10, king, queen, jack, 9, 8, 7 – note the position of the 10.

The two packs are thoroughly shuffled together and the players cut for deal. The dealer gives eight cards to each player, dealing three cards, then two cards, then three cards at a time. The remaining cards are placed face down on the table to form a stock. The top card is turned over and placed face up beside the stock – the suit of this card determines the trumps for this deal. If this card happens to be a 7 the dealer scores 10 points.

The play is in two stages and the first stage consists of 24 tricks. The non-dealer leads to the first trick, and thereafter the winner of each trick leads to the next. After each trick the winner may declare any one of a number of combinations, and then both players replenish their hands by drawing a card from the stock, the winner drawing first. In this stage of the game it is not necessary to follow suit – the second player to a trick may follow suit, trump or discard just as he pleases. A trick is won by the highest card of the suit led, unless it is trumped, and if two cards of the same value are played then the leader wins the trick.

The combinations that may be declared and scored by the winner of a trick are as follows:

(a) **Common Marriage** – **K** and **Q** of the same suit (not trumps) – scoring 20 points.
(b) **Royal Marriage** – **K** and **Q** of the trump suit – scoring 40 points.
(c) **Bézique** – **Q** of spades with **J** of diamonds – scoring 40 points.

(d) **Double Bézique** – both **Q** of spades and both **J** of diamonds – scoring 500 points.
(e) **Four Jacks** – 40 points.
(f) **Four Queens** – 60 points.
(g) **Four Kings** – 80 points.
(h) **Four Aces** – 100 points.
(i) **Sequence** – **A, 10, K, Q, J** of trumps – scoring 250 points.

A player declares a combination by laying the appropriate cards face up on the table in front of him and marking the score. Cards declared in combinations stay on the table until played – they still form part of the player's hand and may be played to tricks as and when required.

The same cards may also be used in later declarations, provided the declarations are of different kinds. For example, a king could be used for a Marriage and then later for Four Kings, but not for another Marriage. A king and queen of the trump suit may be used for a Royal Marriage, and may subsequently be used for a sequence with the addition of the A, 10, J. It is also permissible to use the two cards forming a Bézique as part of a subsequent Double Bézique, though neither card could be used as part of another single Bézique.

A player who holds the 7 of trumps may declare it and exchange it for the exposed trump card, scoring 10 points. The player holding the second 7 of trumps also scores 10 points when he plays it.

After the twenty-fourth trick has been taken there will be only one card left in the stock, plus the exposed trump card. The winner of that trick draws the stock card and the loser takes the exposed trump card. This is the last trick which allows the winner to make a declaration.

The second stage of the game now begins. The players gather any face-up cards in front of them into their hands, and play the last eight tricks. The rules for this stage are different. A player must, if he can, play a higher card of the suit that was led; if he cannot do so, he must nevertheless follow suit if he can; if he cannot follow suit he must play a trump if he has one; otherwise he may discard. No declarations may be made at this stage of the game, but the winner of the last trick scores 10 points.

When the last trick has been won, each player examines the cards in the tricks he has taken, to determine how many Brisques he has won. Brisques are every ace and every 10 included in a trick, and they each score 10 points.

A game is usually played to 1000 or 2000 points.

Cassino

No. of players: 2, 3 or 4
Equipment: Standard pack of 52 cards
Complexity: ★★

Cassino may be played by two players, by three players, or by four
players playing either individually or in partnerships. It is, however,
best with two players and this is the version described here.

The objective of the game is to score points by capturing cards, in
accordance with the following scoring system:

For capturing the 10 of diamonds ('Big cassino')	2 points
For capturing the 2 of spades ('Little cassino')	1 point
For capturing more cards than one's opponent	3 points
For capturing more spades than one's opponent	1 point
For each ace that is captured	1 point

In addition, 1 point is scored each time a player makes a 'sweep',
which means taking in any one turn all the face-up cards in the layout.

Apart from the scoring values shown above, the suits are
disregarded. Court cards have no numerical value, being used only for
matching, but other cards count their face value, aces counting as one.

The dealer deals two cards to his opponent, two cards face up on the
table (the 'layout'), then two cards to himself. He then repeats this
process, so that each player has four cards and there are four in the
layout. When both players have played all the cards in their hands, each
is dealt another four cards in two lots of two – but no more cards are dealt
to the layout. This continues until all the cards have been dealt.

Each player in turn, commencing with the non-dealer, plays one
card from his hand. In his turn a player may perform one of four actions –
taking, building, calling and trailing.

Taking

A player may 'take' face-up cards in the layout if he has a card of the same
value in his hand. He does this by placing his card on top of the layout
card and then placing both cards face down in front of him. With a court
card a player may take only one card of the same face value in the layout.
For example, if there are two kings in the layout he may take only one of
them with a king from his hand. But with a card other than a court card
he may capture two or more cards of the same face value with one card
from his hand. A player may also take cards which in combination add

up to the same value as a card in his hand. For example, if the layout contains a 2, 3, 5 and 10 then a player with a 10 in his hand could take all of them – the 10 (being of the same face value) and the 2, 3 and 5 as a group (totalling 10).

Building

In 'building' a player places a card on one of the cards in the layout if the sum of the face values is equal to the face value of another card in his hand. For example, if he holds a 2 and a 7 and there is a 5 in the layout, he may place the 2 on the 5 and announce 'Sevens'. Then on his next turn he may take the 2 and 5 with the 7 – unless his opponent forestalls him by taking the 2 and 5 with a 7 of his own. Cards which have been built on may not be taken separately, only as a group – so in this example the 5 in the layout could no longer be taken on its own. However, a build may be 'raised' – so the opponent could, for example, place another 2 on top of the 2 and 5 and announce 'Nines'.

If the build is not taken or raised a player may be able to make another build of 7. He would then place this second build on top of the first build of 7 and announce 'Building sevens'. This forms a multiple build. Multiple builds may not be raised – the two builds in this example may now only be taken by a 7.

Calling

If a player has two cards in his hand of the same face value as a combination of cards in the layout he may claim the layout cards for his next turn by playing one of the cards from his hand. For example, if the layout contains a 3 and a 6 and he has two 9s in his hand he may play a 9 to the layout, announcing 'Nines', with the intention of taking all these cards on his next turn. But of course his opponent, if he has a 9 of his own, may capture the cards for himself.

Trailing

If a player is unable to take, build or call he must 'trail' by adding a card from his hand to the layout..

The game ends when all the cards have been played. Any cards left in the layout are collected by the last player to 'take'. This does not count as a sweep.

The players then add up their scores for the cards they have taken – and for any sweeps they may have made in the course of the play. Each deal may be reckoned as a separate game – the player with the greater number of points being the winner – or play may be to a previously agreed number of points such as 21.

Pontoon

No. of players: 4 or more
Equipment: Standard pack of 52 cards
Complexity: ★

Pontoon (also known as *Vingt-et-Un* or, as they say in France, *Twenty-one*) is a gambling game which, in its own way, is every bit as skilful and exciting as *Bingo*.

The players draw cards to decide who will be the banker, and the object of the game is for the other players (the 'punters') to obtain hands better than that of the banker. The suits of the cards are disregarded – all that matters is their numerical value. Court cards count 10; aces count either 1 or 11 at the option of the holder; other cards count their pip value.

A hand in which the cards add up to a total greater than 21 is 'bust' and loses. A hand in which the total value of the cards is between 16 and 21 beats the banker if the value of his hand is lower or if it is bust. A 'pontoon' is a hand totalling 21 in two cards – an ace and a ten or court card – and this beats the banker unless he also has a pontoon. A 'five card trick' is a hand containing five cards totalling 21 or less, and beats the banker unless he also has a five card trick. 'A 'royal pontoon' is a hand consisting of three 7s and beats the banker whatever cards he holds. The banker may not count a royal pontoon – if his hand consists of three 7s it counts only as a normal 21.

Stakes are won from or paid to the banker, and for this purpose coins, counters or other suitable means of exchange are usually employed.

The banker deals one card face downwards to each punter and then one to himself. Each punter (but not the banker) looks at his card, and then stakes any amount up to an agreed maximum. The banker then deals a second card to each punter and one to himself. Each player looks at his second card. At this point the banker may look at his cards.

If any player has a pontoon he declares it. If the banker has a pontoon the deal ends and he collects from any punter who also has a pontoon the stake he has wagered and from any other punter double the stake he has wagered. Otherwise the banker offers extra cards to each of the punters in turn, beginning with the player on his left. A punter has three options:

(a)   to 'stand' (or 'stick') – that is, to take no more cards from the banker.
      A player may stand only if the total value of his hand is 16 or more.

(b) to 'buy' a card – that is, to lay an additional stake (not less than the amount for which he bought any previous card and not greater than his existing stake) and to obtain an extra card face down from the banker.

(c) to 'twist' – that is, to be dealt an extra card face upwards without increasing the stake.

The banker finishes dealing with one player before proceeding to the next. Five cards is the maximum that a player can hold, and a player's fifth card, even if it is bought, is always dealt face upwards. A player who has bought a card may subsequently twist – but not vice versa. A player who goes bust or who gets a royal pontoon must declare the fact.

When all the punters have been given the cards they have asked for, it is the banker's turn to play. He turns his cards face up and deals himself as many extra cards as he wishes.

Settlement is then made, with the banker paying those players with better hands than he has and collecting from the others. The following table summarises the normal scale of payments. Positive numbers represent payment from banker to punter; negative numbers represent payment from punter to banker. 1, 2 and 3 represent single, double and treble stakes.

Banker's Hand	Bust	16	17	18	19	20	21	Five Card	Pontoon	Royal Pontoon
Bust	−1	+1	+1	+1	+1	+1	+1	+2	+2	+3
16	−1	−1	+1	+1	+1	+1	+1	+2	+2	+3
17	−1	−1	−1	+1	+1	+1	+1	+2	+2	+3
18	−1	−1	−1	−1	+1	+1	+1	+2	+2	+3
19	−1	−1	−1	−1	−1	+1	+1	+2	+2	+3
20	−1	−1	−1	−1	−1	−1	+1	+2	+2	+3
21	−1	−1	−1	−1	−1	−1	−1	+2	+2	+3
Five Card	−2	−2	−2	−2	−2	−2	−2	−1	+2	+3
Pontoon	−2	−2	−2	−2	−2	−2	−2		−1	

A change of banker occurs when a punter wins with a pontoon, the winning punter becoming the next banker. If two or more punters win with a pontoon then the player nearest to the left of the banker becomes the new banker.

An additional rule sometimes encountered is that when a punter is dealt a pair as his first two cards (e.g. two queens) he may 'split' the hand to form two separate hands, staking on each card the amount he originally staked on his first card. The banker then deals a second card face down to each of the two hands, which are thereafter dealt with independently.

Poker

No. of players: 2 to 10
Equipment: Standard pack of 52 cards; betting chips
Complexity: ☆☆☆

Poker originated and developed in the United States in the nineteenth century, and is now one of the most popular games in the world. It is, of course, very much a gambling game – and must be played for real stakes. But a gambling game is not necessarily the same thing as a game of chance – *Poker* is a game requiring a great deal of skill.

There are countless hundreds of variations of the game of *Poker* and it would be impossible to describe them all here. These variations differ, however, only in detail and all share certain basic principles. A player familiar with these basic principles should have no difficulty in playing any of the variations when he comes across them. The basic principles will be described briefly in this section and some of the most common variations will be presented in the following sections.

A standard pack of 52 cards is used for *Poker* – though sometimes with a joker added. The cards rank from ace high to 2 low, but the ace also ranks low in the sequence 5, 4, 3, 2, A. There is no ranking of suits.

When *Poker* is played seriously, counters or betting chips are used rather than cash, and chips of different colours are used to represent different values – e.g. white, 1 unit; red, 5 units; blue, 10 units; yellow, 25 units. It is customary for each player to buy chips from the banker (i.e. the person organising the game). During the game each player must keep all his chips on the table in front of him, in full view of the other players. The chips are then cashed in at the end of the game.

The first dealer of the game is chosen as follows. One player takes the shuffled pack and deals one card face up to each player until a jack is dealt. The player receiving the jack becomes the first dealer for the game itself, and thereafter the deal always passes to the next player to the left.

In all variations of *Poker* the cards are dealt one at a time in a clockwise direction, beginning with the player to the left of the dealer. Usually each player receives five cards, but in some variations each player may receive more than five cards, some face up – 'upcards' – and some face down – 'hole cards' – from which he selects five to be his playing hand. In other variations each player may receive fewer cards and some cards may be dealt in the middle to be shared by all the players. A playing hand, however, always consists of five cards.

The objective of the game is to win the highest possible stakes by betting as to which player holds the best hand. This involves calculation and bluff – the winner is not necessarily the player holding the best hand. All bets are made by players putting chips into a pile – the 'pot' – in the middle of the table, and the pot may be won in one of two ways. The game may proceed to a 'showdown' in which all the players left in the game show their hands – in this case the player with the best hand does win. Alternatively one player may make a bet that none of the other players is willing to meet – that player automatically wins, without having to show his hand, and this is where bluffing plays a part.

The card combinations that determine which player has the best hand are common to all the variations of *Poker*. These combinations are as follows:

(a) **Straight Flush**
    Five cards in sequence in the same suit. An ace may be considered high as in A-K-Q-J-10 (which is known as a Royal Flush) or low as in 5-4-3-2-A. If two or more players have a straight flush, the one with the highest-ranking top card wins – e.g. K-Q-J-10-9 beats J-10-9-8-7. A tie is possible.

(b) **Four of a Kind**
    Four cards of the same rank (the fifth card being unmatched). If two or more players have Four of a Kind, the highest-ranking hand wins – e.g. four aces will beat four kings.

(c) **Full House**
    Three cards of one rank and two of another. As between two hands of this type, the one with the higher-ranking three of a kind wins – e.g. K-K-K-2-2 beats Q-Q-Q-J-J.

(d) **Flush**
    Five cards all of the same suit but not in sequence. As between two hands of this type, the one with the higher ranking top card wins, or if the top cards are equal the one with the higher-ranking second card, and so on – e.g. K-J-10-9-4 beats K-J-10-8-6. A tie is possible.

(e) **Straight**

Five cards in sequence though not all belonging to the same suit. An ace may be either high or low. As between two hands of this type the hand with the higher-ranking top card wins. A tie is possible.

(f) **Three of a Kind**

Three cards of the same rank (the other two cards being unmatched). As between two hands of this type the higher-ranking three of a kind wins – e.g. K-K-K-7-2 beats Q-Q-Q-J-9.

(g) **Two Pairs**

Two cards of one rank and two cards of another rank (the fifth card being unmatched). As between two hands of this type, the hand with the higher-ranking pair wins, or if they are equal the hand with the higher-ranking second pair, or if both pairs are equal the hand with the higher-ranking unmatched card – e.g. J-J-10-10-3 beats J-J-9-9-K and J-J-10-10-4 beats J-J-10-10-3. A tie is possible.

(h) **One Pair**

Any two cards of the same rank (the other three cards being unmatched). As between two such hands, the hand with the higher-ranking pair wins, or if they are equal the hand with the highest-ranking unmatched card – e.g. 10-10-Q-5-3 beats 10-10-9-8-6.

(i) **High Card**

Five unmatched cards. As between two such hands, the hand with the higher-ranking top card wins, or if they are equal the higher-ranking second card, and so on – e.g. A-Q-J-5-4 beats A-Q-10-6-5.

The players may agree to designate certain cards to be 'wild'. A wild card is one that may represent any card that the player holding the wild card wants it to represent. Sometimes a joker (or two jokers) can be added to the pack as wild cards, but more often cards of a particular rank are designated wild cards – usually 2s ('deuces wild'). With wild cards two additional poker hands are possible:

(j) **Five of a Kind**

Four cards of the same rank plus a wild card. This hand beats all the other hands.

(k) **Double Ace Flush**

An ace-high flush plus a wild card. This hand ranks higher than a flush but lower than a full house.

In all variations of the game there will be at least one round of betting (known as a 'betting interval') and usually there will be two or more. The number of betting intervals and when they take place will depend on the variation being played, as will the method for deciding which player starts the betting. After one player has started or 'opened' the betting, each of the other players in turn has three options:

(a)   to drop out (or 'fold' or 'pass'). This means that he discards his hand and takes no further part in the play. A player may drop out at any stage and he forfeits any stakes that he may already have paid into the pot.

(b)   to stay in (or 'call' or 'see'). This means that he pays into the pot just enough to make his total stake exactly equal to the greatest total stake put into the pot by any other player.

(c)   to raise (or 'up' or 'go better'). This means that he puts into the pot enough to stay in plus an extra amount – the 'raise'. The other players, to stay in, must then put into the pot enough to make their total stakes equal to his, or drop out, or raise again

In some *Poker* games, players may be allowed to 'check'. This means that, at the beginning of a betting interval, a player may stay in but bet nothing. But once any player makes a bet, the betting interval continues as normal and checking is not allowed.

A betting interval ends when all the players have checked, or when all but one of the players have dropped out – the player left in being, of course, the winner – or when all the bets have been equalised – that is, all the players have bet the same amount and the turn has come round again to the last player to raise.

For example:

Player	Action	Bet	Total bet
A	checks	0	0
B	checks	0	0
C	checks	0	0
D	opens for 5	5	5
E	stays in	5	5
F	drops out	0	0
A	stays in	5	5
B	raises 5	10	10
C	stays in	10	10
D	stays in	5	10
E	raises 10	15	20

A	drops out	0	5
B	stays in	10	20
C	stays in	10	20
D	drops out	0	10

B, C and E remain in and the betting has been equalised.

There may be various limits placed on the size and number of raises allowed, and these are always agreed before the game begins.

As mentioned previously, there are innumerable variations of *Poker*, but the two main forms are *Draw Poker* and *Stud Poker* (each of which has its own numerous variations).

In *Draw Poker*, a player is dealt all his cards face down and they are not seen by his opponents. There is a betting interval, after which the players left in discard any cards they do not want and are dealt replacements from the pack. This is followed by a second betting interval, after which – if more than one player is left in – there is a showdown and the player with the best hand wins.

In *Stud Poker* a player is dealt some of his cards face up and some face down. Normally the first deal is a face-down card and a face-up card. There follows a betting interval. Then each player is dealt one more card, there is a betting interval, each player is dealt another card, there is a betting interval, and so on. The last betting interval is followed by a showdown if more than one player is left in. Because this form requires more skill than *Draw Poker* and because the pot is usually larger (since there are more betting intervals) this is the form of the game preferred by the really expert gamblers.

Another way in which *Poker* is often played is *Dealer's Choice*, in which the dealer specifies the variation to be played. This may be a standard form, any known variation – or any variation he cares to devise, provided the other players agree.

Draw Poker

No. of players: Preferably 5 to 7
Equipment: Standard pack of 52 cards
Complexity: ✰✰✰

Before each deal an agreed stake – the 'ante', usually a chip of the lowest value – is put into the pot by each player. The dealer then deals five cards to each player, one card at a time and face down.

The deal is followed by the first betting interval, which starts with the player to the left of the dealer. He may either check or bet. If he checks, each player in turn after him has the same two options until one player opens by making the first bet. Thereafter players must call, raise or fold until the betting interval is completed. In one popular form of *Draw Poker* called *Jackpots* a player may not open unless he has a pair of jacks or a better hand.

When the first betting interval is over the draw takes place. The dealer takes the pack of cards left over from the original deal and asks each active player in turn (i.e. each player who is still in the game, not having folded) whether he wants to exchange any of his cards. A player may 'stand pat' – retain all the cards he was dealt originally – or may discard from one to three cards from his hand, placing them face down on the table and receiving the same number dealt from the top of the pack. Three cards is usually the maximum number of cards that may be discarded, but in some variations a player may discard any number, even all five.

The second betting interval then takes place, starting with the player who opened the first.

If, after the second betting interval, all the players but one have folded, that player takes the pot without being required to show his hand. Otherwise there is a showdown and each player 'in on the call' must place all five of his cards face up on the table. The player with the best hand wins the pot.

Spit in the Ocean

No. of players: Preferably 5 to 7
Equipment: Standard pack of 52 cards
Complexity: ✩✩✩

This is normally played in the same way as *Draw Poker* except that each player is dealt four cards and an extra card (the 'spit') is dealt face up in the centre of the table. This card is considered to be the fifth card in every player's hand.

Five Card Stud

No. of players: Preferably 7 to 10
Equipment: Standard pack of 52 cards
Complexity: ✩✩✩

The dealer deals each player a face-down card (the 'hole card') and then deals each player a face-up card. Each player then examines his hole card without revealing it. There is then a betting interval, which begins with the player who has the highest face-up card – if two or more players tie for highest face-up card the betting begins with the first to the left of the dealer. In this first betting interval players may stay, raise or fold, but no checking is permitted.

Each active player is then dealt another face-up card. There is another betting interval, beginning with the player whose face-up cards form the highest-ranking *Poker* combination. In this and the subsequent intervals players may check until one of the players opens the betting. A fourth, and then a fifth card is dealt in the same way, each being followed by a betting interval which is begun by the player whose face-up cards show the best *Poker* combination.

If, at any stage of the game, there is only one active player left, all the others having folded, then that player wins the pot. Otherwise the final betting interval is followed by a showdown, in which each active player turns up his hole card, and the player with the best hand wins the pot.

Six Card Stud

No. of players: 5 to 8
Equipment: Standard pack of 52 cards
Complexity: ✩✩✩

This is very similar to *Five Card Stud* except that each active player is dealt a sixth card, face down, and this is followed by one more betting interval. Each player selects any five of his six cards to be his final hand for the showdown.

Seven Card Stud

No. of players: 5 to 7
Equipment: Standard pack of 52 cards
Complexity: ✩✩✩

This, again, is very similar to *Five Card Stud*. Each player is dealt two face-down cards and one face-up. There is a betting interval. There are three more rounds of dealing in which each active player receives a face-up card, each round being followed by a betting interval. Then each player is dealt another face-down card and there is a final betting interval, followed by the showdown.

Brag

No. of players: 3 or more
Equipment: Standard pack of 52 cards
Complexity: ✩✩✩

The game of *Brag* has a very long history and it is a forerunner of *Poker* with which it shares many general features.

Brag hands, in descending order of value, are as follows:

(a) **Prial**
Three cards of the same rank (e.g. 9-9-9).

(b) **Running Flush**
Three cards of the same suit in sequence (e.g. 10-J-Q of hearts).

(c) **Run**
Any three cards in sequence (e.g. 5-6-7).

(d) **Flush**
Any three cards of the same suit (e.g. 2-6-J of diamonds).

(e) **Pair**
Two cards of the same rank, the third card being unmatched.

(f) **High Card**
Three unmatched cards. As between two hands of this type, the hand containing the highest card wins.

Cards rank from ace high to 2 low, but an ace may also count low in the run A-2-3.

Before the game, limits for stakes and raises are agreed, as in *Poker*. To begin the game the dealer antes (i.e. puts an initial stake into the pot). Three cards are then dealt, one at a time and face down, to each player. Thereafter each player in turn has the option of calling, raising or folding. As in *Poker*, there can be an element of bluff. If all but one of the players fold the remaining player wins automatically, otherwise there is a showdown and the player with the best hand wins.

Suits

Everyone is familiar with the modern card suits of clubs, diamonds, hearts and spades. But in the evolution of the playing card there have been several different packs with various other suits.

The oldest surviving playing cards are believed to be a set in the Bibliothèque Nationale in Paris. These cards, dating from the fourteenth or early fifteenth century, have suits of Chalices, Swords, Coins and Staves which are thought to represent the four classes of mediaeval society – the clergy, the aristocracy, merchants and peasants. These same suits were used for playing cards in Spain and Northern Italy as well as in Southern France. In the north and centre of France the suits were usually Hearts, Pikes, Clover leaves and Paving tiles, while in Germany the usual suits were Hearts, Acorns, Bells and Leaves.

Incidentally, the 'spades' on our modern packs are not digging implements but spears (*spade* being Italian for spears).

5   **BOARD GAMES**

Horseshoe
Madelinette
Nine Holes
Achi
Four Field Kono
Alquerque
Nine Men's Morris
Mu-Torere
Hex
Fox and Geese (1)
Fox and Geese (2)
Fox and Geese (3)
Wolf and Goats
Halma
Chinese Checkers
Backgammon
Dutch Backgammon
Plakato
Gioul
Acey Deucey
Russian Backgammon
Wari
Draughts
Losing Draughts
Diagonal Draughts (1)
Diagonal Draughts (2)
Italian Draughts
Spanish Draughts
German Draughts
Russian Draughts
Polish Draughts
Canadian Draughts
Turkish Draughts
Lasca
Reversi
Chess

Losing Chess
Randomised Chess
Refusal Chess
Pocket Knight Chess
Two Move Chess
Progressive Chess
Kriegspiel
Go
Go-Moku

Horseshoe

No. of players: 2
Equipment: Board and 4 counters
Complexity: ✱

Horseshoe is a very simple game which is played in many parts of the world (in China it is known as Pong Hau K'i). It is played on a board which may easily be drawn on a piece of paper, and each player starts with two counters positioned as shown in the illustration. For an impromptu game coins serve very well as counters, with one player's coins placed heads up and other player's placed tails up.

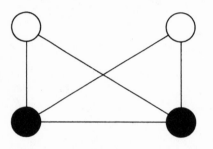

The first player starts by moving one of his counters along a line to the empty point in the centre. The second player then moves one of his counters along a line to the new vacant point. The play continues alternately, each player in turn moving one of his counters along a line to the vacant point. The objective is to block one's opponent so that he cannot move either of his counters.

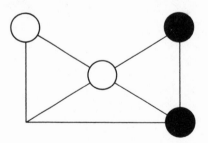

White can now move into a winning position

Madelinette

No. of players: 2
Equipment: Board and 6 counters
Complexity: ✭✩

Madelinette is played in exactly the same way as *Horseshoe*, and the objective is the same – to block the counters of one's opponent so that they cannot be moved. The game is slightly more challenging than *Horseshoe* since the board contains more lines, and each player starts the game with three counters which are positioned as shown in the diagram.

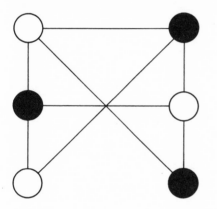

Nine Holes

No. of players: 2
Equipment: Board and 6 counters
Complexity: ✭✭

Nine Holes is played on a simple board which looks like this:

The counters are played on the points formed where the lines intersect. Each player starts with three counters, and they take it in turn to place a counter on any one of the nine points that is vacant, until all six counters are on the board. Then each player in turn may move one of his counters to an adjacent empty point. The first player to get his three counters in a straight line is the winner.

Achi

No. of players: 2
Equipment: Board and 8 counters
Complexity: ☆☆

Achi, a game which is played by Ghanaian schoolchildren, is very similar to *Nine Holes*, but each player starts with four counters and the board has diagonal lines added.

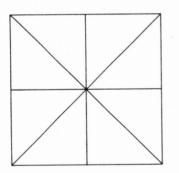

The players take it in turn to place one of their counters on an empty point. When the eight counters are on the board, each player in turn may move one of his counters along a line to an empty point in an attempt to get three counters in a row. The first player to do so is the winner.

Four Field Kono

No. of players: 2
Equipment: Board and 16 counters
Complexity: ★★

Each player starts with eight counters, set out on the board as shown in the illustration.

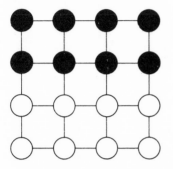

The object of the game is to capture all the counters of one's opponent or to block them so that they cannot move. The players take it in turn to move. To capture one of the opponent's counters, a counter has to jump over another counter of the same colour as itself and land directly on the opponent's counter. The captured counter is then removed from the board. When such a capturing move is not possible, a counter may only be moved along one of the lines one point at a time.

Alquerque

No. of players: 2
Equipment: Board and 24 pieces
Complexity: ★★

Alquerque is a very old game which was a forerunner of the game of *Draughts*. Each player starts the game with twelve pieces which are set out on the board like this:

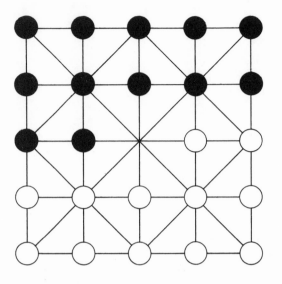

The players have alternate moves. A piece may be moved along a line in any direction to any adjacent point that is empty, or if an adjacent point is occupied by an enemy piece and the point beyond it is empty then the enemy piece may be captured by being jumped over and removed from the board. Two or more captures may be made in this way in one move, changes of direction being permitted. A player who may make a capture must do so, and he must capture all the pieces possible in that move, otherwise he is 'huffed' and the offending piece is removed from the board.

The game is won by capturing all the opponent's pieces.

Nine Men's Morris

No. of players: 2
Equipment: Board and 18 counters
Complexity: ★★

Nine Men's Morris is played on a board that looks like this:

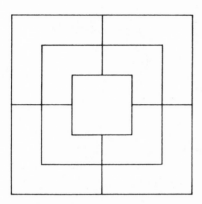

At the start of the game each player has nine pieces or 'men'. Each player in turn places one of his men on any vacant point on the board. The objective is to get three men in a row along any line, thus forming a 'mill'–and to prevent one's opponent from doing so. Each time a player forms a mill he is able to remove from the board any one of his opponent's men that he chooses–but not one which forms part of a mill unless there are none other available. After both players have placed all their men on the board they continue playing alternately, now moving one man at a time along a line to any adjacent point that is empty in an attempt to form further mills.

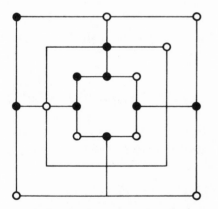

As before, forming a mill entitles a player to remove one of his opponent's men from the board.

The game is won when one's opponent is left with only two men or when his men are blocked so that they cannot be moved.

Mu-Torere

No. of players: 2
Equipment: Board and 8 counters
Complexity: ☆☆

Mu-Torere is a game from New Zealand – it is the only known board game of Maori origin. The board consists of an eight-pointed star with a circle in the middle. The eight points are known as the 'kewai' and the circle in the middle is called the 'putahi'. Each player starts with four counters, placed on four adjacent kewai.

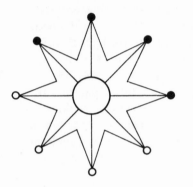

The players move alternately, with Black having the first move. There are three types of move:

(a) A counter may be moved from one of the kewai to the putahi, but only if there is one of the opponent's counters on one (or both) of the kewai on either side of it.
(b) A counter may be moved from the putahi to any of the kewai.
(c) A counter may be moved from any of the kewai to the next on either side.

All of the moves are, of course, subject to the rule that the point being moved to must be unoccupied – only one counter is allowed on each point.

The objective of the game is the block one's opponent so that he cannot move, and the first player to succeed in this objective is the winner.

The scope for strategy might seem rather limited – a player's move is often forced and he has at other times a choice of only two moves – yet this is still quite a challenging and fascinating game.

Hex

No. of players: 2
Equipment: Board and 122 counters
Complexity: ✩✩

The game of *Hex* was invented in the 1940s by the Danish mathematician, inventor and poet, Piet Hein. It is a game which is very simple in principle but which is really intriguing.

The board is diamond-shaped and is made up of adjoining hexagons. The standard board has eleven hexagons along each edge, but boards with a greater or lesser number of hexagons may be used. The two opposite sides of the board belong to Black and the other two belong to White. The four corner hexagons belong to both players.

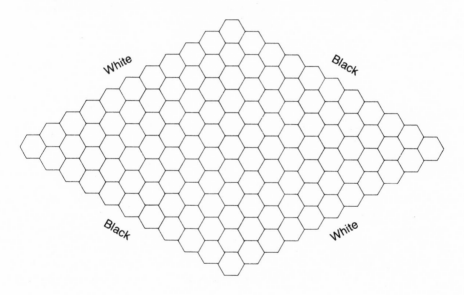

Two sets of counters are required, one black and one white. Using the standard board, the highest number of counters a player will need is 61 but usually he will not need to use all of them.

The game begins with the board completely empty, and the players take turns to place one of their counters in any vacant hexagon, with Black playing first. The objective for each player is to form a continuous line of counters connecting his two sides. The winning line does not have to be straight – provided it has no gaps it may twist and turn and may be any length.

Although the game is simple in principle, analysis of strategy can be quite complex. For example, though it is clear that Black, having the first move, has an advantage – especially if he places his first counter in the centre hexagon – no one has yet been able to work out how he should use this advantage to ensure a win. Nevertheless some players insist that Black should be handicapped by not being allowed to place his first counter in the centre hexagon.

Instead of a board composed of hexagons, a board may be used which is composed of equilateral triangles. The counters are then placed on the intersections – not in the spaces. This is the exact equivalent of the original game. The advantage is that it is much simpler to produce a home-made board of this type. Here is an illustration of such a board, showing the final position in a game that has been won by Black.

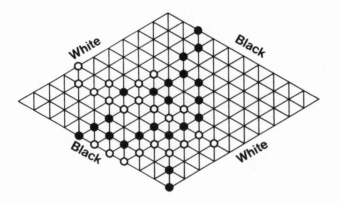

Fox and Geese (1)

No. of players: 2
Equipment: Board and 14 pieces
Complexity: ☆☆

The game of *Fox and Geese* originated in Scandinavia in the Viking era. Since then it has spread all over the world and there are countless variations. The distinctive features of the game in all its variations are that (unlike most other board games) the two players have unequal numbers of pieces, with different powers of movement, and they have different objectives.

The most common variation today is played on a board like the one illustrated here. One player has thirteen pieces – the 'Geese' – and the other player has one piece – the 'Fox'. At the beginning of the game the pieces are placed on the board like this:

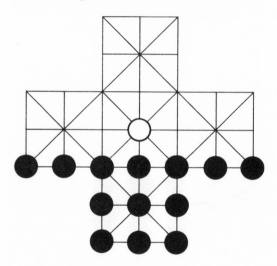

The players take it in turn to move, with the Fox having the first move. Fox and Geese move in the same way – one step in any direction along a line to an adjacent empty point. But the Fox may also capture Geese – if a Goose is on the next point to the Fox and the point immediately beyond is empty, the Fox may jump over the Goose and remove it from the board. The Fox may make several such jumps in one move, capturing a Goose with each jump. The Geese, however, are not allowed to jump over the Fox or over one another.

The Geese win the game if – by surrounding him or forcing him into a corner – they block the Fox so that he cannot move. The Fox wins the game if he captures so many Geese that there are not enough of them left to block him.

Fox and Geese (2)

No. of players: 2
Equipment: Board and 13 pieces
Complexity: ✰✰

A slightly different (and earlier) variation of the game of *Fox and Geese* is played on a board resembling that for the previous game, but without the diagonals. At the beginning of the game the Fox and twelve Geese are placed on the board as illustrated.

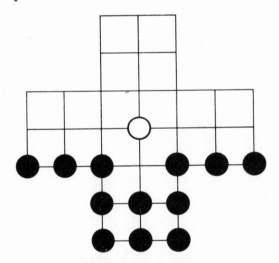

The Fox may move one step forwards, backwards or sideways to an empty point. He may also capture a Goose by jumping over it on to an empty square immediately beyond. The Geese may move one step forwards or sideways only – they are not allowed to move backwards. The Geese win the game if they block the Fox so that he cannot move. The Fox wins if he can break through the Geese to the bottom end of the board – where, of course, the Geese may not pursue him.

Fox and Geese (3)

No. of players: 2
Equipment: Board and 5 pieces
Complexity: ★★

This version of the game is played on an ordinary checkerboard as used for *Chess* or *Draughts*. At the beginning of the game the four Geese are placed on the black squares at one end of the board. The player with the Fox positions him on any other black square that he might choose.

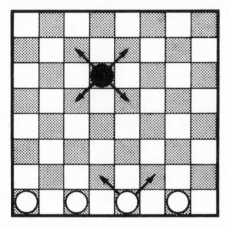

The players move alternately. The Geese may only move diagonally forwards, one square at a time, keeping to the black squares. The Fox also moves only one square at a time, on the black squares, but he may move diagonally forwards or diagonally backwards. There is no jumping and capturing in this version of the game. The Geese win if they block the Fox so that he cannot move. The Fox wins if he can break through the line of Geese to the bottom end of the board.

Wolf and Goats

No. of players: 2
Equipment: Board and 13 pieces
Complexity: ✩✩

Don't let the name fool you – *Wolf and Goats* is really yet another variation of *Fox and Geese* masquerading (like a wolf in sheep's clothing?) under a change of style.

An ordinary checkerboard is used for the game. The twelve Goats are initially placed on the black squares of the first three rows, and the Wolf is placed on either of the black corner squares at the other end of the board.

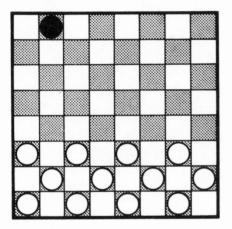

The Goats may move diagonally forwards one square at a time. The Wolf may move diagonally forwards or backwards and may capture Goats by jumping over them. The aim of the Goats is to block the Wolf so that he cannot move, while the Wolf aims to break through them, wreaking havoc on the way, to the other end of the board.

Halma

No. of players: 2 or 4
Equipment: Board and 64 pieces
Complexity: ★★★

Halma was invented in the 1880s. It is played on a chequered board with sixteen squares on each side. Each corner has a section bounded with heavy lines, containing thirteen squares. Two opposite corners have an additional heavy line bounding an area with nineteen squares. These areas are the starting and finishing positions.

There are four sets of pieces, each set being of a different colour. Two sets contain 13 pieces and the other two sets contain 19 pieces.

If there are four players, each starts with thirteen pieces, placed in the marked-off section in his corner of the board. If there are two players, each starts with nineteen pieces in one of the corners with the larger marked-off sections. The aim is to transfer one's pieces to the corner which is diagonally opposite, and the first player to do so is the winner.

Each player in turn is allowed to move one of his pieces. There are two types of move – steps and hops. A piece may step one square in any direction to a vacant square. Alternatively, a piece may hop over any other piece (whether or not it is of the same colour) if there is a vacant square immediately beyond it. In one move a piece may make several such hops, provided that each hop is over one piece into a vacant square. Steps and hop may not be combined in one move. There is no capturing and no pieces are removed from the board.

Successful play consists of forming 'ladders', thus providing a series of hops for one's own pieces to take them a good distance across the board in one move – and blocking ladders formed by one's opponents.

Chinese Checkers

No. of players: 2 to 6
Equipment: Board and 90 pieces
Complexity: ✩✩✩

Chinese Checkers (which is neither Chinese nor Checkers) is a modern game based on the same principles as *Halma*.

The board is in the form of a six-pointed star, each point being of a different colour. The pieces are usually plastic pegs which fit into holes

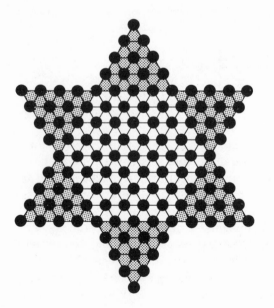

on the board, and there are six sets of 15 pieces – each set being of the same colour as one of the points of the star.

If there are two players, each starts with 15 pieces in the appropriately coloured point. If there are more than two players, each player starts with 10 pieces. The aim is to transfer all one's pieces to the opposite point, the first player to do so being the winner. The moves consist of steps and hops as in *Halma*.

Backgammon

No. of players: 2
Equipment: Board and 30 men; four dice; doubling die (optional)
Complexity: ✩✩✩

Backgammon is one of the great games of the world. It is also claimed sometimes that it is one of the oldest games in the world and that its history may be traced back thousands of years – but this is not strictly true. *Backgammon*, as we know it, first appeared in England in the seventeenth century (though the use of the doubling die was not introduced until the 1920s, in the USA). It had some features in common with a variety of earlier games, all of which shared the same name of *Tables*, and which had reached Europe from the Middle East in the eleventh century. Earlier games – played by the Romans or by the ancient Egyptians – which are claimed to be the ancestors of *Backgammon* had little in common with the game that we know apart from the fact that they were race games using counters and dice.

Although backgammon does not have the depth and complexity of *Chess* or *Go*, it makes up for this in being exciting and fast-moving. It is a paradox that although the moves in *Backgammon* are dependent on the throw of the dice it is a game of almost pure skill. This is because, although the outcome of a single game may to some extent be determined by luck, over a number of games the element of luck will 'cancel out', so to speak, and the more skilful player will triumph.

Each player has fifteen men, and the players are conventionally called Black and White (though their sets of men may be any two contrasting colours). Each player also has two dice.

The board is divided into four sections, known as 'tables'. Each table contains six long, tapering points which are coloured alternately red and white. There is no particular significance to this alternate colouring – it merely serves as an aid to visualising moves. The two inner tables are separated from the two outer tables by a strip which is known as the 'bar'.

Backgammon is a race game and the objective is to be the first player to move all one's men round the board into one's inner table and from there to remove them from the board. The diagram below shows how the men are set out on the board at the beginning of the game. The points are numbered here for reference only – they are not normally printed on the board.

White's outer table   White's inner table

W12 W11 W10 W9 W8 W7   W6 W5 W4 W3 W2 W1

B12 B11 B10 B9 B8 B7   B6 B5 B4 B3 B2 B1

Black's outer table   Black's inner table

White moves in this direction
Black moves in this direction

To decide who moves first, each player rolls one of his dice. If both players throw the same number they roll again until two different numbers are thrown. The player throwing the higher number has the first move, and he moves his men according to the numbers on the two dice. For example, if White throws a 6 and Black throws a 1, then White has the first move and his throw is considered to be 6-1. After that the players move alternately, each player rolling his own two dice to determine his move. As a matter of etiquette, each player, after throwing, lets his dice stand until the other player has thrown his dice and made his move.

Each player advances his men a number of points – towards his own inner table – according to the numbers thrown with the dice. The numbers shown by the two dice are not added together but are taken separately. For example, if a player throws a 6-1 he may advance one man six points and advance another man one point, or he may advance one man six points and then advance the same man another one point (or advance the same man one point and then six points).

If a player can use only the number shown by one of his dice (because of closed points, as described further on) then the other numbered is disregarded. If it is possible for him to use one number or the other but not both, then he must use the higher number.

When a double is thrown, a player moves twice the values shown. For example, a double 6 gives a player four moves of six points each.

If a point is unoccupied it is said to be 'open' and either player may play a piece on to that point. If a player has two or more men on a point that point is said to be 'made' or 'closed'. A player may play further men on to a point that he has made but he may not play any pieces on to a point that has been made by his opponent.

If a point is occupied by a single man that man is known as a 'blot'. A player may play one of his men on to a point occupied by an enemy blot. The blot is then said to be 'hit' – it is removed from the point and placed on the bar.

A player who has a man on the bar must 'enter' it into the opponent's inner table by throwing a number corresponding to an open point or a blot. While he has a man on the bar he may not move any other of his men. If, for example, White has a man on the bar and he throws a 2-3 and the points B2 and B3 have been made by Black then White's throw is void and he may not move. But if Black had a blot on B2, White could enter on that point, hitting the Black blot and sending it to the bar, and he could then use the 3 to move the same man or another man. Both players may have any number of men on the bar at the same time.

When a player has moved all his men into his own inner table – but not before – he may begin 'bearing off' (that is, removing his men from the board). A man may be borne off each point indicated by the number on either of the dice. For example, if White throws a 4-2 he may bear off a man from W4 and another from W2. He may, alternatively, use all or part of the throw to move men inside his inner table. On a throw of 4-4, for example, White might move a man from W6 to W2, move another from W5 to W1 and bear off two men from W4.

It is not always necessary to throw the exact number to bear off a piece from a point. If a number is thrown that is higher than any point on which the player has men left, then he may bear off from the highest occupied point. For example, if Black is left with men only on the points B4, B2 and B1 and he throws a 6-2 he may bear off from B4 and B2.

If a player has a blot that is hit while he is bearing off, that man must be re-entered from the bar into his opponent's inner table and be moved round the board into his own inner table before he can continue bearing off.

The winner is the first player to bear off all his men. If the loser has borne off one or more of his men he loses a single game. If he has not borne off any men he loses a 'gammon' or double game. If he has not borne off any men and in addition he has one or more men left on the bar or in the winner's inner table then he loses a 'backgammon' or triple game.

The doubling die is a modern introduction to increase further the value of a game and is used when the game is played for stakes. Its faces show the numbers 2, 4, 8, 16, 32 and 64. Either player, at any stage in the game when it is his turn to play, and if he thinks that he has an advantageous position, may propose the first double by saying 'I double'. His opponent then has the option of declining the double – thereby conceding the game and paying the original stake – or accepting the double, in which case the game proceeds for double stakes. If he accepts the double the doubling die is placed, with the 2 uppermost, at his side of the board and he is said to be in control of the die. As long as he has control of the doubling die his opponent may not double again, but he may redouble if the balance of the game shifts (as it often does) and he thinks that he now has the better chance of winning. If the redouble is accepted the die is turned to show the 4 and passed to the first player, otherwise the game is conceded by the first player who pays double stakes. The doubling die may be passed back and forth in this way several times in the course of the game, each player alternately having the right to double.

The result of the game – whether it is a single win, gammon or backgammon – acts as a multiplier of the value of the doubling die. Thus if the basic stake is £100, the doubling die shows 32 and you win a backgammon, your opponent has to hand over £9600. Though many players play without using the doubling die there is no doubt that its use adds extra zest to the game.

Some players also allow automatic doubling of the stake each time the same number is thrown by both players at the start of the game when throwing for first play. The number of automatic doubles is usually limited by agreement to one or two.

Dutch Backgammon

No. of players: 2
Equipment: Board and 30 men; four dice
Complexity: ★★☆

Dutch Backgammon is the same as the standard game, except for the following differences:

(a)   At the start of the game all the men are placed on the bar. A player must enter all 15 of his men before making any other move.

(b)   A player is not allowed to hit a blot until he has moved at least one man around the board into his own inner table.

Plakato

No of players: 2
Equipment: Board and 30 men; four dice
Complexity: ★★☆

Plakato is a form of *Backgammon* which is very popular in Greece. It is played in the same way as *Backgammon* except for the following differences:

(a)   At the start of the game each player has all his men positioned on the number 1 point in his opponent's inner table.

(b)   There is no bearing off. Instead, each player has to move all his men right round the board to his own number 1 point.

(c)   Blots are not hit and sent to the bar. Instead, they are blocked, and may not be moved while one of the opponent's men is on the same point.

Gioul

No. of players: 2
Equipment: Board and 30 men; four dice
Complexity: ☆☆☆

Gioul is another form of *Backgammon*, that is popular in the Middle East. It differs from *Backgammon* in the following respects:

(a) At the start of the game each player has all his men positioned on the number 1 point in his opponent's inner table.
(b) Blots are not hit and sent to the bar. Instead, they are blocked, and may not be moved while one of the opponent's men is on the same point.
(c) When a double is thrown, a player is allowed to move according to that double – and then for each subsequent double up to double 6. For example, if he throws a double 3, he has moves for double 3, double 4, double 5 and double 6.
(d) If a player is unable to use any of the moves resulting from the throw of a double, these moves may be claimed by his opponent.

Acey Deucey

No. of players: 2
Equipment: Board and 30 men; four dice
Complexity: ☆☆☆

Acey Deucey is a variant of *Backgammon* that is popular in the US Navy. It differs from the standard game in the following respects:
(a) The game starts with no men on the board.
(b) The players throw single dice, as usual, to decide who will play first, but the first player then throws both his dice for his first throw.
(c) Throws may be used to enter additional men on to the board or to move those already entered. Blots are hit and sent to the bar in the normal manner. Men may be moved before all 15 men have been placed on the board but – as in the normal game – may not be moved while a man that has been hit remains on the bar.

(d) A throw of 1-2 (Acey Deucey) has special status. Having moved a 1 and a 2, the player throwing 1-2 may then name any double he chooses and move his men accordingly. He then has an extra turn and is allowed to throw both dice again. However, if he cannot use any part of the throw, he forfeits the rest. If, for example, he can use the 1 but not the 2, he forgoes the double and the extra throw.

(e) There are a number of sub-variations (no pun intended – these apply on battleships and cruisers as well as on submarines) concerning doubles and scoring. Some allow automatic doubles every time a 1-2 is thrown. Some replace the standard doubling and tripling for gammon and backgammon by a system whereby the loser pays one unit of the stake for each man left on the board or for the number of points needed to bear it off.

Russian Backgammon

No. of players: 2
Equipment: Board and 30 men; four dice
Complexity: ★★★

Whereas in all other variations of *Backgammon* the players move their men in opposite directions around the board, in *Russian Backgammon* (owing, no doubt, to their collectivist philosophy) both players move in the same direction.

The game starts with no men on the board. Both players enter their men on to the same inner table, and once a player has entered two men he may use his throws to enter further men or to move those already on the board.

Blots may be hit and must be re-entered before any other man may be moved, as in the standard game.

When a double is thrown a player moves as normal according to that double but then moves also according to the complement of that double – the complement of a number being its difference from 7. For example, a player throwing a double 2 may move four 2s and then four 5s – but he may use the 5s only if he can use all four 2s. Provided that he can use all the eight moves he has an extra turn and is allowed to throw both dice again.

Wari

No. of players: 2
Equipment: Board and 48 counters
Complexity: ☆☆☆

Wari is one of a group of basically similar games known as *Mancala*
games, which are played all over Asia and Africa and also in America
where they were introduced by slaves from Africa.

The 'board' may be a wooden dish with two rows of six shallow
depressions carved in it, or two similar rows of depressions scooped out
of the earth, or two rows of six saucers, or (more simply) a piece of paper
or card with two rows of six 'holes' drawn on it. The 'counters', to be
authentic, should be seeds or small stones, but coins, buttons or any
other small objects may be used.

At the start of the game four counters are placed in each hole.

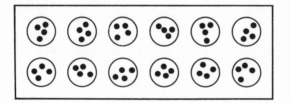

The players sit on either side of the board, and the six holes nearest
to each player form his row. The first player begins by picking up the
four counters from any hole in his row and 'sowing' them one by one, in
an anti-clockwise direction, in the next four holes. For example:

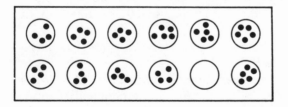

The other player then takes the counters from any hole in his row
and sows them one by one in an anti-clockwise direction. And so the
game continues, each player in turn sowing the counters from any one of
the holes in his row.

If in any player's turn the last counter to be sown goes into one of the opponent's holes and that hole now contains either two or three counters, then he wins all the counters in that hole, and he removes them from the board. He also wins the counters in any adjacent holes that contain either two or three counters.

If, after a while, a hole contains twelve or more counters then a sowing from that hole will take more than one complete circuit of the board. When this happens, the original hole from which the twelve or more counters were taken is left empty and it stays empty for the remainder of the game.

If a player has no counters left in his row when it is his turn then the game is over. However, when an opponent's row is empty a player must, if possible, making a sowing which will leave at least one counter in his opponent's row. If he cannot do so the game is finished and he takes all the counters left on the board and adds them to those he has already won.

The game may also end by agreement if there are only a few counters left on the board and they are just being moved round the board with neither player being able to win any more counters. In that case each players takes the counters from his own row and adds them to the counters he has already won.

Each player then counts the number of counters he has won, and the player with the greatest number is the winner.

Draughts

No. of players: 2
Equipment: Board and 24 pieces
Complexity: ★★☆

Draughts, or *Checkers* as it is known in America, is a game of skill for two players. There are a large number of national variations, of which the game as played in Britain and America is but one. For obvious reasons, however, we will consider the British and American game as the standard version, and the other variations will be described later in this chapter in terms of their differences from this game.

Draughts is played on a square board which is divided into 64 smaller squares. The squares are alternately black and white. The pieces or 'men' are thick flat discs, normally made of wood. One player has twelve white pieces, and the other has twelve black pieces. (Actually the squares and the pieces may be of any light and dark colours – red and white or green and buff, for example – but whatever the actual colours they are always referred to as 'black' and 'white').

The player with the black pieces always has the first move. To determine which player should have the black pieces the usual procedure is for one player to pick up a black piece and a white piece and, holding his hands under the table or behind his back, to conceal a piece in each hand. He then holds out his fists to the other player, who chooses one or the other. The colour of the piece in the fist he chooses determines the colour of the pieces he will play with.

At the start of the game the board is positioned so that each player has a black square at his left-hand corner, and each player's pieces are set out on the black squares of the three rows nearest to him.

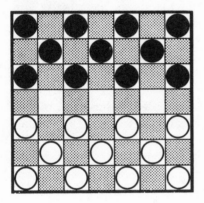

The player with the black pieces makes the first move and thereafter the players move alternately. The objective is to remove all the opponent's pieces from the board by capturing them, or to block them so that they cannot be moved.

The pieces are moved only on the black squares, so they must move diagonally, and they may be moved only to an empty square.

When not capturing an opposing piece, a piece can move only one square at a time. A capture consists of a piece jumping over an opposing piece on an adjoining square into an empty square beyond. The piece that is captured is then removed from the board. Several pieces may be captured in this way in one move, so long as each piece that is captured has an empty square beyond it.

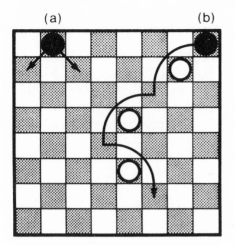

(a) Non-capturing move
(b) Capturing move

Initially the pieces may only be moved forwards – that is, away from the player making the move. However, when a piece reaches one of the four squares at the far edge of the board it is promoted to a 'king'. It may then move either forwards or backwards. A king is recognised by being 'crowned' – that is, it has another piece of the same colour (from among those previously captured and removed from the board) placed on top of it to form a sort of double-decker piece. A player's turn always ends when a piece is crowned, even though the newly-made king may then be in a position to capture opposing pieces.

If a player can make a capturing move then he must do so, even if it is to his disadvantage. Where he has a choice of moves which will capture opposing pieces – a move which will capture two pieces, for example, or another which will capture three pieces – then he may choose which move to take, but he must make all the captures that are possible on that move.

If a player fails to capture a piece when he could do so, then his opponent has three options before making his own move:

(a) He can accept the offending move and do nothing.
(b) He can insist that the move be taken back and replayed to make the possible capture.
(c) He can 'huff' the other player by removing from the board the piece which made the offending move.

As stated previously, a game is won by capturing all the opponent's pieces or by blocking them so that they cannot move. A tied game results when neither player is able to force a win. If one player is in a stronger position he may be required to win the game within his next 40 moves or else be able to demonstrate a clear advantage over his opponent. If he fails to do so the game is declared a draw.

There are a number of other rules which are mainly matters of etiquette:

(a) **Time Limits**

A play is only allowed five minutes in which to make a move. If he takes longer than this the other player (or the referee, in tournament play) may call 'Time'. If the player does not complete his move within one minute after that he loses the game.

(b) **Adjusting Pieces on the Board**

If a player wishes to adjust any pieces properly on the squares he must announce his intention before doing so. The first time a player breaks this rule he may be cautioned, and if he does it again he forfeits the game.

(c) **Touch and Move**

If a player, when it is his turn to move, touches one of his pieces then he must move that piece if it can make a legal move. If it cannot make a legal move, the same penalties apply as for the previous rule.

(d) **False and Improper Moves**

A player making any false or improper move immediately forfeits the game. If a piece is moved so that any part of it goes over one of the corners of the square on which it is positioned then the move must be completed in that direction – playing it in any other direction constitutes an improper move.

Although *Draughts*, in contast to *Chess*, might be regarded by very many people as literally 'child's play', there are many players who take it very seriously indeed and who consider it to be the equal of *Chess* (if not superior) in terms of skill and complexity. The openings, traps and combinations, the end-game, general strategy and tactics are all analysed in great detail. *Draughts* problems are composed and studied in the same way as *Chess* problems. National and International tournaments are organised, as well as National and World Championships.

Losing Draughts

No. of players: 2
Equipment: Board and 24 pieces.
Complexity: ★★☆

As the name might lead you to expect, in *Losing Draughts* the winner is
the first player to get rid of all his pieces. The rules are the same as those
for the normal game of *Draughts* except that huffing is not allowed. A
player must always capture all the pieces that he possibly can. If he fails
to do so, his opponent may insist that he take the move back and play it
again to capture the pieces that he missed.

Diagonal Draughts (1)

No. of players: 2
Equipment: Board and 24 pieces
Complexity: ★★☆

This is an interesting and enjoyable variation of *Draughts*. The rules are
almost exactly the same as for the standard game. The only differences
are the way the pieces are positioned at the start of the game – they are
lined up across the corners as shown in the diagram – and the squares on
which kings are made are the four squares nearest to the opponent's
corner of the board.

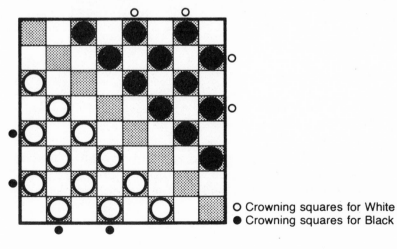

○ Crowning squares for White
● Crowning squares for Black

Diagonal Draughts (2)

No. of players: 2
Equipment: Board and 18 pieces
Complexity: ✫✫✫

This is very similar to the previous game, except that each player starts with only nine pieces, which are set out as shown in the diagram. The squares on which kings are made are the three squares nearest to the opponent's corner.

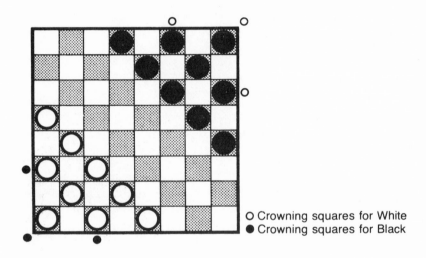

O Crowning squares for White
● Crowning squares for Black

Italian Draughts

No. of players: 2
Equipment: Board and 24 pieces
Complexity: ✫✫✫

Italian Draughts is similar to the standard game of *Draughts* played in Britain and America, except that the board is usually positioned so that each player has a white square at his left-hand corner, and the rules relating to captures are rather different.

(a) A king may not be captured by an uncrowned piece.

(b) A player who is able to make a capturing move must do so.

(c) If a player has a choice of capturing moves he must choose the move which captures the greatest number of pieces. If a king may capture either another king or an uncrowned piece, then it must capture the other king.

Spanish Draughts

No. of players: 2
Equipment: Board and 24 pieces
Complexity: ★★☆

Spanish Draughts is in most respects similar to *Italian Draughts*. The difference is that kings are much more powerful, having what is known as the 'long move'. This means that a king may be moved any number of squares along a diagonal, as long as it is unobstructed (in much the same way as a Bishop moves in *Chess*).

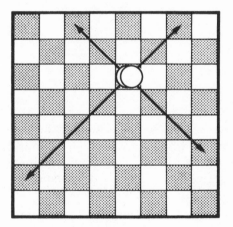

A king may capture an opposing piece anywhere on the same diagonal provided that there are no pieces in between and there are one or more empty squares immediately beyond it. The jump may end in any of the empty squares beyond the captured piece. If the king, having made a capture, can then capture another piece on a different diagonal he must do so. The move continues until the king has captured all the pieces that it can. Only when the move is complete are the captured pieces removed from the board, but they may not be jumped over more than once.

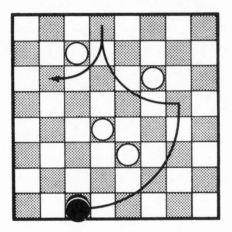

German Draughts

No. of players: 2
Equipment: Board and 24 pieces
Complexity: ☆☆☆

German Draughts is played in the same way as *Spanish Draughts* but has two additional features. First, in *German Draughts*, although ordinary (uncrowned) pieces may only move forwards when not capturing, they may make capturing moves either forwards or backwards. Second, a piece may only be crowned if its move *ends* when it reaches the last row on the far side of the board. If its move takes it to the last row and it is then in a position to capture other pieces by jumping backwards in the same move, it must do so. It does not become a king on that move.

Russian Draughts

No. of players: 2
Equipment: Board and 24 pieces
Complexity ★★☆

Russian Draughts is very similar to *German Draughts*, i.e. when a piece reaches the last row at the far side of the board it must jump backwards to capture other pieces, if it may do so. In *Russian Draughts*, however, it does become a king on that move. The other difference is that when a player has a choice of capturing moves there is no compulsion to make the move that captures the highest number of pieces.

Polish Draughts

No. of players: 2
Equipment: Board and 40 pieces
Complexity: ★★☆

Polish Draughts is played with the same rules as *German Draughts*. It is, however, played on a larger board consisting of 100 squares. Each player starts the game with 20 pieces set out on the first four rows.

Canadian Draughts

No. of players: 2
Equipment: Board and 60 pieces
Complexity: ★★☆

Canadian Draughts is another game that is played with the same rules as *German Draughts*. It is played on an even larger board consisting of 144 squares, and each player starts the game with 30 pieces set out on the first five rows.

Turkish Draughts

No. of players: 2
Equipment: Board and 32 pieces
Complexity: ★★★

Turkish Draughts is played on a standard chess board. Each player starts the game with 16 pieces which are set out on *both* black *and* white squares of each player's *second* and *third* rows. The distinctive features of Turkish Draughts are that the pieces move forwards or sideways but not diagonally and thus they move on both black and white squares.

A piece becomes a king when it reaches the last row at the far end of the board. It may then move any number of squares forwards, backwards or sideways.

The method by which a king captures other pieces is similar to that in *Spanish Draughts* except, of course, that the jumps are not diagonal. The captured pieces are removed from the board immediately after each capture – they are not left on the board until the end of the move, and thus do not block further captures.

A player who is able to make a capturing move must do so. If he has a choice of capturing moves, he must choose the move that captures the greatest number of pieces.

The game is won by capturing all the opponent's pieces or by blocking them so that they cannot be moved. The game is also won by a player with a king if his opponent is left with just a single uncrowned piece.

Lasca

No. of players: 2
Equipment: Board and 22 pieces
Complexity: ★★

Lasca was invented by Edward Lasker, an American chess master. It is played on a square board which is divided into 49 smaller squares, alternately black and white, with a white square in each corner. Play is on the white squares only.

One player has eleven white pieces and the other player has eleven black pieces. The pieces are flat discs, like *Draughts* pieces – but each piece is marked with a spot on one side. When the unmarked side is uppermost the piece is known as a 'soldier'. When the piece is turned over so that the marked side is uppermost the piece is known as an 'officer'.

At the beginning of the game each player sets up his pieces on the white squares of the three rows nearest to him. All the pieces start as soldiers.

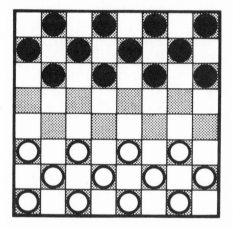

White has the first move and after that the players move alternately.

The manner in which the pieces move and capture other pieces is similar to the manner in which they move and capture in *Draughts*. The distinctive features of *Lasca*, however, are 'columns' and 'guides'. A column may be a single piece or it may be a pile of pieces, one on top of another. The top piece of the column is the guide. The colour of the guide determines to which player the column belongs. The rank of the guide – soldier or officer – determines the way in which the column moves.

At the beginning the the game each piece is a single column with a soldier as a guide. A column guided by a soldier may move diagonally forward, one square at a time (just like an ordinary piece in *Draughts*). When the column reaches the far end of the board, the guide is turned over to become an officer. A column guided by an officer may move one square in any direction (just like a king in *Draughts*).

Pieces are captured by one column jumping over an enemy column into an empty square beyond (just like a capture in *Draughts*). In *Lasca*, however, no pieces are removed from the board, and only the guide is captured, not the whole column. The captured guide is added to the bottom of the column that captured it.

For example, suppose a column of two white pieces jumps over a column of two black pieces. The guide of the black column is added to the bottom of the white column. The other black piece that was on the bottom of its column remains on its original square. If the white column in this example was guided by an officer then it could jump back over the remaining black piece, adding it to the bottom of its column and ending up on its original square.

A player who is in a position to capture an enemy piece must do so, and if he can capture several enemy pieces one after the other in the same move, he must capture all of them. If he has a choice of capturing moves he can choose which one he wants to take. A move ends when no more pieces can be captured or when a soldier reaches the far end of the board and becomes an officer.

The objective of the game is to make it impossible for one's opponent to move. This is achieved either by having all the columns guided by one's own pieces or by blocking the remaining enemy columns so that they cannot move.

Reversi

No of players: 2
Equipment: Board and 64 pieces
Complexity: ★★☆

Reversi – like *Halma* – was invented in the 1880s. It is played using all the squares of an ordinary chessboard. The pieces are coloured white on one side and black on the other. Each player has thirty-two pieces, one player playing them with the black side uppermost and the other playing them with the white side uppermost.

Black always begins the game, and the first four moves are taken up by each player in turn placing one of his pieces on one of the four central squares of the board.

After the four central squares have been filled, the players continue playing alternately, but each move has to be a taking move – a player who cannot make a taking move has to pass until he can do so.

A taking move consists of a player trapping one or more enemy pieces between two of his own. To do this a piece must be placed on the board next to an enemy piece and it must trap one or more enemy pieces between itself and another of the player's own pieces in a straight line – horizontally, vertically or diagonally – with no empty spaces in between. It is often possible in one move to take several pieces in different lines simultaneously.

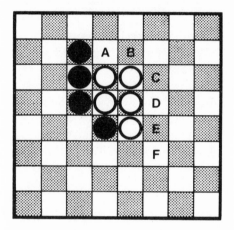

For example, in the position illustrated here Black may play a piece in any of the lettered squares. Playing in square B he will take one white piece, playing in squares A, D or F he will take two white pieces, but playing in squares C or E he will capture three white pieces.

Pieces that are taken are turned over to displayed the colour of the player that took them. Thus pieces once played are never removed from the board or moved from their original squares, but they may be turned over to transfer ownership several times in the course of the game.

The game ends when all sixty-four pieces have been played or when neither player can move. The winner is the player with the greater number of pieces of his colour on the board at the end of the game.

Chess

No. of players: 2
Equipment: Board and 32 pieces
Complexity: ☆☆☆☆

The first recorded description of the game of *Chess* comes from eighth-century India. From India the game seems to have spread to Persia and then to the Arabs, and to have been introduced into Europe during the Moorish occupation of Spain. During this period of the game's history it was gradually evolving, and the features of the game that we know today were finally determined in the sixteenth century.

    Chess, like *Draughts*, is played on a square board consisting of 64 smaller squares coloured alternately black and white. The board is always positioned so that each player has a white square at his right hand side.

    At the beginning of the game the pieces are set out on the board like this:

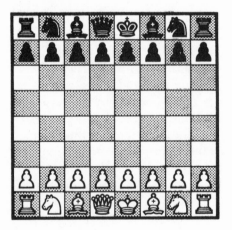

Each player has sixteen pieces, consisting of:

1 king		2 knights	
1 queen		2 rooks	
2 bishops		8 pawns	

Note that the white queen always starts the game on a white square, and the black queen on a black square.

The player with the white pieces always make the first move, after which the players move alternately. A piece may be moved to an empty square or may capture an enemy piece by occupying the square on which that piece stood – the captured piece being removed from the board. At no time may a square be occupied by more than one piece.

The objective of the game is to checkmate the opponent's king. If the king is threatened with capture on the next move it is said to be 'in check'. When a player makes a move that threatens the opposing king with capture it is customary for that player to say 'Check'. The player whose king is in check must on the next move rescue it in one of these three ways:

(a) by moving the king to another square where it is not threatened,
(b) by capturing the piece that is giving check,
(c) by interposing another piece between the king and the piece that is giving check.

If the king cannot be rescued from check then the situation is called 'checkmate' (or simply 'mate') and the player whose king is checkmated loses the game.

Each of the different chess pieces has different powers of movement.

The king may move only one square at a time, in any direction. Of course, it may not move to a square that is threatened by an enemy piece – in other words, the king is not allowed to move into check.

A bishop moves diagonally, and may move any number of squares as long as it is unobstructed. Thus a bishop which starts the game on a black square is restricted to the black squares for the rest of the game. Each player starts the game with one bishop on a black square and another on a white square.

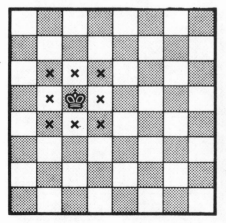 

A rook (sometimes called a castle) may move any number of squares along a row (usually called a 'rank') or column (usually called a 'file') so long as it is unobstructed.

The queen may move any number of squares along a rank, file or diagonal – that is, it combines the powers of movement of a rook and a bishop. The queen is the most powerful piece on the board.

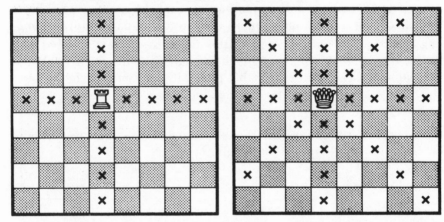

The knight's move differs from that of the other pieces in that it does not move in a straight line and it may jump over other pieces. The knight in a single move moves one square along a rank or file and then one square diagonally – if necessary jumping over any intervening pieces.

The normal move for a pawn, except when capturing, is one square forward along a file. On its first move, however, a pawn may move either one square or two squares. When a pawn reaches the opposite side of the board (the eighth rank) it is promoted and becomes a queen, rook, bishop or knight. Naturally, players usually choose to promote pawns to queens but there may be circumstances in which it is preferable to promote a pawn to a rook, bishop or knight.

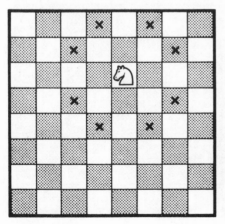

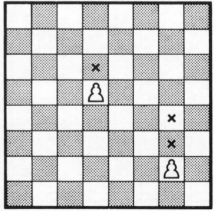

All the pieces, with the exception of the pawn, capture in the same way as they move normally. A pawn captures by moving one square diagonally forward.

There is, in addition, one special type of pawn capture: the capture *en passant* (in passing). If a pawn moves two squares on its initial move, and there is an enemy pawn on an adjacent file which could have captured it had it moved only one square, then it can be captured exactly as if it had only moved one square – the capturing pawn moves one square diagonally forward and the captured pawn is removed from the board. The *en passant* capture, if it is to be made, must be made *immediately* after the opposing pawn has made its two-square move.

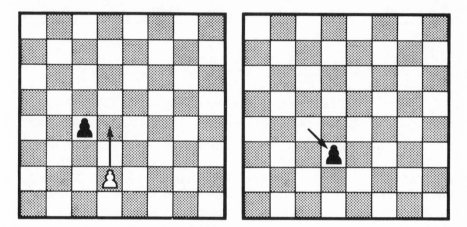

There is one more special type of move to be described, and that is *castling*. This differs from every other move in that two pieces are moved at the same time – the king and a rook. Castling consists of moving the king two squares to the right or left from its starting position and moving the rook to the square the king has just passed over. Castling may not be performed in any of the following circumstances:

(a) if there are any pieces between the king and the rook,
(b) if the king is in check,
(c) If the square that the king passes over or moves to is threatened by an enemy piece,
(d) if either the rook or the king has previously been moved.

Castling has two main purposes – to tuck the king safely in the corner where it is more easily protected, and to bring the rook more quickly into play.

As described previously, a game is won by checkmating the opponent's king. Often a game is won before that stage – when a player resigns because he can see that checkmate is inevitable. Sometimes, also, a game is drawn. A draw may occur in the following circumstances:

(a) Lack of material – when there are not enough pieces left on the board to win the game for either player. For example, if one player is left with only his king and the other player is left with only his king and a bishop, the game is drawn since checkmate cannot be forced.

(b) Perpetual check – when one player can continue giving check indefinitely to his opponent's king but cannot checkmate it.

(c) Stalemate – when one player, it being his turn to move, can make no legal move, but his king is not in check.

(d) Repetition – when exactly the same position occurs three times with the same player having the next move. Either player may then claim a draw.

(e) Fifty-move rule – when no capture or pawn move has been made by either player during his past fifty moves.

(f) Agreement – when both players agree to a draw.

Learning the moves of the different pieces is, of course, only the first step in learning how to play the game. Obviously a thorough description of strategy and tactics is beyond the scope of this book, but the following general principles should be helpful to the beginner and the occasional player.

Successful play often hinges on control of the centre squares. It is therefore advisable to begin by moving at least one of the centre pawns forward two squares. As many pieces as possible should then be brought into play as quickly as possible. A common mistake made by beginners is to bring out the queen very early and to move it aimlessly around the board, attempting attacks that are easily countered, meanwhile leaving the other pieces on their original squares. In general, the knights and bishops should be brought into play before the queen, and the knights, if possible, should be placed on safe squares near the centre of the board rather than at the edges where they are less effective. It is also usually good policy to castle fairly early in the game.

Before making any move you should check whether your opponent's previous move poses any threats that you have to counter, whether his previous move has left any weaknesses in his position that you can exploit, and whether your proposed move leaves any of your own pieces in a vulnerable position. If there are no immediate threats and you are not sure which move to make, decide which of your pieces is least usefully placed and move that piece to a square where it is more useful.

The best and quickest way of improving one's game is to play as often as possible against an opponent slightly better than yourself. If you always play inferior players or players who are very much better than you are, then you will learn little if anything from them. It also helps to play as many different opponents as possible.

For recording games there are two systems of notation in general use – the Descriptive, or English, system and the Algebraic, or Continental, system.

In the Descriptive system, the pieces are represented by their initial letters (Kt or N being used to represent a knight) and the squares are numbered according to the pieces which stand at the end of the files at the start of the game. For example, the square on which the queen stands is Q1 and the squares in front of it are Q2, Q3 and so on to Q 8. Pieces are differentiated according to whether they are on the king's side of the board or on the queen's side – for example QR (queen's rook) and KR (king's rook). Each square has two names – depending on whether it is being regarded from White's point of view or from Black's point of view. For example, White's king's rook starts the game on his square KR1, which is Black's KR8.

A move is described by writing the piece which is moved and the square it is moved to. If, for example, White's first move is to move the pawn in front of his queen two squares forward, this would be written P-Q4 (read as 'Pawn to queen four'). Captures are shown by an 'x' – e.g. QRxP (read as 'Queen's rook takes pawn'). Other symbols used are: ch (check) e.p. (en passant) 0-0 (castles, king's side) 0-0-0 (castles, queen's side) !(good move) ?(dubious move).

BLACK

QR8	QN8	QB8	Q8	K8	KB8	KN8	KR8
QR7	QN7	QB7	Q7	K7	KB7	KN7	KR7
QR6	QN6	QB6	Q6	K6	KB6	KN6	KR6
QR5	QN5	QB5	Q5	K5	KB5	KN5	KR5
QR4	QN4	QB4	Q4	K4	KB4	KN4	KR4
QR3	QN3	QB3	Q3	K3	KB3	KN3	KR3
QR2	QN2	QB2	Q2	K2	KB2	KN2	KR2
QR1	QN1	QB1	Q1	K1	KB1	KN1	KR1

WHITE

White's point of view

BLACK

QR1	QN1	QB1	Q1	K1	KB1	KN1	KR1
QR2	QN2	QB2	Q2	K2	KB2	KN2	KR2
QR3	QN3	QB3	Q3	K3	KB3	KN3	KR3
QR4	QN4	QB4	Q4	K4	KB4	KN4	KR4
QR5	QN5	QB5	Q5	K5	KB5	KN5	KR5
QR6	QN6	QB6	Q6	K6	KB6	KN6	KR6
QR7	QN7	QB7	Q7	K7	KB7	KN7	KR7
QR8	QN8	QB8	Q8	K8	KB8	KN8	KR8

WHITE

Black's point of view

The moves are conventionally recorded in two columns, White's moves in the first column and Black's in the second column. Here, as an example, is a famous game played in 1854 between G. A. Anderssen and J. Dufresne:

	Anderssen *White*	**Dufresne** *Black*		*White*	*Black*
1	P-K4	P-K4	13	Q-R4	B-N3
2	N-KB3	N-QB3	14	QN-Q2	B-N2
3	B-B4	B-B4	15	N-K4	Q-B4
4	P-QN4	BxNP	16	BxQP	Q-R4
5	P-B3	B-R4	17	N-B6 ch	PxN
6	P-Q4	PxP	18	PxP	R-N1
7	0-0	P-Q6	19	QR-Q1	QxN
8	Q-N3	Q-B3	20	RxN ch	NxR
9	P-K5	Q-N3	21	QxP ch	KxQ
10	R-K1	KN-K2	22	B-B5 ch	K-K1
11	B-R3	P-N4	23	B-Q7 ch	K-Q1
12	QxP	R-QN1	24	BxN mate	

In the Algebraic system each square is represented according to the rank and file it is on – the eight files being represented by the letters a to h, and the eight ranks by the numbers 1 to 8. The squares are always described as from White's point of view.

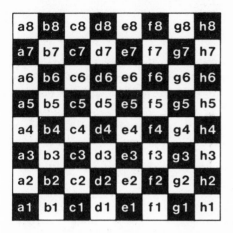

Moves are recorded by writing the piece which is moved and the square it is moved to, thus Be4. Other abbreviations are generally the same as for the Descriptive notation.

Losing Chess

No. of players: 2
Equipment: Board and 32 pieces
Complexity: ★★★☆

This game is one of a number of unorthodox variations of *Chess*. In *Losing Chess* the objective is to lose all one's pieces. The king has no special status and can be taken like any other piece. A player who is able to capture an opposing piece must do so. The first player to get rid of all his pieces is the winner.

Randomised Chess

No. of players: 2
Equipment: Board and 32 pieces
Complexity: ★☆☆☆

Randomised Chess is played in the same way as conventional *Chess* except that at the beginning of the game the pieces on the first rank are arranged in a random manner (provided that it is the same for both players), e.g. king, knight, rook, bishop, rook, knight, bishop, queen. Thus the result is like a game of *Chess* without conventional Opening theory.

Refusal Chess

No. of players: 2
Equipment: Board and 32 pieces
Complexity: ★★☆☆

Refusal Chess is played in the same way as normal *Chess* except that at each move a player has the right to refuse his opponent's choice of move and to insist that he play some other move instead. The right of refusal may be exercised as often as one likes during the game – but only one refusal per move.

Pocket Knight Chess

No. of players: 2
Equipment: Board and 32 pieces plus 2 extra knights
Complexity: ★★☆☆

This is played in the same way as normal *Chess* except that each player starts the game with an extra knight in his pocket. At any stage of the game, when it is his turn to move, a player may place his extra knight on any vacant square on the board. This counts as his move, and thereafter the extra knight functions as a normal piece.

Two Move Chess

No. of players: 2
Equipment: Board and 32 pieces
Complexity: ★★☆☆

In this variation of *Chess* the normal rules apply except that each player has two moves at a time instead of one. A player giving check on his first move forfeits his second move. A player who is in check must get out of check on his first move.

Progressive Chess

No. of players: 2
Equipment: Board and 32 pieces
Complexity: ★★☆☆

This is a tremendously challenging *Chess* variation and it requires great ability to think ahead. White has one move, then Black has two moves, White then has three moves, then Black has four moves, and so on. When a player gives check this ends his turn and he forfeits the rest of his moves. A player who is in check must get out of check on his first move.

Kriegspiel

No. of players: 2 plus referee
Equipment: 3 boards and 3 sets of chess pieces
Complexity: ★★★★☆

Kriegspiel is a very challenging variation of *Chess* in which neither player sees the pieces of his opponent or knows exactly what moves his opponent is making.

Each player has his own board, as does the referee. Neither player is allowed to see the board of his opponent – normally the two players sit back to back. The referee's board must also be concealed from both players though he must be able to see their boards.

At the start of the game White sets out the white pieces on his board in the normal way, and Black does the same with the black pieces on his board. The referee sets up his own board with both black and white pieces and he duplicates the moves on this board throughout the game.

The players move alternately. If no capture or check is involved and the move is legal, the referee will announce 'White has moved' or 'Black has moved' as appropriate. No information is given about the piece that has moved or the square it has gone to.

If a player – White, let us say – moves a piece to a square that is occupied by one of his opponent's pieces (other than the king) the referee announces 'White captures' and he removes the captured piece from Black's board. Thus Black knows that there is now a white piece on that square but he does not know what piece it is or which square it was moved from. White, on the other hand, knows that he has captured a black piece but does not know which piece he has captured.

A move that gives check is announced as such, identifying the line of attack – rank, file, long diagonal or short diagonal – e.g. 'White has moved, giving check on the seventh rank', or 'Black has moved, giving check on the short diagonal', or 'White has moved, giving check with a knight'.

Of course, since each player can see only his own pieces, many of the moves he tries will be illegal. When this happens the referee announces 'Illegal' and the player must withdraw that move and try another.

A player, at any time when it is his turn to move, may ask the referee if he has any possible captures *with a pawn*. The referee answers either 'Yes' or 'No'. If the reply is 'Yes', the player must attempt at least one pawn capture before trying another move.

Kriegspiel obviously requires a very high level of *Chess* skill, since the referee is the only person who really knows what the position is on the board. A player, however, may gather information about the disposition of his opponent's forces by attempting moves which he knows are quite likely to be illegal, and by attempting long-ranging moves with bishops, rooks and queen. Information may also be provided by announcements concerning checks and pawn captures.

Go

No. of players: 2
Equipment: Board and 361 pieces
Complexity: ★★★★

The game of Go is believed to have originated in China about 2000 BC. It was later introduced into Japan, and the Japanese are now the world's foremost exponents of the game.

Go is just as complex and demanding a game as *Chess*, and as with *Chess* whole books can be, and have been, written which are devoted to just a single aspect of the game. Obviously only the basic principles can be presented here.

The board is ruled with 19 horizontal lines and 19 vertical lines, forming a total of 361 points where the lines intersect. The pieces are called 'stones' — one player starts with 181 black stones and the other player starts with 180 white stones.

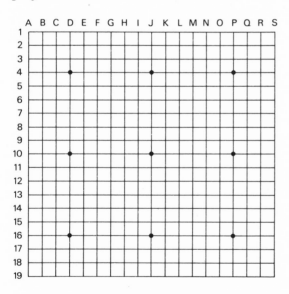

At the beginning of the game the board is empty. Each player in turn places one of his stones on a vacant point, the objective of the game being to surround vacant territory. Points are also scored for capturing enemy stones. Stones once placed on the board are not moved unless they are captured — in which case they are removed from the board. The board is thus gradually filled up with stones until the game ends when all vacant territory has been surrounded by one player or the other. Each player then counts the number of points he has surrounded and the number of enemy stones he has captured – the player with the higher total being the winner.

The player with the black stones normally has the first turn. Since this confers an advantage the weaker player is usually allowed to play with the black stones. There is a further handicapping system, whereby if one player is markedly weaker than the other he may be allowed, on his first move, to place two or more stones on the board – on the marked handicap points.

Handicap	Handicap points used
2	P4,D16
3	P4,D16,P16
4	D4,P4,D16,P16
5	D4,P4,J10,D16,P16
6	D4,P4,D10,P10,D16,P16
7	D4,P4,D10,J10,P,10,D16,P16
8	D4,J4,P4,D10,P10,D16,J16,P16
9	D4,J4,P4,D10,J10,P10,D16,J16,P16

Vacant points that are adjacent – horizontally or vertically – to a stone are known as its 'liberties'. When all of a stone's liberties are occupied by enemy stones it is captured and removed from the board. A group of stones of the same colour connected horizontally or vertically is known as an 'army'. Armies may be captured in the same way as single stones. In the diagram below, white stones played on any of the points marked with a cross will capture black stones. Stones such as the black stones in this diagram which are liable to be captured on the next move are said to be in 'atari'. It should be noted that it is not necessary for the attacking stones to be connected horizontally or vertically.

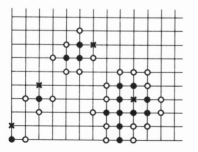

Note that in the fourth example above the black army is captured by playing a white stone in an internal liberty – such as internal space is known as an 'eye'. If the external liberties of the black army had not previously been completely occupied by white stones, a white stone could not be played in the eye – as it would itself immediately be captured. Such a move is illegal. Therefore, when capturing an army which has an eye, the final move which captures the army must be within the eye.

An important principle, which follows from this, is that whenever an army has two or more separate eyes it can never be captured.

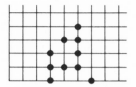

The next diagram illustrates what is known as a 'ko' situation. If White were to play on the point indicated in the first position this would lead to the second position, and if Black were then to play on the point indicated in the second position this would lead back to the first position. Obviously this could continue indefinitely. To prevent this happening there is a rule that the second player may not recapture in a ko situation until he has made at least one other move elsewhere on the board.

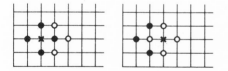

It is important to understand how captures may be made but it is more important to realise that surrounding vacant points is the primary objective and capturing enemy stones is secondary to this. A general principle to follow is that stones should not be played inside territory which is securely held by the opponent as they are sure to be captured eventually. Another general principle is that, since the scoring is based on the *vacant* points that one has surrounded, stones should not be played unnecessarily within one's own territory, as they merely reduce one's score.

The game ends when both players agree that there are no more points to be gained. If only one player considers the game to be ended he says 'Pass' and is not allowed to make any further moves. The other player may then continue playing until he, too, judges that he can secure no further points.

Each player counts the number of vacant points in his territory and adds to this the number of enemy stones he has captured in the course of the game. The player with the higher total is the winner.

Go-Moku

No. of players: 2
Equipment: Go board and 200 pieces
Complexity: ★★★

One player has 100 white pieces (or 'stones') and the other player has 100 black pieces. Each player in turn places one of his stones on any vacant point on a Go board, the objective being to get five pieces of one's own colour in a row, horizontally, vertically or diagonally – while at the same time, of course, trying to prevent one's opponent from doing so. The first player to get five in a row is the winner.

If both players have played all their stones without getting five in a row, the game continues with each player in turn moving one of his stones horizontally or vertically to an adjacent vacant point until one player succeeds in forming a row of five.

6 DOMINO GAMES

Introduction:
General Principles and Terminology
Fours
Ends
Blind Hughie
Round the Clock
Maltese Cross
Block
Partnership Block
Tiddly-wink
Sebastopol
Cyprus
French Draw
Draw or Pass
Bergen
Matador
Fives
Threes
Sniff
Muggins
Five Up
All Fives
Fives and Threes
Forty-two
Bingo

Introduction: History, General Principles and Terminology

It is generally agreed by the experts that dominoes originated in China, perhaps as many as 2000 years ago, and that they were introduced into Europe by Venetian traders in the fourteenth or fifteenth century. From Italy they were subsequently introduced into France, and it is believed that the English may first have learned about dominoes from French prisoners-of-war during the Napoleonic Wars.

Dominoes, for nearly all their history, have been especially popular among working men. In the days when paper was an expensive commodity, dominoes, carved from bone, were more easily made and more durable then the playing cards which were popular among the upper classes.

Dominoes are rectangular tiles, made usually from bone, ivory, wood or plastic. A standard European set consists of 28 tiles. The face of each tile is divided by a central line into two equal squares, each of which is either blank or marked with pips from one to six in number. This set is also known as the Double-6 set, as the double-6 is the top domino in the set. All the games described in this chapter are played with this set.

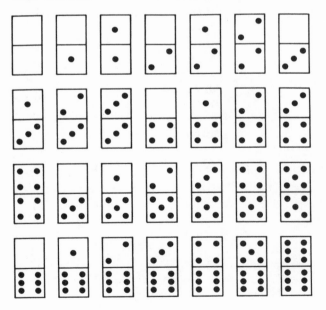

In some games reference is made to the 'suit' of a domino. The domino suits are as follows:

Blank suit:	Double-blank, 6-blank, 5-blank, 4-blank, 3-blank, 2-blank, 1-blank.
1 suit:	Double-1, 6-1, 5-1, 4-1, 3-1, 2-1, 1-blank.
2 suit:	Double-2, 6-2, 5-2, 4-2, 3-2, 2-1, 2-blank.
3 suit:	Double-3, 6-3, 5-3, 4-3, 3-2, 3-1, 3-blank.
4 suit:	Double-4, 6-4, 5-4, 4-3, 4-2, 4-1, 4-blank.
5 suit:	Double-5, 6-5, 5-4, 5-3, 5-2, 5-1, 5-blank.
6 suit:	Double-6, 6-5, 6-4, 6-3, 6-2, 6-1, 6-blank.
Double suit:	Double-6, Double-5, Double-4, Double-3, Double-2, Double-1, Double-blank.

It may be noted that every domino belongs to two suits – for example, the 6-5 belongs to the 6 suit and the 5 suit, and the double-3 belongs to the 3 suit and to the double suit.

There are larger sets of dominoes than the Double-6 set. There is a Double-9 set, consisting of 55 dominoes up to double-9, and a Double-12 set, consisting of 91 dominoes up to double-12. These sets are not very common, but almost all the games for a double-6 set may be played with these larger sets, with in some cases a slight modification of the rules.

Dominoes offer hours of fun and fascination. Most of the games are quite easy to learn, and a novice can quickly reach an acceptable level of play, though real expertise, of course, is only acquired after much practice.

Although there is a tremendous range and variety of domino games, certain general principles apply. These principles are described here to avoid constant repetition in the descriptions of the games that follow. Domino novices are urged to acquaint themselves thoroughly with the information in this section before studying the descriptions of the individual games.

The Players
Some of the games are for two players, some for four, and some for any number from two to five. Where there are four players they may play individually or two may play in partnership against the other two. Partners should sit on opposite sides of the table, as for bridge or whist.

Shuffling
Before each game or each hand, the dominoes are all placed face down on the table and are moved around until they are thoroughly mixed. It is customary for all players to take part in the shuffle.

Drawing a Hand

After the dominoes have been shuffled, each player selects the number of dominoes required for the game being played. Except in games such as *Blind Hughie*, in which the players are not allowed to look at the dominoes they have drawn, the player may hold his dominoes in his hand, place them in a rack, or stand them on edge before him on the table, so that they are visible to him but concealed from the other players. The dominoes that are left when all the players have drawn their hands are known as 'the boneyard'. The dominoes in the boneyard are usually moved to one side of the table, still face down, and depending on the game being played they may remain out of play for that hand or they may form a pool from which later draws may be made.

Leading

In some games the lead (i.e. the first turn) goes to the player who has drawn the double-6. If no player holds this domino then the lead goes to the player holding the next highest double. In other games the lead is decided by lot before the hands are drawn. Each player picks up one domino, and the lead goes to the player picking up the domino with the highest number of pips – in the event of two players tying those players select again. The dominoes are shuffled before and after this draw for lead.

Direction of Play

After the first player has led, play always proceeds to the left (in a clockwise direction) around the table.

The Play

In a few games – those based on card games – the dominoes are played so that tricks may be taken.

The basic characteristic of most domino games, however, is that the dominoes are played so that matching ends are adjacent.

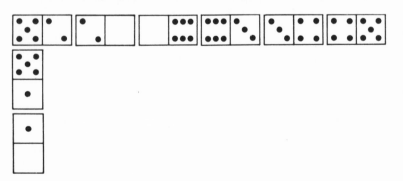

In most games the players may build on either end of such a row, which is known as 'the line of play'. Note that the row may bend at right angles (particularly when nearing the edge of the table!).

Doubles are usually played *across* the line of play, whereas the other dominoes are played *with* the line of play.

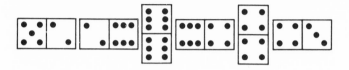

Usually one can play only against the sides of the doubles, as in the illustration above, but in a few games one may play against the ends as well, like this:

Passing
In some games, if a player cannot match a domino from his hand with either end of the line, he is said 'to pass' or to be 'knocking', and it is customary for the player to knock on the table when this happens. Play immediately passes to the next player.

In some games the player who is unable to play a matching domino must draw a domino from the boneyard.

End of Play
A hand ends when one player has played all his dominoes (this is known as 'going out') or when all the players are unable to play from their hands and have all passed in turn (this is known as a 'blocked game').

Scoring
There are various scoring systems, depending on the particular game

being played. Most games, however, consist of a number of 'hands' or rounds, and are played until one player attains an agreed number of points such as 100. The scoring is usually based on the number of pips on the dominoes remaining in the players' hands. A cribbage board may be used to record the score, in which case the game is usually played to 61 points or 121 points.

General Rules

(a) If, in the course of play, a player realises that he has drawn too many dominoes, one of his dominoes must be chosen at random by another player and returned to the boneyard.

(b) If, in the course of play, a player realises that he has drawn too few dominoes, he must draw from the boneyard to make up the right number.

(c) If a player accidentally exposes one of his dominoes so that it is seen by one of the other players then it must be shown to all the other players.

(d) If a player misplays (for example, if he joins a 5 on to a 6, or if he plays out of turn) then he must take the domino back and play correctly if the misplay is discovered before the next player takes his turn. If the misplay is not discovered before the next player takes his turn then the misplay must be accepted and if any points were scored on the misplay they, too, are allowed to stand.

(e) Once a domino has been played, provided it is not a misplay, the player may not change his mind and take the domino back.

Variations

Many of the games described in this chapter have a tremendous number of variations. Ask a number of *Block* players, for example, what rules they play by and the likelihood is that you will be given several slightly different versions.

While the basic formula of any game will be agreed on by (almost) everyone, versions of the game may differ in the following respects:

(a) The number of dominoes drawn by each player.

(b) The lead player – he may be chosen by lot or he may be the player holding the highest double.

(c) The domino played by the lead player – it may be the highest double in his hand or it may be any domino he chooses.

(d) Whether dominoes are drawn from the boneyard if a player cannot play a domino from his hand.

(e) Whether the boneyard is drawn upon till only two dominoes remain or whether it is drawn upon until it is empty.
(f) The way in which points are scored at the end of a hand, and the number of points a game is played to.

It would be an impossible task to describe all the possible variations of each game. The best method – the one adapted here – is to describe one generally accepted version of each game, and to advise readers that, although they might encounter other variations, the basic principles remain the same.

Fours

No. of players: 3, 4 or 5
Equipment: Set of dominoes
Complexity: ☆

Fours is a simple domino game which is eminently suitable for young players, and is usually the first domino game they learn to play.
The lead player is chosen by lot, and each player then draws his dominoes. If three are playing each draws nine dominoes, if four are playing each draws seven dominoes, if five are playing each draws five dominoes. Any dominoes left over are put to one side and are not used in the game.
The object of the game is to be the first player to get rid of all his dominoes. Each player in his turn is allowed to continue playing dominoes from his hand for as long as he can match either end of the line of dominoes already played, after which the turn passes to the next player on the left.
The first player leads with any domino that he chooses from his hand. Naturally he will take care to choose the domino that allows him to get rid of as many other dominoes as possible. He will continue playing his dominoes until he can no longer do so. If he is very lucky he will be able to play all his dominoes in one turn and will win the game.
This does not happen very often, however – it usually takes at least two turns to get rid of all one's dominoes. Each player plays in turn until one player wins the game by getting rid of all his dominoes. In some cases it may happen that the game becomes blocked and all the

players are left with dominoes that cannot be played. When this happens, each player adds up the number of pips on the dominoes left in his hand, and the winner is the player with the lowest total.

Ends

No. of players: 4
Equipment: Set of dominoes
Complexity: ✭

Ends is a simple but fascinating domino game, which can be enjoyed equally by children and adults.

Each player draws seven dominoes, and the game is started by the player with the double-6 placing it face upwards in the centre of the table. Each player in his turn is now allowed to play one domino that matches either end of the line of dominoes already played, the turn always passing to the next player on the left around the table. If a player cannot go when it is his turn, he must ask the player on his left for a suitable domino. If that player has a domino that can be played he gives it to the player who asked for it, who then plays it. The player on the left then has his turn as usual.

If the player on the left does not have a playable domino, he must ask the next player on *his* left. If that player does not have a playable domino, he again must ask the player on *his* left. The first player in this chain who *does* have a playable domino gives it to the player who first requested it. The player who asked for the domino plays it and the game proceeds as normal.

If the request passes right round the table and no player has a playable domino, then the player who first asked for it is allowed to play *any* domino from his hand on either end of the line, without making a match.

The winner is the first player to get rid of all his dominoes.

Blind Hughie

No. of players: 2 to 5
Equipment: Set of dominoes
Complexity: ☆

This is purely a game of chance, and is popular with children. The lead player is chosen by lot. With two or three players, each draws seven dominoes; with four or five players, each draws five dominoes. A player is not allowed to look at the dominoes he has drawn – they must remain face down on the table in a row in front of him.

The lead player begins by turning over the leftmost domino of his row and placing it in the centre of the table. Each player in his turn then looks at the leftmost domino of his row. If he can match it to either end of the line of play then he plays it, otherwise he replaces it, face down, at the rightmost end of his own row.

Play continues around the table until one player wins by playing all his dominoes, or until the game is blocked because none of the players can play their remaining dominoes, in which case nobody is the winner.

Round the Clock

No. of players: 2 to 5
Equipment: Set of dominoes
Complexity: ☆☆

A leader is chosen by lot and the players then draw their hands – seven dominoes each for two players, six dominoes each for three players, five dominoes each for four or five players.

Play begins with the player who has the double-6 in his hand laying it face up in the centre of the table. If none of the players has the double-6 then the leader must draw a domino from the boneyard. If it is the double-6 he plays it, otherwise the next player must draw from the boneyard. This continues around the table until the double-6 is drawn and played or until there are only two dominoes left in the boneyard. If the double-6 happens to be one of these two dominoes left in the boneyard then the game is abandoned and new hands are drawn for a fresh game.

Once the double-6 has been played, the next four dominoes must be played against the sides and ends of double-6. If a player cannot play from his hand and there are more than two dominoes in the boneyard he may draw one of them. If he still cannot play then he must pass.

When these dominoes have been played, the next four dominoes played must be the doubles for the four ends.

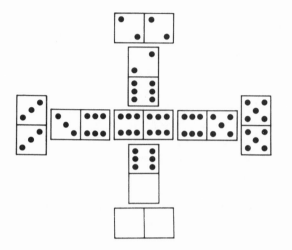

The next four dominoes must be played against the doubles on the ends, and so on.

The winner is the first player to get rid of all his dominoes or, if the game is blocked, the player left with the lowest number of pips in his hand.

Maltese Cross

No. of players: 4
Equipment: Set of dominoes
Complexity: ✰✰

Maltese Cross is somewhat similar to *Round the Clock*. Each of the four players draws seven dominoes, and the player with the double-6 leads. Dominoes may be played to both ends and both sides of the double-6 so that a four-ended line of play results. However, there is one rule that gives *Maltese Cross* its distinctive character. This rule is that, until a double has been played, all ends with that number are blocked.

Take this situation as a example:

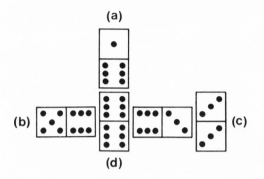

The player whose turn it is may play any matching domino at (c) or (d) since the double-6 and double-3 have been played. But only the double-1 may be played at (a) and only the double-5 at (b).

If a player in his turn is unable to play a domino from his hand then he must pass.

The first player to get rid of all his dominoes is the winner. If the game is blocked, then the winner is the player who has the lowest number of pips left in his hand.

Block

No. of players: 2, 3 or 4
Equipment: Set of dominoes
Complexity: ★★

Block is probably the most popular of all domino games. If there are two players each draws seven dominoes. If there are three or four players each draws five dominoes. The lead player, who is chosen by lot, plays any domino from his hand. The next player must play a domino which matches either end of the starter, or if he does not have a matching domino he must pass. Play progresses round the table in this way with each player adding a domino to either end of the line or passing. Doubles are placed across the line of play.

The aim is to be the first player to play all the dominoes in your hand, and to do this you should to attempt to play dominoes that will block your opponents and force them to pass. Therefore a good hand is one which contains a preponderance of one suit. For example, if the line looks like this:

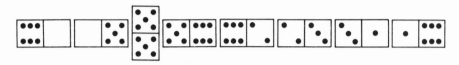

and you hold the double-6, 6-3 and 6-4, then your opponents are fully blocked since all the sixes have either been played or are in your hand. You may play the double-6 and your opponents will still be knocking. You can then play either the 6-3 or the 6-4 and your opponents will be restricted to playing on that one end – you still hold a block on the other.

Play continues until one player has played all his dominoes – in which case he is the winner and he scores one point for each pip in his opponents' hands – or until all the players are blocked – in which case the winner is the player with the lowest number of pips in his hand and his score is the total number of pips in his opponents' hands minus the number of pips in his own hand.

The winner of one hand is given the lead in the next hand, and the game is played to an agreed number of points.

Partnership Block

No. of players: 4
Equipment: Set of dominoes
Complexity: ★★

This is the same as the previous game, except for the following differences:

(a) Two players play as partners against the other two and score jointly.
(b) When one player has played all his dominoes, the partnership scores the number of pips in the hands of the opposing partnership.
(c) When the game is blocked, the partnership with the lowest total of pips in their two hands scores the difference between the number of pips in their opponents' hands and the number of pips in their own.

Tiddly-Wink

No. of players: 2, 3 or 4
Equipment: Set of dominoes
Complexity: ★★

Tiddly-Wink is a variation of *Block* with the following differences:

(a) The dominoes are shared equally between the players, any left-over dominoes remaining in the boneyard.
(b) The player with the highest double always leads.
(c) Any player who plays a double may, if he wishes, play another matching domino on the free side of that double within the same turn.

Sebastopol

No. of players: 4
Equipment: Set of dominoes
Complexity: ★★

Each player draws seven dominoes, and the player who holds the double-6 leads. The next four dominoes must be played against the sides and ends of the double-6 to form 'the star' as in this example:

If a player does not have a 6 in his hand, he must pass until the star has been completed. Thereafter play proceeds as for *Block* except that

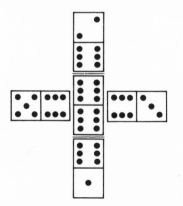

there are four ends to play on instead of two. Scoring is the same as for
Block.

Cyprus

No. of players: 4
Equipment: Set of dominoes
Complexity: ✫✫

Cyprus is similar to *Sebastopol* except that after the double-6 has been
led the next six dominoes must be played against it to form a star with six
ends like this:

If a player does not have a 6 in his hand, he must pass until the star has
been completed. Therafter play proceeds as for *Block* except that there
are now six ends to play on.

Cyprus is sometimes played with a double-9 set of dominoes, and in
that version the double-9 is led and the star is formed with eight ends.

French Draw

No. of players: 2, 3 or 4
Equipment: Set of dominoes
Complexity: ★★

This is basically the same game as *Block* except that dominoes may be drawn from the boneyard in the course of play.

With two or three players each draws seven dominoes; with four players each draws six dominoes. The lead player, who is chosen by lot, plays any domino he chooses from his hand. Subsequently any player, if he is unable to play a matching domino from his hand or if he simply does not wish to do so, must draw a domino from the boneyard and continue doing so until he draws one that he is able and willing to play or until only two dominoes are left in the boneyard. A player who cannot play a domino from his hand when only two dominoes remain in the boneyard must pass.

Play continues until one player goes out (in which case he is the winner) or until the game is blocked (in which case the winner is the player with the lowest number of pips left in his hand).

The winner, as in *Block*, scores points equal to the total number of pips left in his opponents' hands minus the number of pips (if any) left in his own hand. The game is played to an agreed number of points.

Draw or Pass

No. of players: 2, 3 or 4
Equipment: Set of dominoes
Complexity: ★★

The lead player is chosen by lot and the players then draw their dominoes – seven dominoes each if there are two players, and five dominoes each if there are three or four players.

The lead player plays any domino he chooses from his hand. After that each player in his turn can choose to do one of three things:

(a) He can play a domino from his hand to match either end of the line of play.

(b)   He can draw as many dominoes as he likes from the boneyard (provided that two always remain there). If he chooses to draw he cannot also play a domino in that turn.

(c)   He can pass – and is allowed to do this even though he may have a domino that he could play if he wished.

Play continues round the table in the normal way, each player in turn choosing one of these three options. Play ends when one player goes out or when all the players pass in succession.

The winner is the player who goes out or who has the lowest number of pips left in his hand. He scores points equal to the number of pips left in his opponents' hand minus the number of pips (if any) left in his own hand. The game is played to an agreed number of points (usually 100).

Bergen

No. of players: 2, 3 or 4
Equipment: Set of dominoes
Complexity: ★★

If there are two or three players each draws six dominoes; if there are four players each draws five dominoes. The objectives are to be the first player to play all one's dominoes, to block one's opponents, and to score special points by playing so that the same number appears at both ends of the line of play. When the same number does appear at both ends of the line, as in this example, this is known as a 'double-header'.

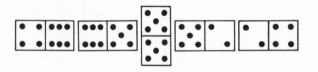

When the same number appears three times at the ends (i.e. when one end is a double) this is known as a 'triple-header'.

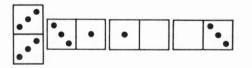

The player with the highest double leads and immediately scores two points for a double-header, or if none of the players has drawn a double the player with the lowest domino leads that but does not score. Play proceeds as for *French Draw* except that whenever a player plays a domino to form a double-header he scores two points and whenever he forms a triple-header he scores three points.

The winner of a hand, who also scores two points, may be the player who first plays all his dominoes or, in a blocked game, the player left with no doubles, the fewest doubles or the lowest number of pips in his hand.

A game is usually played for ten or fifteen points.

Matador

No. of players: 2, 3 or 4
Equipment: Set of dominoes
Complexity: ✭✭

Matador is an intriguing game in which dominoes are played not so that joined ends match, but so that joined ends add up to seven. Doubles (except the double-blank) are not played across the line of play but are treated as ordinary dominoes.

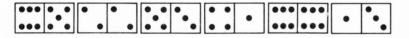

There are, however, four dominoes – the 'matadors' – which have special features. The matadors are the double-blank and the three dominoes which have pips adding up to seven – the 6-1, the 5-2 and the 4-3. A matador is a sort of joker or wild card that can be played anywhere on the line of play. When they are played the join does not have to add up to seven. Matadors are placed across the line of play.

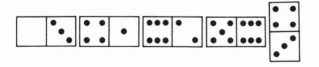

Against the 4-3 matador one could play a four (making a join of seven with the 3 of the matador) or a three (making a join of seven with the 4) or, of course, another matador.

Note the blank at the end of the line illustrated above. Only a matador may be played next to a blank, since so other domino can make a join adding up to seven.

When the first player has been chosen by lot, the players draw their dominoes. If there are two players each draws seven dominoes; if there are three players each draws six dominoes; if there are four players each draws five dominoes.

The first player leads with any domino he chooses from his hand, and play proceeds to the left around the table in the usual fashion. Any player, in his turn, who is unable to play a domino from his hand or simply does not wish to do so must draw a domino from the boneyard – and continue doing so until he draws one that he is able and willing to play, or until only two dominoes remain in the boneyard. When there are only two dominoes left in the boneyard a player must play a domino if he can, and must pass if he has no playable domino.

Play continues until one player has played all his dominoes – in which case he is the winner, scoring one point for each pip in his opponents' hands – or until none of the players can play any more dominoes – in which case the player with the lowest number of pips in his hand is the winner, and his score is the total number of pips in his opponents' hands minus the number of pips in his own.

A game is played to an agreed number of points.

Fives

No. of players: 2, 3 or 4
Equipment: Set of dominoes
Complexity: ☆☆

Fives is the simplest of a group of domino games in which the object of the game is not only to be the first player to get rid of all his dominoes but also to score points by making the ends of the line of play add up to certain numbers.

In *Fives* dominoes are played so that joined ends match. If the pips at the ends of the line of play then total five the player scores one point; if they total ten he scores two points; if fifteen he scores three points; if twenty he scores four points. If the ends do not add up to the multiple of five no points are scored. Doubles are always played across the line of play and both halves of the double are counted in the number of pips. For example, the last player in the game shown here would have scored two points, since the ends add up to ten.

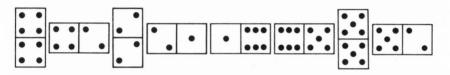

The first player is chosen by lot, and the players then draw their dominoes. If there are two players each draws seven dominoes; if there are three players each draws six dominoes; if there are four players each draws five dominoes.

The first player leads with any domino he chooses from his hand. Each player then follows on in his turn, trying, of course, to score as many points as possible and to prevent his opponents from scoring points.

If a player, in his turn, is able to play a matching domino then he must do so. If he cannot play any of his dominoes then he must draw from the boneyard until he is able to play, or if there are no dominoes left in the boneyard he must pass.

Play continues in this way until one of the players has played all his dominoes, in which case he is the winner, or until the game is blocked, in which case the winner is the player left with the lowest number of pips in his hand. The winner adds together the number of pips left in his opponents' hands, subtracts the number of pips (if any) left in his own hand, and scores one point for every five pips in this total.

A game is usually played to 61 points.

Threes

No. of players: 2, 3 or 4
Equipment: Set of dominoes
Complexity: ★★

Threes is played in exactly the same way as *Fives* except that the scoring is based on multiples of three instead of on multiples of five. Thus a player scores one point if the ends of the line of play add up to 3, two points if they add up to 6, three points if they add up to 9, and so on. At the end of the hand, the winner scores one point for every three pips left in his opponents' hands.

Sniff

No. of players: 2, 3 or 4
Equipment: Set of dominoes
Complexity: ★★

The playing and scoring in *Sniff* is like that in *Fives*, being based on scoring points for ends that add up to multiples of five. In *Sniff*, however, the line of play may have up to four ends, so higher scores may be achieved.

The first player is chosen by lot, and the players then draw their dominoes. If there are two players each draws seven dominoes; if three players each draws six dominoes; if four players each draws five dominoes. The first player leads with any domino he chooses from his hand, and the turn passes round the table in the usual way.

Until the first double is played, the line of play has two ends, as in *Fives*. The first double to be played is called 'the Sniff' and it may be placed *across* the line of play or *with* the line of play, as the player chooses. If the Sniff is played with the line of play, dominoes can be played on the sides of the Sniff, but only after the open end has been played on. If the Sniff is played across the line of play, dominoes can be played on the ends of the Sniff, but only after the open side has been played on. The subsequent doubles are always played across the line of play, and only their sides can be played on.

As in *Fives*, a player must play a domino if he can. If he cannot, he must continue drawing from the boneyard until he draws a domino that he can play. If the boneyard is empty he must pass.

Play continues until one player goes out or until the game is blocked. The points scored at the end of play are the same as in *Fives*, with the winner scoring one point for every five pips left in his opponents' hands. The game is played to an agreed number of points, usually 61.

Muggins

No. of players: 2, 3 or 4
Equipment: Set of dominoes
Complexity: ★★

Muggins is another game, like *Fives* and Sniff, in which the aim is to play so that the ends of the line of play add up to multiples of five. In *Fives* there are only two ends to be counted, in *Sniff* there may be up to four – in *Muggins* there may be even more – but in other respects the method of scoring is exactly the same as for the other two games.

Each player draws his dominoes – seven dominoes if there are two players; six dominoes if there are three players; five dominoes if there are four players.

The player who has the highest double in his hand leads with that domino (and if it happens to be the double-5 – because the double-6 is in the boneyard – he will immediately score two points). Play then proceeds around the table in the usual way, with each player playing matching dominoes on the ends of the line of play. A player must play a domino if he can, otherwise he must draw from the boneyard until he draws a playable domino. If the boneyard is empty then he must pass.

Doubles are always played across the line of play. The ends of any double may be played on once the open side has been played on.

As for *Fives* and *Sniff*, the winner at the end of a hand scores one point for every five pips left in the hands of his opponents.

Five up

No. of players: 2, 3 or 4
Equipment: Set of dominoes
Complexity: ★★

Five Up is a variant of *Muggins* and is played in the same way except for the following differences: (a) The lead player for the first hand is chosen by lot, and he may play any domino he chooses from his hand. The lead passes to the next player on the left for each subsequent hand. (b) Regardless of the number of players, each draws only five dominoes.

All Fives

No. of players: 2, 3 or 4
Equipment: Set of dominoes
Complexity: ★★

All Fives is another variant of *Muggins*, with the following differences:

(a) The lead player for the first hand is chosen by lot, and he may play any domino he chooses from his hand. The lead passes to the next player on the left for each subsequent hand.
(b) Regardless of the number of players, each draws only five dominoes.
(c) When a player plays a double or a domino from which he scores points he immediately has an extra turn. If he does not have a playable domino for his extra turn he must draw from the boneyard until he draws a playable domino or until the boneyard is empty.
(d) A player may not go out by playing a double or a domino that scores points. When such a domino is the last one in his hand he must play it and then draw from the boneyard until he draws a domino that he can play or until the boneyard is empty. If the boneyard is already empty when it is his turn to play his last domino he may not play it and must pass.

Fives and Threes

No. of players: 2, 3 or 4
Equipment: Set of dominoes
Complexity: ★★

Fives and *Threes* is a very popular domino game. As its name suggests, it is a combination of the game of *Fives* and the game of *Threes*. In the version usually played, however, the rules of *Fives* and *Threes* are slightly different from the rules of the other two games.

The lead player is chosen by lot and the players then draw their dominoes. The draw is seven dominoes for two players, six dominoes for three players, and five dominoes for four players. The lead player plays any domino he chooses from his hand, and the other players follow on in their turn as usual. If a player does not have a domino he can play then he knocks and the turn passes to the next player on his left. There is no drawing of extra dominoes from the boneyard.

Points are scored when the number of pips at the ends of the line of play add up to a multiple of three or a multiple of five thus:

Pip Total	Score
3 or 5	1
6 or 10	2
9	3
12 or 20	4
18	6
15	8 (5 threes and 3 fives)

As you can see, the best score is when the pips add up to 15 – that is, when the ends are a 5 and the double-5 or a 3 and the double-6. The next best score is when the pips add up to 18 – that is, when the ends are a 6 and the double-6. Therefore, if you have the double-6 or double-5 in your hand, it should be played with care so that you, and not your opponents, get the high scores.

Play continues until one player has played all his dominoes or until the game is blocked. If a player has played all his dominoes he scores one extra point. No extra points are scored if the game is blocked.

A cribbage board is often used to record the scores, and a game is played to 61 points.

Forty-Two

No. of players: 4
Equipment: Set of dominoes
Complexity: ⋆⋆

Forty-two could be described as a card game that is played with dominoes. Two players play in partnership against the other two, they bid for the number of tricks they think they can win, score points for winning tricks, and can score bonus points. From this you can see that there is some resemblance to the game of *Bridge* – but rest assured, *Forty-two* is a good deal less complicated than that noble game.

There are five points-scoring dominoes, known as 'honours', in *Forty-two*. The three dominoes which have five pips – the 5-blank, the 4-1, and the 3-2 – are worth five points each. The two dominoes which have ten pips – the double-5 and the 6-4 – are worth ten points each.

The maximum number of points that can be scored in a round is 42 (hence the name of the game), made up as follows:

(a)   One point for each trick taken (7 points altogether).
(b)   Bonus points for tricks containing the honours (35 points altogether).

To begin a game the players draw for partners and to see who will lead the bidding. Each player draws one domino. The player who draws the highest domino will lead the bidding, and his partner is the player who draws the next highest domino. The players arrange themselves around the table so that partners sit opposite each other.

Each player then draws seven dominoes, and examines his hand in an attempt to guess how many points he and his partner will be able to score.

The player who won the draw to lead the bidding makes the first bid and the other players then bid in turn, the bidding going round the table only once. A bid must be for 30 points or more and must be higher than any previous bids. If a player does not wish to bid then he may pass.

The player who makes the highest bid has then, together with his partner, to attempt to take tricks to the value of the bid (or more).

The player who made the highest bid leads with any domino he chooses from his hand, and this domino determines which suit is trumps for the round. Since every domino belongs to two suits, he declares which of the two is the trump suit. For example, if he leads the 5-4 he may declare either fives or fours as trumps. The other players each play one domino in turn, and the player who plays the highest trump wins the trick.

For subsequent tricks, unless a trump is led, the suit is determined by the highest number on the domino that is led. Thus if threes are trumps and the 5-2 is led, the suit being led is fives.

Players must follow suit if they can. If they cannot, they may play any suit they choose, including trumps. A trick is won by the highest domino of the suit that was led or, if a trump was played, by the highest trump.

The player who wins a trick puts the four dominoes face down in front of him, and he leads the first domino for the next trick.

When all seven tricks have been taken, the scores for the round are worked out. If the partnership who made the highest bid were successful in winning tricks equal to or greater in value than their bid they score the number of points bid plus the value of their tricks. If they were unsuccessful, however, then their opponents score the number of points bid plus the value of the tricks that *they* have won.

Further rounds are played until the score of one partnership reaches some agreed figure such as 150 or 250.

Bingo

No. of players: 2
Equipment: Set of dominoes
Complexity: ★★★

Bingo is another domino game that bears some resemblance to a card game – in this case the resemblance is to Bézique. The scoring system in *Bingo* is quite complicated, but you should not let this deter you from playing what many consider to be the best of all domino games.

Points are scored in two ways – by winning tricks that contain certain dominoes, and by having doubles in one's hand.

The dominoes that score points in a trick are as follows:

(a) The double of the trump suit, which scores 28 points.
(b) The double-blank (called 'bingo') which scores 14 points – except, of course, when blanks are trumps and it scores 28.
(c) The other doubles, which score their pip value.
(d) The dominoes of the trump suit (other than the double) which score their pip value, with a blank counting as seven.
(e) The 6-4 and the 3-blank, which each score 10 points.

A player, when it is his turn to lead, may claim points if he has two or more doubles in his hand. To claim these points a player must lead one of the doubles and show the others to his opponent. The calls and the points claimed are as follows:

(a) For two doubles, the player calls 'Double', claiming 20 points.
(b) For three doubles, the player calls 'Triplets', claiming 40 points.
(c) For four doubles, the player calls 'Double doubles', claiming 50 points.
(d) For five doubles, the player calls 'King', claiming 60 points.
(e) For six doubles, the player calls 'Emperor', claiming 70 points.
(f) For all seven doubles, the player calls 'Invincible', claiming 210 points.
   The player must win the trick in order to gain the points he has claimed.

Each player should record the points he has gained from tricks and doubles at the time the tricks are taken.
   There is a bit more than this to the scoring system, but the rest is better left until we have looked at the way in which the game proceeds.
   The first player is chosen by lot. Each player then draws seven dominoes, the remaining fourteen forming the boneyard. The second player determines trumps by turning over one domino in the boneyard so that it is face upwards. The higher pip value on that domino is the trump suit (a blank, being worth seven, is higher than any other pip value).
   The initial phase of play begins with the first player leading any domino he chooses from his hand. The higher pip value of this domino determines the suit being led.
   The second player then plays any domino he chooses from his hand – he does not have to follow suit. If he plays a higher domino of the suit that was led, or a trump (when a trump was not led), or the double-blank ('bingo', which wins any trick in which it is played) then he wins the trick. Otherwise the first player wins the trick.
   The winner of the trick leads the next domino, but before that both players draw a domino from the boneyard (the winner of the trick drawing first).
   The first phase proceeds in this way until all the dominoes have been drawn from the boneyard. The last domino to be drawn must always be the domino that was turned up to establish trumps.
   In the second phase the remaining tricks are played with a change in the rule about the dominoes the second player may play. From this point the second player *must* always follow suit if he can. If he cannot follow

suit he must play a trump or 'bingo' if he can. Only if he does not have a domino of the suit being led, a trump or 'bingo', may he play any other domino.

It is possible to go from the first phase into the second phase before all the dominoes have been drawn from the boneyard. If a player, after he has won a trick, thinks that his hand is good enough to score at least 70 points from tricks and doubles without drawing any more from the boneyard, then instead of drawing from the boneyard he turns the trump domino face down. This is known as 'closing' and, from that point on, the rules of the second phase apply – there is no further drawing from the boneyard, and the second player must follow suit if he can.

The object of the game is to score seven 'sets', and the first player to do so is the winner. Sets are scored as follows:

(a) One set is scored for every 70 points gained from tricks and doubles.
(b) One set is scored by the first player to score 70 points – if his opponent has scored 30 points or more.
(c) Two sets are scored by the first player to score 70 points – if his opponent has won a trick but has scored less than 30 points.
(d) Three sets are scored by the first player to score 70 points – if his opponent has not yet won a trick.
(d) Two sets are scored by the opponent of a player who 'closes' and then fails to score 70 points.
(f) One set is scored for taking the double of the trump suit with 'bingo'.

7   **DICE GAMES**

Going to Boston
Fifty
Chicago
Beetle
Pig
Twenty-one
Round the Clock
Centennial
Everest
Hearts
Drop Dead
Craps
Shut the Box
Crag
Yacht
Poker Dice
Liar Dice

Going to Boston

No. of players: 2 or more
Equipment: 3 dice
Complexity: ★★

The first player rolls all three dice at once. He then leaves the die which shows the highest number (if two are equally high, he leaves only one of them) and he rolls the other two again. Of these two he again leaves the die showing the higher number and rolls the other die again. This completes his turn, and his score is the total shown by the three dice. When all the players have done the same in their turn, the player with the highest score is the winner of that round.

An agreed number of rounds are usually played, and the player who has won the most rounds is the winner of the game.

Fifty

No. of players: 2 or more
Equipment: 2 dice
Complexity: ★★

Fifty is a very simple dice game, in which the objective is to be the first player to score (would you believe it?) fifty points. Each player in turn throws the two dice once and he scores only if a double is thrown. A double 6 scores 25 points. A double 5, double 4, double 2 or double 1 scores 5 points. But when a player throws a double 3 he loses all the points he has scored so far and has to start all over again.

Chicago

No. of players: 2 or more
Equipment: 2 dice
Complexity: ☆

This simple game, which is all luck and no skill, is based on the eleven possible totals which can be obtained from throwing two dice – that is, totals from 2 to 12.

The dice pass around the table eleven times, and each player in his turn throws the two dice once. On the first round each player who throws the dice to make a total of 2 scores two points, the others scoring nothing. On the second round each player who throws the dice to make a total of 3 scores three points, the others scoring nothing. The game proceeds in this way, on successive rounds the players having to throw a total of 4, 5 and so on up to 12, and scoring accordingly. The player who obtains the highest total score is the winner.

Beetle

No. of players: 2 to 6
Equipment: One die; paper and a pencil for each player
Complexity: ☆

Beetle is the most popular family dice game. The objective is to be the first player to complete the drawing of a beetle. Artistic talent, however, is not absolutely necessary, as you may see from this example:

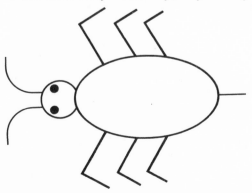

The beetle consists of thirteen parts: body, head, tail, two eyes, two feelers and six legs. The right value must be thrown with the die before each part may be drawn.

Special 'beetle dice' are obtainable for playing this game, with the faces marked B (body), H (head), T (tail), E (eye), F (feeler) and L (leg). A standard die, however, serves just as well, with the numbers corresponding to the parts of the beetle as follows:

> 1 for the body
> 2 for the head
> 3 for each leg
> 4 for each eye
> 5 for each feeler
> 6 for the tail

Thus, to complete his beetle, a player must throw a 1, a 2, six 3s, two 4s, two 5s and a 6.

Player take it in turn to throw the die, each player throwing it only once in each round.

Before a player can start drawing his beetle he must throw a 1. This permits him to draw the body. Once the body is drawn, he may start adding the head, legs and tail when he throws the appropriate numbers with the die. The feelers and eyes, however, cannot be added until after he has thrown a 2, enabling him to draw the head.

The game is sometimes played for points. A round ends when one player has completed his beetle. He scores 13 points, and each of the other players scores one point for each part he has drawn. Further rounds are played and the game is won by the first player to score 51 points.

Pig

No. of players: 2 or more
Equipment: One die
Complexity: ☆

Before the game begins a preliminary round is played in which each player throws the die once. The player who throws the lowest number begins the game. He then throws the die and scores the value shown by the die. He throws again and adds this score to his previous score. He may continue doing this as many times as he likes, on each throw adding to his previous score, until he decides to stop. However, if at any time he throws a 1 his turn ends and he loses his whole score for that turn. The play passes around the table, each player in his turn throwing the die until he decides to stop or until he throws a 1.

The scores are recorded for each turn and the first player to attain a total score of 101 is the winner.

Twenty-One

No. of players: 2 or more
Equipment: One die; a supply of counters (or coins or whatever)
Complexity: ☆

This is a version of the card game *Pontoon* that is played with dice. The 'stakes' may be counters, buttons, matchsticks, pennies, £10 notes or whatever you wish. We will assume that counters are being used.

The players each put one counter into the kitty. Each player in turn then throws the die as many times as he likes, adding up the numbers thrown, in an attempt to get a total of twenty-one or near as possible to it. A player whose total goes over twenty-one is 'bust' and is out of the game.

When all the players have had a turn the player whose total is nearest to twenty-one collects the kitty. If two or more players get equally high totals they may share the kitty or there may be a play-off between them.

Play may continue until one player has won all the counters, or for an agreed number of games after which the player with the highest number of counters is the winner.

Round the Clock

No. of players: 2 or more
Equipment: 2 dice
Complexity: ⋆

The object of the game is to roll, in the correct sequence, a 1, then a 2, then a 3, and so on up to 12. Each player in turn rolls the two dice. For the numbers up to 6 either of the individual dice values or the total value of the two dice may be counted. For instance, if a player needs a 4 he will be successful if either of the dice shows a 4 or if the dice show a 3 and a 1. For the numbers from 7 to 12 obviously only the total value of the two dice is counted. The first player to reach 12 is the winner.

Centennial

No. of players: 2 or more
Equipment: 3 dice; paper and a pencil;
a counter for each player
Complexity: ⋆

Centennial is essentially an extended version of *Round the Clock*. The players' positions are recorded on a simple board which may be drawn on a piece of paper. It consists of a row of twelve numbered squares, which should be large enough to place the counters on.

1	2	3	4	5	6	7	8	9	10	11	12

The objective is to move one's counter, according to the numbers thrown with the dice, from 1 to 12 and then back to 1 again. The first player to do so is the winner.

Each player in his turn throws the three dice. His throw must contain a 1 before he can place his counter on square 1, then he will need a 2 or two 1s in order to move to square 2, and so on. In each throw the value of any individual die, or the combined values of any two dice, or the total value of all three dice may be counted.

In one turn a player may be able to move his counter several places. If a player, for example, on his first turn is lucky enough to throw a 1, a 2, and a 4, then the 1 will take him to square 1, the 2 to square 2, the 2 plus 1 to square 3, the 4 to square 4, the 4 plus 1 to square 5, the 4 plus 2 to square 6, and finally the 4 plus 2 plus 1 to square 7. Not bad for one throw!

The players continue throwing the dice in turn until one player wins by completing the round trip from square 1 to square 12 and back down to square 1 again.

There is one extra rule which makes it worthwhile for a player to watch his opponents' throws carefully. This rule is that if a player throws a number that he needs but overlooks it and does not use it then that number may be claimed by any other player who needs it. The number must be claimed as soon as the dice are passed on and the player claiming it must be able to use it immediately.

Everest

No. of players: 2 or more
Equipment: Paper and a pencil for each player; 3 dice
Complexity: ☆

Everest is similar to Centennial, but whereas in Centennial the numbers from 1 to 12 and back to 1 have to be scored in the right sequence, in Everest they may be scored in any sequence. Because of this difference, each player needs his own sheet of paper marked with two rows of 12 squares, one numbered from 1 to 12 and the other numbered from 12 to 1.

1	2	3	4	5	6	7	8	9	10	11	12

12	11	10	9	8	7	6	5	4	3	2	1

Each player in turn throws the three dice. He may then cross off any numbers on his chart, in any order and using either row, according to the values of the dice.

The values of the dice may be used singly or in any combination, but (unlike the scoring in Centennial) each value may be counted only once. Thus if a player throws a 1, a 2 and a 4 he has the choice of crossing off the following numbers on his chart:

(a) a 1, a 2 and a 4, or (b) a 1 and a 6, or (c) a 2 and a 5, or (d) a 3 and a 4, or (e) a 7. The first player to be able to cross off all his twenty-four numbers is the winner.

Hearts

No. of players: 2 or more
Equipment: 6 dice
Complexity: ⭐

This game in its original form is played with six special dice, each of which has its faces marked with the letters H, E, A, R, T, S. These 'hearts dice' may be bought, but the game may be played just as well with ordinary dice.

There is a preliminary round to select the first player (usually the player who obtains the highest score from throwing the six dice). Then each player in his turn throws the six dice. Points are scored for throwing the following combinations of numbers:

1,2	= five points
1,2,3	= ten points
1,2,3,4	= fifteen points
1,2,3,4,5	= twenty points
1,2,3,4,5,6	= twenty-five points

If two dice of the same value are thrown, only one of them counts. However, if the throw contains three 1s then the unfortunate player loses all the points he has scored so far. The winner is the first player to score 100 points.

Drop Dead

No. of players: 2 or more
Equipment: 5 dice
Complexity: ⭐

Each player in turn throws the five dice. If any of the five dice show a 2 or a 5 he scores nothing, otherwise his score is the total of the numbers shown by the five dice. Any dice showing a 2 or a 5 are put to one side and he throws the remaining dice again. Again, if any of the dice show a 2 or a 5 they are put aside and he scores nothing, otherwise the total of the dice is added to his previous score. He continues in his way, throwing with an ever-decreasing number of dice, and increasing his score whenever a throw does not include a 2 or a 5. His turn ends when his last die shows a 2 or a 5 and he is said to have 'dropped dead'.

When all the players have had their turn the player with the highest score is the winner.

Player 1		**Player 2**		**Player 3**	
Throw	*Total Score*	*Throw*	*Total Score*	*Throw*	*Total Score*
1,1,3,4,5	0	1,1,3,6,6	17	2,2,3,5,5	0
3,3,4,6	16	1,2,2,4,6	17	2	0
2,4,4,5	16	1,3,6	27		
1,6	23	2,3,4	27		
2,3	23	1,4	32		
1	24	2,5	32		
6	30				
5	30				

Craps

No. of players: 2 or more
Equipment: 2 dice; a supply of counters (or buttons or whatever) for use as stakes
Complexity: ☆

Craps is of course a gambling game and is often played with great earnestness for considerable stakes. Each player takes a turn to be the 'shooter' (that is, the person who throws the dice). He places on the table whatever stake he is prepared to wager. All or part of this stake may be matched (or 'covered') by the other players.

The shooter throws the two dice. If the total value is 7 or 11 this is known as 'a natural', and the shooter immediately wins all the stakes that have been wagered. If the total of the two dice is 2, 3 or 12 this is known as 'craps' and the shooter immediately loses.

If the shooter throws any other total on his first throw (that is, 4, 5, 6, 8, 9 or 10) this number is known as his 'point'. He continues throwing until he either throws his point again or until he throws a 7 (any other totals thrown being disregarded). If his point comes up first then he wins. If a 7 comes up first then he loses.

As long as the shooter wins, he retains the dice, places a new stake and shoots again. As soon as he loses he passes the dice to the next player who then becomes the shooter.

Shut the Box

No. of players: 2 or more
Equipment: 2 dice; paper and pencil; 9 counters
Complexity: ★★

This is a traditional dice game from the North of France, where it is played on a special wooden board consisting of a tray in which the dice are thrown and a row of nine numbered boxes with sliding lids which can cover or disclose the numbers.

To play the game at home you will need a sheet of paper on which is drawn a row of nine squares, numbered from 1 to 9, and nine counters (or coins or buttons or whatever) with which you can cover the numbers.

| 1 | 2 | 3 | 4 | 5 | 6 | 7 | 8 | 9 |

The objective is to cover as many numbers as possible.

At the beginning of each player's turn all the numbers are uncovered. He throws the two dice and adds together their values. He must then choose numbered squares which add up to the same total and cover them. For example if he threw a 6 and a 4, the total would be 10 and he could choose to cover squares 6 and 4, or 7 and 3, or 8 and 2, or 9 and 1, or 6 and 3 and 1, and so on. He then throws the dice again. Again he must choose numbers to cover that will add up to the same total as the dice. Of course, they must be numbers that have not already been covered.

A player is allowed to throw with only one die, if he wishes, once the three top numbers (7, 8 and 9) have been covered. He continues throwing until he fails to find a combination of numbers to cover that will match the dice total. The numbers that remain uncovered are added together to form the player's score.

When all the players have had their turn the winner is the player with the lowest score.

Crag

No. of players: 2 or more
Equipment: 3 dice; score sheet and pencil
Complexity: ☆☆

To play Crag you will need a score sheet drawn like this:

	Player 1	Player 2	Player 3
Ones			
Twos			
Threes			
Fours			
Fives			
Sixes			
Odd Straight			
Even Straight			
Low Straight			
High Straight			
Three of a kind			
Thirteen			
Crag			
Totals			

There is a preliminary round to determine who will be the first player. Each player throws the dice once, and the player with the highest score will start the game.

The game itself starts with the first player throwing the three dice. He may then, if he wishes, throw one, two or all three dice again. His objective is to obtain one of the following scoring patterns:

1   **Ones** (scoring one point for each 1 thrown – maximum 3 points)
2   **Twos** (scoring two points for each 2 thrown – maximum 6 points)
3   **Threes** (scoring three points for each 3 thrown – maximum 9 points)
4   **Fours** (scoring four points for each 4 thrown – maximum 12 points)
5   **Fives** (scoring five points for each 5 thrown – maximum 15 points)
6   **Sixes** (scoring six points for each 6 thrown – maximum 18 points)
7   **Odd Straight** (the 1, 3 and 5 – scoring 20 points)
8   **Even Straight** (the 2, 4 and 6 – scoring 20 points)
9   **Low straight** (the 1, 2 and 3 – scoring 20 points)
10 **High Straight** (the 4, 5 and 6 – scoring 20 points)
11 **Three of a kind** (all three dice showing the same value – scoring 25 points)
12 **Thirteen** (a total of thirteen without a double – 2, 5 and 6, or 3, 4 and 6 – scoring 26 points)
13 **Crag** (a total of thirteen including a double – 1, 6, 6 or 3, 5, 5 or 5, 4, 4 – scoring 50 points)

His score is recorded on the chart and the dice are passed to the next player. Each player in his turn throws the three dice and may decide to score with the dice as thrown or to throw one or more again in an attempt to obtain a better score. His score is then recorded and the play passes round the table.

A player may or may not have a choice as to which pattern he scores. Let us say, for example, he has thrown two 4s and a 6. He may choose to score 8 points for Fours or 6 points for Sixes if he has not already scored for either of these patterns. If he has already scored for one of them then he is obliged, this time, to score for the other. If he has already scored for both of these patterns then he must choose some other pattern for which to score nought.

When the dice have passed thirteen times around the table the players will have filled in all thirteen spaces on the score sheet. The player with the highest total score is the winner.

Yacht

No. of players: 2 or more
Equipment: 5 dice; score sheet and pencil
Complexity: ★★

To play *Yacht* you will need a score sheet drawn like this:

	Player 1	Player 2	Player 3
Ones			
Twos			
Threes			
Fours			
Fives			
Sixes			
Little Straight			
Big Straight			
Full House			
Four of a Kind			
Choice			
Yacht			
Totals			

A preliminary round is played to select the first player. Each player throws the dice once, and the player with the highest score will start the game. The dice pass around the table twelve times, and each player in his turn will be attempting to obtain one of these twelve patterns:

1 **Ones** (scoring one point for each 1 thrown – maximum 5 points)
2 **Twos** (scoring two points for each 2 thrown – maximum 10 points)
3 **Threes** (scoring three points for each 3 thrown – maximum 15 points)

4   **Fours** (scoring four points for each 4 thrown – maximum 20 points)
5   **Fives** (scoring five points for each 5 thrown – maximum 25 points)
6   **Sixes** (scoring six points for each 6 thrown – maximum 30 points)
7   **Little Straight** (1,2,3,4,5 – scoring 15 points)
8   **Big Straight** (2,3,4,5,6 – scoring 20 points)
9   **Full House** (three of any number and two of another – scoring pip value – for example, 1,1,1,2,2 would score 7 points and 6,6,6,5,5 would score 28 points)
10   **Four of a Kind** (four of any number – scoring the pip value of the four dice – for example, 1,1,1,1,6 would score 4 points and 6,6,6,6,1 would score 24 points)
11   **Choice** (no pattern is required and the score is the total pip value of the five dice – the aim is to obtain as high a total as possible – for example, 3,5,5,6,6 would score 25 points)
12   **Yacht** (all five dice showing the same number – scoring 50 points)

Each player in his turn throws the five dice. He must then declare which one of the twelve patterns he is going to aim for. This must be a different pattern for each of his turns. Having declared the pattern he is trying to achieve, he is then allowed two further throws, each time throwing any or all of the five dice again (but he is not obliged to use all three throws if he obtains the required pattern on his first or second throw). If he achieves the pattern he has declared then his score is entered on the score sheet, otherwise a score of nought is entered.

Although luck plays a large part in the game, if high scores are to be achieved good judgement and calculation of probabilities are also required.

When the dice have passed around the table twelve times the players will have filled in all twelve spaces on the score sheet. The totals are calculated and the player with the highest total score is the winner.

Poker Dice

No. of players: 2 or more
Equipment: Set of 5 poker dice (or 5 standard dice)
Complexity: ✫✫

This game is usually played with a set of five special poker dice, each of which has its faces marked (rather like miniature playing cards) with

Ace, King, Queen, Jack, 10, 9. It may be played, using the same rules, with standard dice, but then the game loses something of its flavour.

Each player in turn throws the five dice. His objective is to get the best possible poker 'hand'. The hands, in descending order of value, are:

1 **Five of a Kind** (five aces ranking highest and five 9s lowest)
2 **Four of a Kind** (ranking as for Five Of a Kind)
3 **Full House** (three of a kind and a pair – ranking according to the three of a kind – for example, K, K, K,9,9 ranks higher than Q,Q,Q,J,J)
4 **Straight** (five consecutive values – A,K,Q,J,10 ranking higher than K,Q,J,10,9)
5 **Three of a Kind** (three aces ranking highest and three 9s lowest)
6 **Two Pairs** (the higher pair determines the value – for instance A,A,10,10,0 beats K,K,Q,Q,10)
7 **One Pair** (a pair of aces ranking highest and a pair of 9s lowest)
8 **Ace High** (ranking according to the value of the highest 'backers' – for example, A,K,J,10,9 beats A,Q,J,10,9)

If a player is not satisfied with his hand on the first throw he may throw any number of the dice a second time (and, in some versions of the game, a third time) in an attempt to improve his hand.

When all the players have had their turn, the player who obtained the best hand is the winner.

Liar Dice

No. of players: 3 or more
Equipment: Set of 5 poker dice (or 5 standard dice);
dice cup (optional); 3 counters for each player.
Complexity: ★★☆

Liar Dice is a fascinating game of deceit, deception, bluff and counter-bluff, and is considered by many to be by far the best of all dice games. Like *Poker Dice* the game is best played with a set of special poker dice but may be played with ordinary dice. The hands and their relative values are the same as described for the game of *Poker Dice*.

Each player starts the game with three counters – these are his 'lives' and when he loses all three he is out of the game.

A preliminary round is played to determine who will be the first player. Each player throws the five dice, and the player who obtains the highest hand starts the game.

The game starts with the first player throwing the five dice, concealing them with the dice cup or with his hands so that he, but none of the other players, may see what he has thrown. He then declares his hand (e.g. 'Pair of Queens' or 'Full House, Nines and Jacks'). This call may actually be the hand he has thrown or it may be a complete and utter lie. If he lies, he may declare a hand higher than or lower than the hand he has really thrown.

The next player on the left may either accept or challenge the call. If he accepts the call, the first player passes the dice to him, taking care that they remain concealed from the other players and that none of the dice get turned over accidentally. This is more easily performed if a dice cup (or other container) is used to cover the dice.

The second player examines the dice. He may then decide to throw none, some or all of the dice again. He must declare truthfully how many dice he is throwing. At all times the dice must remain concealed from the other players. He then has to declare a hand better than the hand declared by the previous player. This may be either a higher type of hand or a higher-ranking hand of the same type. If the first player had declared 'Pair of Queens' then he could, for example, declare 'Three Tens' or 'Pair of Aces'. Again, this may be true or bluff – equal to, higher than or lower than the actual hand.

The next player then has the choice of accepting the hand or challenging it. If he accepts it, he may throw any number of the dice again and must then declare a higher hand.

The play continues around the table in this way until a challenge is issued. The player being challenged exposes the dice. If the declarer can refute the challenger by showing that his declaration was equal to or less than the actual hand, then the challenger must pay one counter into the pool. If, on the other hand, the declarer has called a hand that was better than the actual hand then it is the declarer who must pay a counter into the pool.

After a challenge a new round is started by the challenger (or by the next player if the challenger has lost his last life).

The game continues until all but one of the players have lost their three lives and have been eliminated. The last player left in is the winner.

8 **MATCHSTICK GAMES**

Match Tower
Take the Last
Garden Path
Nim
One Line Nim
Odd or Even
Kayles
Tac Tix
Matchboxes
Maxey

Match Tower

No. of players: 2 or more
Equipment: An empty bottle and a good supply of matches
Complexity: ✶

The empty bottle should be one with a narrow neck, such as a wine bottle. If the only available wine bottle is full, it is *not* a good idea to drink the contents merely to provide an empty bottle for this game – a steady hand is required.

The number of matches required depends upon the dexterity of the players. For clumsy players only a few dozen matches will be needed while expert players may need several hundred. The aim is to build up layer after layer of matches over the mouth of the bottle, each player in turn adding one match. The first four matches are laid across the mouth of the bottle, the next four are laid across the first four, the next four across the previous four, and so on.

There are no winners, but the loser is the player who first dislodges the structure and sends it tumbling down. He must pay whatever penalty is decided by the other players.

Take the Last

No. of players: 2 or more
Equipment: 50 matches
Complexity: ✶

Place the fifty matches in a heap on the table. Each player in turn has to take matches from the heap, and may take any number he pleases between one and six. The player who takes the last match is the winner.

Alternatively the game may be played·as follows. Each player has three lives. As before, each player in his turn takes up to six matches from the heap. But this time the player who takes the last match loses a life. When a player loses all his lives he drops out of the game. The winner is the last player left when all the others have dropped out.

Garden Path

No. of players: 2
Equipment: Board, and about 15 matches for each player
Complexity: ☆☆

Each player's matches should be clearly distinguishable from those of
his opponent. You could use matches with heads of two different
colours or else use ink, paint or crayon to colour them. You also need a
board, which can be drawn on card or paper. The board consists of a grid
of 25 squares as in the diagram. The sides of the squares should be just a
fraction greater than the length of the matches being used. The sides of
the grid should be labelled North, South, East and West as shown.

Each player in turn puts one of his matches on any vacant line on the
board. One player's objective is to form a continuous path from North to
South, and the other player's objective is to form a continuous path from
East to West. Each player, of course, will attempt to block his opponent
while at the same time trying to complete his own path. The first player
to complete his path is the winner.

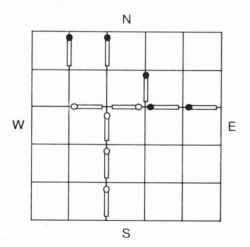

Nim

No. of players: 2
Equipment: 15 matches (or possibly more)
Complexity: ★★

Nim is a very old game and is believed to have originated in China. The basic version of the game starts with three rows of matches – three matches in the first row, five in the second row, and seven in the third row.

Each player in turn has to pick up any number of matches from any one of the rows. He may pick up only one match or the whole row or any number in between – but only from one row at a time. The player who picks up the last match is the winner.

Variation 1
The game is played exactly as described above, but the winner is the player who forces his opponent to pick up the last match.

Variation 2
The game may start with any number of rows, containing any number of matches. Try it, for example, with five rows containing 4, 5, 6, 7 and 8 matches.

One Line Nim

No. of players: 2
Equipment: 15 matches
Complexity: ★★

The fifteen matches are laid out in a line.

Each player in turn has to pick up one, two or three matches. The winner is the player who forces his opponent to pick up the last match. You may also try playing *One Line Nim* with 21 or 25 matches instead of 15.

Odd or Even

No. of players: 2
Equipment: 25 matches
Complexity: ★★

Place the matches in a line on the table, as for *One Line Nim*. Each player in turn has to pick up one, two or three matches. When all the matches have been picked up the winner is the player with an even number of matches in his hand. Alternatively, the game may be played so that the winner is the player who has picked up an odd number of matches.

Kayles

No. of players: 2
Equipment: About 20 matches
Complexity: ★★

Kayles, in fact, can be played with any number of matches from 5 upwards, but 20 is a reasonable number. You may play with fewer matches than this if you want a shorter game or with more if a longer game is required.

The matches are laid end to end in a long line. Each player in turn takes either one match or two matches which are touching each other. The player who takes the last match is the winner. Alternatively, the game may be played so that the winner is the player who forces his opponent to take the last match.

Tac Tix

No. of players: 2
Equipment: 16 matches
Complexity: ★★☆

The game of *Tac Tix* was invented by Piet Hein, a remarkable Danish mathematician, inventor and poet (among other things) who also invented the board game of *Hex*. The matches are arranged in a square formation, like this:

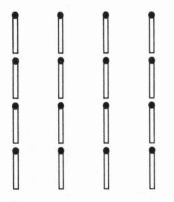

Each player in turn takes one or more matches from any one row or column, but the matches he takes must be adjacent, with no gaps in between.

For example, suppose the first player takes all four matches from the second row. The second player may then take any number of adjacent matches from one of the other rows, but he is now unable to take the three remaining matches from any of the columns, because of the gap – he may only take any one match or the lower two. The winner of the game is the player who forces his opponent to take the last match.

(There is not much point in playing so that the winner is the player who *takes* the last match, because then the second player can always win by playing symmetrically opposite his opponent.) Advanced players might like to try the game using a 5 × 5 or 6 × 6 square instead of the 4 × 4 square shown here.

Matchboxes

No. of players: 2
Equipment: 220 matches
Complexity: ★★

The matches are laid out in a square grid as in the diagram. Each player in turn may remove any one match or he may remove any two matches that are touching (either in a straight line or at right angles). The player who removes the last match is the winner.

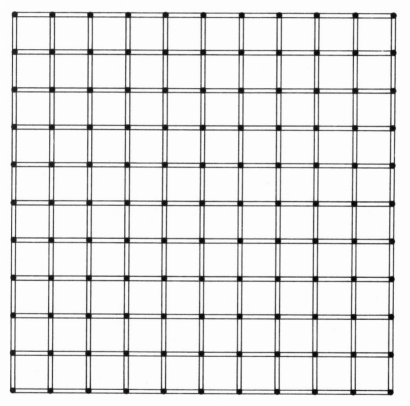

Maxey

No. of players: 2
Equipment: Pencil and paper; 10 matches
Complexity: ★★

The playing area is a piece of paper on which seven parallel lines have been drawn. The lines should be about the same length as a match and a little less than a match-length apart. The players start with five matches each, and each player in turn plays one match. A player may place his match on to one of the parallel lines or, if two adjacent lines are occupied by matches, he may 'bridge' those two matches by playing a match across them. Any pair of matches may only be bridged once.

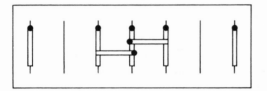

A player scores one point each time he plays a match on to a line next to a line that is already occupied by a match, and two points each time he forms a bridge between two matches.

The player with the most points when all the matches have been played is the winner.

9

Scissors, Paper, Stone
Fingers
Spoof
Crown and Anchor
Put and Take
Fan Tan
Lotto

Scissors, Paper, Stone

No. of players: 2
Equipment: None
Complexity: ☆

Variations of this game are known in many parts of the world. 'Scissors', 'paper' and 'stone' are represented by extending a hand to form different shapes – a hand with two fingers extended (in a sort of horizontal V-sign) represents scissors; a flat hand extended horizontally represents paper; a clenched fist represents stone.

Each player conceals one hand behind his back. Simultaneously both players show their hands, forming whichever of the three shapes they have chosen. The winner is decided by the rule 'Scissors cut paper; paper wraps stone; stone blunts scissors'. Thus scissors wins against paper, paper wins against stone, and stone wins against scissors. If both players choose the same shape, the round is a draw. Any number of rounds may be played to determine the overall winner.

Fingers

No. of players: 2
Equipment: None
Complexity: ☆

This is a guessing game, in which the aim is to guess the total number of fingers (from nought to ten) that will be displayed by the two players.

Each player conceals one hand behind his back. Simultaneously both players show their hands with any number of fingers extended. For the purposes of this game thumbs count as fingers, and a clenched fist represents nought. At the same time as revealing his hand each player calls out a number from nought to ten, which is his guess at the total number of fingers which will be displayed by the two players. If both players guess correctly, or if neither guesses correctly, the round is a draw. Any previously agreed number of rounds may be played.

Spoof

No. of players: 3 or more
Equipment: Three small objects (such as coins or matches)
for each player
Complexity: ✫

Spoof is a game of bluff, in which the objective is to guess the total number of objects concealed in the hands of the players.

Each player has three small objects – coins, matches, paperclips or anything small enough to be enclosed in a clenched fist. He chooses any number of them to conceal in his fist, and holds his fist out in front of him. When all the players are holding out their fists, each player in turn, proceeding in a clockwise direction, has a guess at the total number of objects concealed. Each player's guess must be different. The players then open their fists and the objects are counted. The player guessing correctly or whose guess is nearest to the correct number wins the round.

The player guessing first has the advantage that he can guess any number he likes, but the players guessing subsequently have the compensating advantage that they can deduce information from the guesses already made – if they can tell when another player is bluffing.

Crown and Anchor

No. of players: 7
Equipment: Board; set of 3 dice
Complexity: ✫

Crown and Anchor is a simple gambling game that was at one time popular in the British Navy.

The faces of each of the three dice are marked with a crown, an anchor and four aces. The board is also marked with these symbols. One player is the banker, and the other players place stakes on the board to bet on the symbols of their choice. The banker rolls the dice, and a player may win one, two or three times his stake according to the number of times his chosen symbol appears on the uppermost faces of the dice. The banker, of course, has the odds in his favour, pocketing on average half the stakes. Each player has a session as a banker.

Put and Take

No. of players: Any number
Equipment: Put and Take top
Complexity: ☆

Put and Take is played with a special eight-sided top, of which the faces are marked as follows:

PUT 1   PUT 4
TAKE 1   TAKE 4
PUT 3   PUT ALL
TAKE 3   TAKE ALL

Each player puts an agreed stake into the pot. Then each player in turn spins the top and, according to the face that is uppermost when the top comes to rest, puts the indicated amount into the pot or takes the indicated amount from the pot. PUT ALL means that the player must put into the pot a sum equal the amount already there; TAKE ALL means that he wins the entire pot.

Put and Take tops may be bought in some toyshops, but some searching may be required to find one. A simple home-made substitute may be produced by cutting out an eight-sided shape from stiff card and marking it as in the illustration. A nail is pushed through the centre so that the top can be spun, and the edge on which the top settles determines the action to be taken.

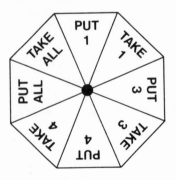

Fan Tan

No. of players: Any number
Equipment: A board, a bowl of beans, and a stick
Complexity: ✯

Fan Tan is a Chinese gambling game, and is incredibly popular not only in Asia but also in Chinese communities throughout the world. Many Chinese people have a passion for gambling, and indeed they must to be so addicted to this game, which is often played in all-night sessions and for very high stakes.

The board, usually improvised, is simply a flat playing surface with the corners marked 1, 2, 3 and 4. Each player places a stake on one of these four numbers. The banker has a bowl of beans (dried beans, that is, not the baked-in-tomato-sauce variety) from which he takes a random handful and places them in the centre of the board. With a stick he counts off the beans in groups of four. It is only the number of beans – from 1 to 4 – in the last group that is important. This is the number that the players have wagered on and that determines whether they win or lose.

Lotto

No. of players: 2 to 6
Equipment: Lotto cards; 90 numbered discs
Complexity: ✯

Lotto (alias *Housey Housey* or *Tombola*), at one time a popular family game in many countries – in the days before television – is the forerunner of modern, commercialised *Bingo*.

Each player has a special card marked with fifteen numbers between 1 and 90. None of the numbers is duplicated on other cards.

12		31		53		72	84
4		24	46		65		87
	19	28		49		68	77

One of the players is the caller, and he has a set of 90 numbered discs which he draws at random, one at a time, from a bag or other suitable container. Each number is called out as it is drawn, and the disc is given to the player on whose card it appears. That player covers the number on his card with the disc. When all the numbers on a player's card have been covered he calls 'Lotto' and wins the game.

Marbles

No. of players: Any small number
Equipment: Marbles
Complexity: ⋆

Marbles (also called taws or alleys or bools) are small, hard balls which are usually made from glass but may also be made of clay, stone, wood or other materials.

There are several schools of thought as to the optimal technique of marble propulsion. Some players merely roll them, but dedicated players usually prefer to flick (or 'knuckle') them. To do this, the back of the hand is placed on the ground with the side of the forefinger at right-angles to the required line of flight. A marble is poised in the crease of the top joint of the forefinger and is flicked smartly with the thumb.

There are many different games which can be played with marbles. With a few exceptions they all share the common principle of shooting a marble to hit another target marble, thus winning it. Some of the more popular games are described here.

Captures

A game for two players. The first player shoots his marble. The second player then shoots his marble in an attempt to hit the first player's marble. If he hits it he keeps it, otherwise the first player shoots his marble again, from its last position, in an attempt to hit the second player's marble. The players continue playing alternately in this way until one hits and wins the other's marble.

Spanners

This is the same as *Captures*, with the additional rule that when a player's marble is less than a hand's span from that of his opponent he may attempt a 'span'. This consists of flicking the two marbles together with finger and thumb. A hit means that he wins his opponent's marble, but a miss means that he loses his own marble to his opponent.

Alleys

This game may be played by any small number of players. The first player places a marble any agreed distance from the throwing-line. The other players in turn shoot their marbles in an attempt to hit this target. Any marbles that miss the target are pocketed by the first player. When a player succeeds in hitting the target he takes the place of the first player and he wins any marbles missing the target.

Dobblers

Another game for any small number of players. A row of marbles is formed, using one or two marbles from each player. The players, each using one throwing marble, shoot in turn and win any marbles they displace from the row. A successful shot entitles a player to an extra shot. A player's throwing marble is always left lying after his turn, and if it is hit by another player's marble he must put an extra marble in the row.

One Step

This game is played in the same manner as *Dobblers* except that each player's first shot is made by taking one step forward and then throwing from an upright position. Subsequent shots must also be made from an upright position but without the step forward.

Spangy

This is a game for 5 players. A square is drawn on the floor and each player places a marble in the square – one in the centre and one at each corner. The players shoot in turn, from a throwing-line about 10 yards from the square. A player wins any marbles that he succeeds in knocking out of the square. If his marble comes to rest within a hand's span of one of the target marbles he may win that marble if he makes a successful span (as in *Spanners*). A player always picks up his marble at the end of his turn, starting his next turn from the throwing-line.

Ring Taw

This game may be played by any small number of players. A circle of about one foot in diameter is drawn on the floor, with an outer circle of about seven feet in diameter. Each player puts one or two marbles in the inner circle.

Shooting from any point outside the outer circle, each player in turn attempts to knock one or more marbles out of the inner circle. If he is successful he wins any that he dislodges and has another shot from the point where his marble came to rest. After a player's turn has finished his marble is left where it is until his turn comes round again. If it is hit by another player's shot he has to give another marble to the player who hit it.

Increase Pound

This is similar to *Ring Taw*, but with the following differences:
(a) Knocking a marble out of the inner circle does not entitle a player to an extra shot.
(b) A player whose marble comes to rest inside the inner circle forfeits it. On his next turn he must shoot with a fresh marble from any point outside the outer circle.
(c) A player whose marble is hit when it lies within the outer circle must hand over to the shooter all the marbles he has won so far.

Fortifications

Four concentric circles are drawn on the floor. Each player places one marble in the outer circle, two in the next circle, three in the next, and four in the inner circle. Each player in turn shoots in an attempt to knock a marble from the outer circle. If he succeeds he wins the marble that he dislodges. If he fails he must place an extra marble in that circle. When, and only when, the outer circle has been cleared, the players may aim for marbles in the next circle – but any player who failed to win a marble from the outer circle is out of the game. When the second circle has been cleared the players proceed to the next circle, and so on. When attacking the second circle a hit entitles a player to an extra shot; when attacking the third circle two consecutive hits entitle a player to an extra shot; when attacking the inner circle three consecutive hits entitle a player to an extra shot.

Hundreds

This is a game for two players. A small circle is drawn on the floor. Each player shoots one marble in an attempt to get it in the circle. If both players get their marbles in the circle they both shoot again. When only one of the players gets his marble in the circle he scores 10 points and shoots again. He continues shooting and scoring 10 points each time he is successful, until he misses or until he has scored 100 points. If he misses before scoring 100 points, his opponent starts shooting, in the same way, until *he* misses or scores 100. Play alternates in this way and the first player to score 100 points wins the game.

Bounce Eye

A circle of about one foot in diameter is drawn on the floor. Each player puts one or more marbles in the circle to form a cluster in the centre. Each player in turn, from a standing position, drops a marble on the cluster, winning any marbles that are knocked out of the circle. If none are knocked out, the unsuccessful player has to add an extra marble to the group in the circle.

Spillikins

No. of players: 4 to 6
Equipment: Set of spillikins
Complexity: ★★

Spillikins (also known as *Jackstraws*) may be played with a set of about fifty straws or strips of plastic, wood, bamboo, ivory or bone. The most common form, however, consists of thin, rounded sticks, 6 to 8 inches long, with points at each end and coloured to indicate various point-values.

One player picks up all the spillikins and drops them on the table or floor to form a heap. The next player then attempts to remove one spillikin from the heap without disturbing any of the others. If he is successful he keeps it and attempts to remove another. The slightest disturbance of any spillikin other than the one he is trying to remove ends his turn, and the next player takes his turn. The game ends when all the spillikins have been successfully removed from the heap. The players' scores are then added up and the player with the highest score is the winner.

A sharp eye and a steady hand are requisites for successful play. Many different techniques may be used – plucking with finger and thumb, pressing down the end of a spillikin and drawing it out gently, pressing down an end sharply to jerk a spillikin off the top of the heap, and so on. In some versions of the game once a spillikin of a particular value has been removed it may be used as a tool to help remove others.

Fivestones

No. of players: 1 or more
Equipment: Five stones
Complexity: ★★

To play *Fivestones* you may use the knucklebones of a sheep, or small
pebbles, but in this age of sophistication the 'stones' are more usually a
set of small wooden or plastic cubes.

The game consists of a series of lesser games to be played with the
stones, in which they are thrown into the air and caught again in various
ways. There is an almost infinite variety of these lesser games and they
may be played in any order. The players should agree beforehand the
games to be played and the sequence (usually in order of increasing
complexity). Each player in turn then goes through the sequence of
games until he fails on one of them, and it then becomes the next player's
turn. When a player's turn comes round again he recommences with the
game in which he failed on his previous turn. The first player to
complete the sequence successfully is the winner.

Many of the games start with the same basic throw. The stones are
thrown up into the air from the palm of the hand, and as many as possible
are caught on the back of the hand. They are then thrown from the back of
the hand and as many as possible are caught in the palm.

Ones

The player performs the basic throw, as described above. If he succeeds
in catching all five he immediately goes on to the next game. If he catches
none, he has failed and the turn passes to the next player. Otherwise, he
transfers all but one of the stones he has caught to his other hand. The
single stone is thrown in the air, one of the fallen stones is gathered in the
throwing hand, and the thrown stone is caught in the same hand. One of
these two stones is transferred to the other hand. This process is repeated
until all the stones on the floor have been gathered.

Twos

The five stones are scattered on the ground. One stone is picked up and
thrown into the air, two of the stones on the ground are gathered into the
throwing hand, and the thrown stone is caught in the same hand. Two
stones are transferred to the other hand. The process is repeated,
gathering the remaining two stones from the floor.

Threes

This is played in the same way as *Twos*, except that three stones are gathered on the first throw and the remaining stone on the second throw.

Fours

This is like *Twos* except that all four stones on the floor must be gathered in one throw.

Pecks

The basic throw is performed, and if all five stones are caught the player immediately goes on to the next game. Otherwise he keeps all the caught stones in his hand, holding one of them between thumb and forefinger. This stone is thrown into the air, one of the stones on the floor is gathered in the throwing hand and the thrown stone is caught in the same hand. This process is repeated until all five stones have been gathered into the throwing hand.

Bushels

The player performs the basic throw. If all five stones are caught he goes on to the next game; if none are caught his turn ends. Otherwise he throws in the air all the stones in his hand, one of the stones on the floor is gathered in the throwing hand, and all the thrown stones are caught in the same hand. This is repeated until all the stones have been gathered in the same hand.

Claws

The game begins with a modification of the basic throw. The player throws the five stones and attempts to catch them on the back of his hand. If none are caught his turn ends. If all five are caught the player attempts to complete the basic throw and if he is successful he goes on to the next game. If one or more, but not all five, are caught on the back of the hand they remain there while the player picks up the remaining stones on the ground between the fingers of his throwing hand – no more than one stone between any two fingers. He then throws the stones from the back of his hand and catches them in his palm. The stones held between the fingers must then be manoeuvred into the palm – without using the other hand.

Ones Under The Arch

The five stones are scattered on the floor. The player forms an arch by touching the thumb and forefinger of the non-throwing hand to the floor. One stone is picked and thrown into the air. Before it is caught again in the throwing hand one of the remaining stones must be knocked under the arch. This is repeated until all four stones have been knocked under the arch. The arch is then removed, the stone is thrown into the air and the other four stones are gathered into the throwing hand and the thrown stone is caught in the same hand.

Twos Under the Arch

This is the same as *Ones Under the Arch* except that two stones must be knocked under the arch on each throw.

Threes Under the Arch

Three stones must be knocked under the arch on the first throw, and the remaining stone knocked under the arch on the second throw.

Fours Under the Arch

All four stones must be knocked through the arch at the same time.

Stables

The five stones are scattered on the floor. The fingers and thumb of the non-throwing hand are spread out and placed so that the fingertips are touching the floor and the palm is raised, the spaces between the fingers forming the four stables. One stone is thrown into the air, and before it is caught one of the other stones must be knocked into one of the stables. In this manner a stone is knocked into each of the four stables in turn. The non-throwing hand is then moved away, the throwing stone is thrown into the air, the four stones are gathered into the throwing hand, and the thrown stone is caught in the same hand.

Toad in the Hole

The five stones are scattered on the floor. The non-throwing hand is placed so that the thumb lies straight on the floor with the fingers curled round to form a hole. One stone is thrown into the air and before it is caught again in the throwing hand one of the remaining stones must be picked up and dropped into the hole. This is repeated until all four stones have been dropped into the hole. The non-throwing hand is moved away, the throwing stone is thrown into the air, the four stones are gathered into the throwing hand, and the thrown stone is caught in the same hand.

Snake in the Grass

Four of the stones are placed in a straight line, about six inches apart. The fifth stone is thrown into the air and before it is caught again in the same hand one of the end stones is moved. The moved stone must follow the path shown round the other stones and back to its starting point.

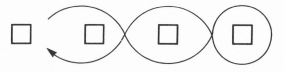

As many throws as required may be taken to complete the manoeuvre, provided that on each throw the end stone is moved part of the way and provided that no other stone is touched.

Tiddlywinks

No. of players: 2, 3 or 4
Equipment: Cup; 6 winks and a squidger for each player
Complexity: ★★

Tiddlywinks may be played on the floor but is best played on a table which is covered with a thick cloth or a piece of felt. The cup, which should be about 1½ inches wide and 1 or 2 inches high, is placed in the centre of the table. Each player has six winks, which are small flat disks of plastic or bone, and a squidger, which is a larger disk. A wink is squidged by pressing the edge of one's squidger against the edge of the wink, thus making the wink jump into the air. The object of the game is to be the first player to squidge all one's winks into the cup.

Each player lines his winks up in front of him at an equal distance from the cup. To determine the order of play each player squidges one wink, and the player who gets his wink nearest to the cup is the first to play. Play proceeds from player to player in a clockwise direction around the table.

A player may squidge only his own winks and has one squidge per turn except that when he succeeds in potting a wink he is entitled to an extra squidge. Winks are always squidged from where they lie (except that, when a wink is accidentally squidged off the table, it may be replaced on the nearest point on the edge of the table).

When a wink is covered by another wink, it is said to be squopped. If a player has a wink that is squopped by an opponent's wink he may not squidge it – he must wait until the opponent removes his wink or must attempt to dislodge it by squidging another of his own winks at it.

Successful play requires not only accurate squidging but also the ability to judge when to pot and when to squop.

Golomb's Game

No. of players: 2
Equipment: Chessboard; set of pentominoes
Complexity: ★★★

This simple yet complex game was invented by Solomon W. Golomb, an American research mathematician.

Pentominoes are described in the chapter on Solo Games. This game for two players requires only a chessboard and a set of pentominoes of which the unit square is the same size as the squares of the chessboard. Each player in turn picks an unplayed pentomino and places it on the board to cover five vacant squares. The last player to be able to place a piece on the board is the winner. That's all there is to it. Try it. It's fascinating.

Calculator 21

No. of players: Any small number
Equipment: 2 dice; a pocket calculator per player
Complexity: ☆

The roll of the dice indicates a calculation to be performed on a player's calculator. The aim is to reach a displayed total of exactly 21, and the first player to do so is the winner.

Each player in turn rolls the two dice. One of the dice determines the number to be entered on his calculator. The other determines the arithmetic operation to be entered – an odd number indicating subtraction and an even number addition. The player may choose which of the dice to use as a number and which to use as an operation. For example, a throw of 5,2 may be entered on the calculator as 5 + or as 2 −.

For example:	Roll	Enter	Display
	4,5	5 +	5
	6,2	6 +	11
	6,5	5 +	16
	4,1	4 −	20
	2,2	2 +	18
	6,4	4 +	22
	3,1	1 −	23
	3,2	2 −	21

Darts

No. of players: Any number
Equipment: Dartboard; set of 3 darts per player
Complexity: ☆☆

The standard dartboard is 18 inches in diameter and is divided into twenty numbered segments, high numbers alternating with low numbers. There is a narrow outer ring, in which a dart scores double the score for the segment, and a narrow ring midway between the centre and the outer ring, in which a dart scores treble. In the centre of the circle there are two concentric rings – known as the bull – the outer bull scoring 25 and the inner bull scoring 50.

Darts may be played by individual players, by pairs or by teams. In singles games the players take alternate turns – a turn consisting of throwing three darts. In pairs or team games the pairs or teams take alternate turns, the players on each side throwing in succession. There is usually a preliminary throw to establish who has the first turn, the player throwing nearest to the bull playing first.

Only darts in the board at the end of a player's turn count in the scoring. Darts that miss the board or that hit the board outside the scoring area or that drop out from the board do not count and may not be re-thrown. The method of scoring is to subtract the score for a player's turn from a target total, which is usually 301 for singles game, 501 for doubles game, and 1001 for team games. But before beginning to score, a side must score a double (by throwing a dart into the outer doubles ring). The starting double is scored as are any darts thrown after it in that turn but not darts thrown before the double. Thus, for example, if a player on his first turn in a singles game throws a 7, a double 20 and an 11 his score for that turn is 51, so his new target is marked as 250 (301 − 51). A player must also finish with a double which brings his score exactly to nought. If the score for a player's turn would take him past nought, or to one, then he does not score at all for that turn.

David	Edward
250	284
240	220
104	159
22	101
–	

Apart from the standard game described above there are a number of other darts games which, although they might be looked down on by serious darts players, may provide a good deal of enjoyment.

Round the Clock

This game is for any number of players, playing all against all. Three darts are thrown in a turn. Starting with a double, each player has to throw a 1, then a 2 and so on up to 20, and has to finish with a treble. The first player to finish the sequence is the winner.

Shanghai

This game is somewhat similar to Round the Clock except that each player on his first turn aims for and scores only 1s, on his second turn aims for and scores only 2s and so on. The player with the highest total score after twenty turns is the winner.

Scram

This is a game for two players, one being the 'stopper', the other being the 'scorer'. Each player in turn throws three darts. The stopper goes first, aiming with his three darts to block the scorer. Each segment of the board that is hit by the stopper is thenceforth closed to the scorer. The scorer aims to score as many points as possible before the stopper closes all the segments on the board. The players then change roles, and the player with the higher number of points as scorer wins the game.

Darts Football

This game is for two players, each throwing three darts in turn. The first player to throw a dart in the bull 'gets control of the ball' and starts scoring one goal for each double he throws – until his opponent gets control of the ball by throwing a bull and *he* starts scoring for each double. The first player must then aim for another bull to recover the ball. The winner is the first player to score ten goals.

Darts Cricket

This is a game for two teams. A coin is tossed to decide which team bats first. The batting team and the bowling team take alternate turns, a turn consisting of three darts. Runs are scored by the batting team for each point scored in excess of 40 in a turn. For example, a member of the batting team getting 60 with his three darts would score 20 runs. The bowling team aims for bulls to take 'wickets', an outer bull taking 1 wicket and an inner bull taking 2 wickets. When 10 wickets have been taken by the bowlers, the teams change over. The game is won by the team with the higher number of runs.

Billiards

No. of players: 2
Equipment: Billiard table; balls; cues
Complexity: ★★★

Billiards has been defined as a game in which balls on a table are poked with a stick. There is, of course, much more to it than that, and it is a game which, although it can be enjoyed by a complete novice, demands great skill if it is to be played well.

The playing area of a standard billiard table measures 12 ft by 6 ft 1½ in (though scaled-down versions may be used) and is of green baize over a bed of slate, being bordered by cloth-covered rubber 'cushions'. There are six pockets – one at each corner and one midway down each of the long sides. Twenty-nine inches from the bottom cushion is the 'baulk line', the space between this line and the bottom cushion being known as 'baulk'. On the baulk line there is a semi-circle known as the 'D'. Down the centre of the table there are four 'spots' – the billiard spot, 12¾ in from the top cushion; the centre spot between the two centre pockets; the pyramid spot, midway between the centre spot and the top cushion; and the baulk spot in the centre of the baulk line.

Three balls are used – a red ball and two white cue balls, one of which is marked with a spot so that they may be distinguished. Each

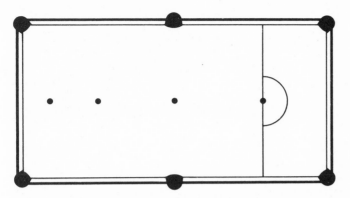

player has a cue – a long, tapered, wooden rod – which he uses to strike his cue ball. One other piece of equipment that may be used is a 'rest' – a cue-like rod with an X-shaped metal end on which the cue may be rested for shots where the cue ball would otherwise be inaccessible.

Each player may strike with the cue only his own cue ball, and points are scored as follows:

(a) Two points if the cue ball hits the opponent's cue ball and 'pots' it (i.e. sends it into a pocket).

(b) Two points if the cue ball is potted 'in off' the opponent's cue ball.

(c) Three points if the cue ball hits the red ball and pots it.

(d) Three points if the cue ball is potted in off the red ball.

(d) Two points for a 'cannon' if the cue ball hits both the other balls.

A player whose cue ball fails to hit either of the other balls forfeits one point, unless the cue ball goes into a pocket, in which case he forfeits three points.

To decide who has the first shot, the players 'string' by playing their cue balls simultaneously from the 'D' to rebound off the top cushion. The player whose ball returns nearer to the bottom cushion has the first shot.

To start the game the red ball is placed on the billiard spot, and the first player plays his cue ball from any point in the 'D'. When the first player's turn is finished, the second player brings his cue ball into play.

A player's turn, known as a 'break', may consist of any number of shots provided that he scores with each shot. Only when a shot fails to score does his turn end, and his opponent follows. When the red ball is potted it is immediately replaced on the billiard spot. When the opponent's cue ball is potted it remains out of play for the remainder of that break. When a player pots his own cue ball it is brought back into play by being placed anywhere in the 'D' before the other player starts his break. A cue ball brought back into play may not strike any other ball in the baulk unless it first strikes a cushion outside the baulk.

The game may be won by the player scoring the greater number of points in an agreed length of time or by the player whose score first reaches an agreed total.

Snooker

No. of players: 2 or more
Equipment: Billiard table; balls; cues
Complexity: ★★☆

Snooker may be played by two players or by a greater number playing either in teams or all against all. Twenty-two balls are used – a white cue ball, fifteen reds and six colours. The points values of the balls are as follows: Red – 1 point, Yellow – 2 points, Green – 3 points, Brown – 4 points, Blue – 5 points, Pink – 6 points, Black – 7 points.

At the start of the game the balls are placed on the table as follows: the red balls in the form of a triangle with its apex on the pyramid spot and its base towards the top cushion; the yellow on the right-hand corner of the 'D'; the green on the left-hand corner of the 'D'; the brown on the baulk spot; the blue on the centre spot; the pink on the pyramid spot; the black on the billiard spot.

The players draw to decide who will play first, and the first player plays the cue ball from anywhere within the 'D' to strike a red. As in *Billiards*, each player's break continues until he plays a shot which fails to score. The first shot of each break must be at a red, as long as any reds remain on the table. If it is potted the player scores 1 point, and then aims to pot any one of the colours that he might choose. Having potted a colour he scores accordingly, and then aims to pot another red. The player's break continues this way, potting reds and colours alternately. Reds that are potted are not replaced on the table. While any reds remain on the table, colours are replaced on their respective spots after being potted. If a player should inadvertently pot the cue ball he forfeits four points, his break ends, and the next player brings the cue ball back into play in the 'D'.

The player who pots the last red then aims to pot any one of the colours as usual. If he is successful that colour is replaced on its spot. Thereafter the colours must be potted in strict order of ascending points value and, when potted, are not replaced on the table.

11 SOLO GAMES

Count Them Out

No. of players: 1
Equipment: Set of dominoes
Complexity: ✫

This is an extremely simple game, in which there is absolutely no element of skill.

The dominoes are shuffled and are all laid out in a straight line, face down. They are then turned over to be face up, without being moved from their original positions in the line. The player begins counting from 0 to 12, moving his finger along the line of dominoes and touching a domino each time he calls a number. Whenever he reaches 12 he starts counting again at 0, and whenever he reaches the end of the line of dominoes he goes back to the beginning of the line. Each time the number he calls matches the pip value of the domino he is touching (e.g. if he calls 0 when touching the double-blank or 9 when touching the 6-3) he discards the domino and pushes the remaining dominoes together to close up the gap. The objective is to discard all the dominoes.

Grace's Patience

No. of players: 1
Equipment: Set of dominoes
Complexity: ✫

The dominoes are shuffled thoroughly and are all laid out, face down and end to end, in a straight line. They are then turned face up without moving them from their original positions in the line.

The objective is to find adjacent matching pairs and discard them, and to continue doing this until all 28 dominoes have been discarded. Two adjacent dominoes may be discarded only if they have matching ends, e.g.

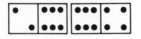

Whenever two dominoes are discarded the remaining dominoes are pushed together to close the gap. Care must be taken when deciding the order in which dominoes are to be discarded.

For example, in the position above, discarding the 2-5 with the 5-6 would block the game – in order to win it is necessary to discard the 3-4 and double-4 and then the 5-6 and 6-blank.

Even exercising the utmost skill, one will not win very often.

Twelves

No. of players: 1
Equipment: Set of dominoes
Complexity: ★★

The dominoes are shuffled and six are drawn to form a hand. Any two dominoes in the hand which have a combined pip value of 12 (e.g. the double-blank and double-six or the 1-3 and 6-2) may be discarded and placed in a discard heap. Each time two dominoes are discarded another two are drawn from the boneyard. The game is won if all 28 dominoes can be discarded in this way.

Five Piles

No. of players: 1
Equipment: Set of dominoes
Complexity: ★★

The dominoes are shuffled and three are drawn and turned face up to form a reserve. The remaining 25 dominoes are arranged in five piles with five dominoes in each. The piles are then turned over so that the dominoes are face up. The top dominoes of the piles are examined, and if any two of them have a combined pip value of 12 they may be removed and placed in a discard heap. The process is then repeated with the dominoes now on top of the piles. At any time, also, a domino from the reserve may be paired and discarded with a domino on top of the pile if they have a combined pip value of 12. The objective is to discard, in this manner, all 28 dominoes.

Sir Tommy

No. of players: 1
Equipment: Standard pack of 52 cards
Complexity: ✭

Patience (in the UK) and *Solitaire* (in the USA) are generic terms for a wide range of different card games for one player. It is said that *Sir Tommy* is the original patience (or solo) game from which all the rest are derived.

The objective is to build up four ascending sequences from ace to king, regardless of suit and colour. Cards are dealt out from the stock one at a time on to any one of four face-up waste piles. The aces when they turn up are used to form four foundations next to the waste piles.

The foundations may be built on, placing any 2 on any ace, any 3 on any 2, and so on. The top card of any waste pile may be played on to a foundation, in this way, but cards may not be transferred from one waste pile to another.

The stock is dealt out only once – there is no second chance. There is a small amount of skill involved in the decision as to which waste pile a card from the stock is dealt, but it is simply a matter of avoiding the necessity of covering a low-ranking card with a high one.

Lady Betty

No. of players: 1
Equipment: Standard pack of 52 cards
Complexity: ☆

This is exactly the same as *Sir Tommy* except that six waste piles are used instead of four, and thus the patience works out more frequently. The sexist implication of the names of these two games is, of course, that the ladies require an easier game than the men.

Puss in the Corner

No. of players: 1
Equipment: Standard pack of 52 cards
Complexity: ☆

The aces are removed from the pack and placed face upwards to make four foundations, arranged in a square. The remainder of the pack forms the stock. The objective is to build up on the foundations ascending sequences of cards of the same colour (though not necessarily of the same suit) from ace to king.

The stock is dealt out, one card at a time. If a card is not playable on to a foundation it is played onto any one of four face-up waste piles which are formed in the course of play at the four corners of the foundation square.

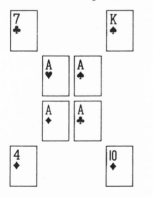

If the patience has not worked out when the last card of the stock has been dealt, one more deal is permitted. The four waste piles are gathered together in any order without shuffling to form a new stock, which is then dealt out again.

Clock Patience

No. of players: 1
Equipment: Standard pack of 52 cards
Complexity: ☆

This is a very simple patience game, requiring no skill or judgement, but it is one which seldom works out.

The pack is dealt out in thirteen piles, with four cards face down in each pile. The piles are arranged in the form of a clock face, with the thirteenth pile in the centre.

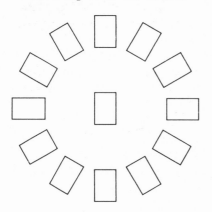

The objective is to end with four cards of the same rank in each pile in its correct place on the clock – i.e. four aces at one o'clock, four 2s at two o'clock, and so on, with four jacks at eleven o'clock, four queens at twelve o'clock and four kings in the centre.

The top card of the centre pile is turned up and is placed face upwards at the bottom of the pile that occupies the space belonging to that card (e.g. a 4 is placed at the bottom of the four o'clock pile). The top card of this pile is turned and placed under the appropriate pile. The player continues moving cards in this manner until all the cards are in the correct piles or until the game is blocked.

Monte Carlo

No. of players: 1
Equipment: Standard pack of 52 cards
Complexity: ☆

This patience game is also known by the names of *Weddings* or *Double And Quits*. It is a simple, straightforward game, in which the cards are matched up in pairs.

The pack is shuffled and twenty cards are dealt out, face upwards, in four rows of five cards each. Any two cards of the same rank that are adjacent in the layout – horizontally, vertically or diagonally – may be discarded, but only two cards may be discarded at a time. The vacated spaces are then closed up by moving cards from right to left and by filling vacant spaces at the right end of a row with cards from the left end of the row below. The order in which the cards were originally dealt should be preserved, and the end result should be two spaces at the right end of the bottom row. Two more cards are dealt to these spaces, and the process of discarding a pair and moving up is repeated. This is continued until the game is blocked because no more pairs can be found to be discarded or until all the cards have been discarded in pairs.

Klondike

No. of players: 1
Equipment: Standard pack of 52 cards
Complexity: ☆☆

This is almost certainly the best known and most popular patience (or solitaire) game. In Britain it is often known as *Canfield,* which in America is the name by which *Demon* is better known.

Twenty-eight cards are dealt out in the following manner. First a row of seven, with the first card face up and the rest face down. Then a row of six, the first card face up and overlapping the second card of the first row and the rest face down and overlapping the cards of the first row. Then a row of five, a row of four and so on, each row overlapping the previous row and starting with a face-up card overlapping the second card of the previous row. Aces as they become available are placed in a row above the layout to form foundations. The aim is to build each suit in the correct sequence from ace to king.

The remainder of the pack is placed face down as the stock. Cards are turned up from the stock one at a time, and if not playable on the foundations or on the layout are placed face up on a discard pile. The top card of the discard pile is always available to be played to the foundations or the layout.

On the columns of the layout descending sequences of cards are built of alternating colour (e.g. red 10 on black J, black 9 on red 10, etc.). The bottom card of each sequence is available to be played to a foundation. A sequence as a whole may be transferred to another column to form a longer sequence. When a face-down card is exposed at the bottom of a column it is turned face up. When a complete column is cleared, the space may be filled only with a king or with a sequence built on a king.

The stock may be played through only once.

Demon

No. of players: 1
Equipment: Standard pack of 52 cards
Complexity: ★★

Thirteen cards are dealt face down to a reserve pile, which is then turned over so that only the top card is visible. The next four cards are dealt face up in a row to the right of the reserve pile, forming the 'tableau'.

The next card is dealt face up above the first card of the tableau to form the first of four foundations. As they become available, the other three cards of the same rank as this card will be placed to form the other three foundations. The objective is to build up each suit in sequence on its foundation. Thus if, for example, the foundation is the 9 of clubs the sequence to be built up will be 9,10,J,Q,K,A,2,3,4,5,6,7,8 of clubs, and similar sequences will be built up for the other suits on their foundations.

The remainder of the pack, when the reserve pile, tableau and first foundation have been dealt out, forms the stock. The stock is turned over in batches of three cards on to a waste pile. If there are less than three

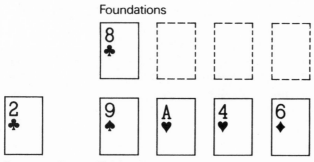

Foundations

Reserve pile   Tableau

cards at the end of the stock they may be turned over singly. The only card in the waste pile that is available for play is the top card though, of course, when it is played it will make the card below available.

The foundations may be built up in suit sequence. Cards may be built on the columns of the tableau in descending sequence of alternate colour (e.g. red jack on black queen, black 10 on red jack, etc.). An entire column may be transferred on to another column, provided that this sequence is maintained. As soon as a tableau column becomes vacant it is filled with the top card of the reserve pile or, if no cards are left in the reserve pile, with the top card of the waste pile (though in this case there is no obligation to fill the space immediately).

When the end of the stock is reached, the waste pile is turned over to form a new stock which is then redealt, without shuffling. This may be performed as often as required until the game is either blocked or won.

The game is very rarely won.

Cribbage Solitaire

No. of players: 1
Equipment: Standard pack of 52 cards; cribbage board
Complexity: ★★

This is a game for the Cribbage enthusiast to play when he cannot find an opponent to play against.

The player deals six cards to himself and two to the crib. He then discards two cards from his hand to the crib, and turns up a start from the top of the pack.

He scores for his hand and then for the crib, as in the show when playing *Cribbage*.

The eight cards in the hand and the crib are then put to one side, and a fresh hand and crib are dealt (using the start as the first card of the new hand) and scored. In this way six hands are dealt and scored, and the objective is to score 120 points or more.

Match Words

No. of players: 1
Equipment: 28 matches
Complexity: ☆

The matches are arranged as shown in the diagram:

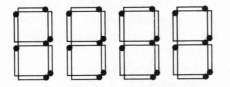

The object of the game is to see how many words can be formed by removing various numbers of matches. It will be found that not many words may be formed by removing less than 5 matches or more than 11 matches, but the numbers in between offer plenty of scope. For example:

Removing 6

Removing 8

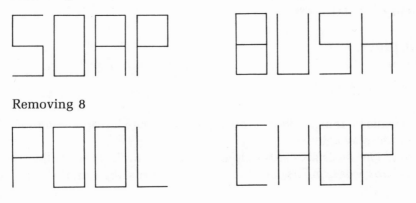

Removing 10

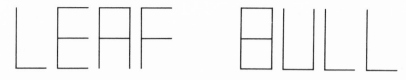

Elimination

No of players: 1
Equipment: Pocket calculator
Complexity: ★★

Any five-digit number is entered into the calculator. The objective is
to reduce that number to zero in four steps, using only the arithmetic
functions − and ÷ with two-digit numbers.
    For example:

14587   *47629*

− 67	=	14520		− 29	=	47600
÷ 60	=	242		÷ 40	=	1190
÷ 11	=	22		÷ 70	=	17
− 22	=	0		− 17	=	0

    A rather more demanding version of the game is to start with a
six-digit number, which has to be reduced to zero in four steps in the
same way.

Tangram

No. of players: 1
Equipment: Seven-piece tangram set
Complexity: ★★

Tangram is an ancient Chinese game-puzzle-recreation. The tangram set is a set of seven pieces formed by the dissection of a square as shown in the diagram.

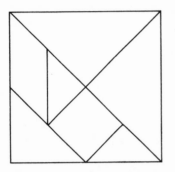

A tangram set may easily be made at home from stiff card or from wood, or a set may be bought (they can sometimes be found in the trendier sort of gift shop).

The object is to arrange the pieces to form various shapes. This may be done free-style, just putting the pieces together in various ways to see what shapes turn up. An amazing variety of aesthetically pleasing designs can be discovered in this way. Alternatively the tangram set can be used in puzzle mode, the objective being to put the pieces together to make some set design, such as this parallelogram.

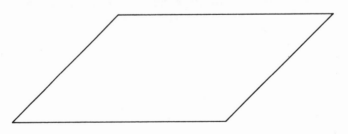

A marvellous puzzle of this type, devised by the great puzzle-setter Henry E. Dudeney, is to use all the tangram pieces to form each of these two figures, which appear to be identical except that one has a foot and the other does not.

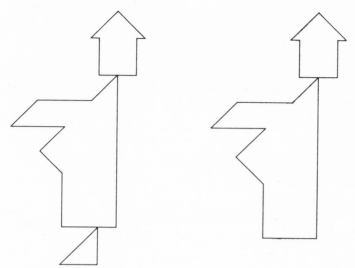

Solitaire

No. of players: 1
Equipment: Board and 33 pieces
Complexity: ☆☆

The *Solitaire* board is normally made of wood or plastic and has 33 holes to hold the pieces (which may be small marbles or pegs).

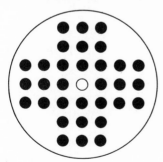

A piece may only be moved by jumping over another piece which is adjacent horizontally or vertically and landing in the next hole, which must be vacant. The piece that was jumped over is then removed from the board.

For the basic game, all the pieces are placed on the board. One piece is then removed, normally from the centre hole but optionally from any other hole. The objective is to make a series of moves that will result in only one piece being left on the board. To provide a greater challenge it may be stipulated that the last remaining piece should be in the centre hole or in any other hole that may be nominated.

Other problems may be set – for example, starting with only nine pieces arranged in the form of a cross in the centre of the board and ending with one piece in the centre hole.

Pentominoes

No. of players: 1
Equipment: Set of pentominoes
Complexity: ★★☆

Pentominoes were introduced to the world by a Californian mathematician, Solomon W. Golomb, in an article published in the *American Mathematical Monthly* in 1954.

Starting from the definition of a domino as two squares 'simply connected' (i.e. joined along their edges) he coined the word polyomino to describe the class of shapes formed by squares thus connected. Thus, a monomino is a single square, a domino 2 squares simply connected, a tromino 3 squares, a tetromino 4 squares, a pentomino 5 squares, a hexomino 6, and so on.

Of all this family of polyominoes, it is the pentomino which has attracted the most interest because of its suitability for games and puzzles.

There are twelve distinct ways in which five squares can be joined together to form a pentomino. These twelve shapes constitute a set of pentominoes. A set may easily be made from stiff card or from wood.

There are a number of problems which may be set, in which the objective is to put the pentominoes together to form various shapes. For

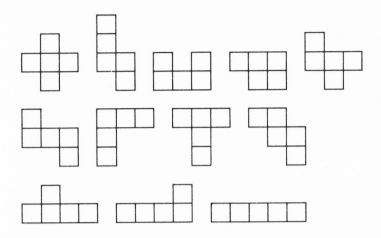

example, all 12 pieces may be used to construct a 5 × 12 rectangle, a 6 × 10 rectangle, a 4 × 15 rectangle or a 3 × 20 rectangle. Of these the 3 × 20 rectangle is by far the most difficult to construct.

Another popular problem (known as 'the triplication problem') is to choose one of the pieces and then to use nine of the remaining eleven to construct a large-scale replica of the chosen piece. This will be three times the height and three times the length of the original. The triplication problem may be solved for each of the twelve pentominoes.

12 CHILDREN'S PARTY GAMES

Some words of caution for parents

Ring a Ring of Roses
The Farmer's in his Den
Three Blind Mice
Oranges and Lemons
Poor Pussy
Squeak, Piggy, Squeak
Pass the Parcel
Musical Chairs
Musical Bumps
Musical Islands
Musical Statues
Hunt the Thimble
Hot and Cold
Hunt the Slipper
Blind Man's Buff
Blind Postman
Cat and Mouse
Hide and Seek
Potato Race
Balloon Race
Blow Ball
Nose Ball
Ankle Race
Plate and Feather Race
Newspaper Race
Back-to-Back Race
Three-Legged Race
Piggy-Back Race
Tortoise Race
Two Minute Race
Pass the Balloon
Egg and Spoon Race
Simon Says

Do This, Do That
On and Off
Card Throwing
Ping-Pong Throwing
Coin on the Plate
Wool Gathering
Balloon Battle
Goodies and Baddies
Handshake
Happy Travellers
Dead Lions
Ghosts

Some Words of Caution for Parents

When organising a children's party it is the responsibility of the adults involved to set the pace. With very young children it is generally not wise to have more than two or three organised games – it is better to provide a selection of toys for the little ones to play with most of the time. With older children one must be careful not to let the fun get out of hand. Children usually love the more active running, chasing and racing games, but they should not be permitted to play too many such games or for too long at a time. Intersperse them with some of the quieter games. Otherwise, with too much excitement and hilarity, 'it will all end in tears'.

With some of the more boisterous games, close adult supervision may be necessary to make sure that nothing gets broken or damaged, that the children don't try to exceed their capabilities and that younger, smaller children don't suffer at the hands of older, bigger ones. But try not to fence the children in with too many prohibitions. Try to achieve a happy balance and the children will enjoy themselves – and so will you.

Ring a Ring of Roses

No. of players: 3 or more
Equipment: None
Complexity: ☆

The players join hands and dance round in a circle, singing:

'Ring a ring of roses,
A pocket full of posies,
A-tishoo, A-tishoo,
We all fall down.'

As the last word is sung, the players all drop down to sit on the floor.
This is repeated as often as required – young children enjoy it

immensely and seldom want to stop. The original verse may be repeated each time, or these other verses may be used as well:

'The king has sent his daughter
To fetch a pail of water,
A-tishoo, A-tishoo,
We all fall down.

The bird upon the steeple
Is singing to the people,
A-tishoo, A-tishoo,
We all fall down.

The wedding bells are ringing,
The boys and girls are singing,
A-tishoo, A-tishoo,
We all fall down.'

The Farmer's in his Den

No. of players: 8 or more
Equipment: None
Complexity: ☆

One of the players is chosen to be the Farmer. The other players form a circle and dance round him, singing:

'The farmer's in his den,
The farmer's in his den,
Heigh-ho, heigh-ho,
The farmer's in his den.

The farmer wants a wife
The farmer wants a wife,
Heigh-ho, heigh-ho,
The farmer wants a wife.'

At this point the Farmer chooses one of the other players to be his

Wife and to join him in the middle of the circle. The players continue singing:

> 'The wife wants a child,
> The wife wants a child,
> Heigh-ho, heigh-ho,
> The wife wants a child.'

The Wife chooses another player to be the Child, who also comes into the middle. The players continue singing:

> 'The child wants a nurse,
> The child wants a nurse,
> Heigh-ho, heigh-ho,
> The child wants a nurse.'

The Child picks a player to be the Nurse, who joins the group in the middle. The players continue singing:

> 'The nurse wants a dog,
> The nurse wants a dog,
> Heigh-ho, heigh ho,
> The nurse wants a dog.'

The player chosen by the Nurse goes into the middle on hands and knees. The players sing the last verse:

> 'We all pat the dog,
> We all pat the dog,
> Heigh-ho, heigh-ho,
> We all pat the dog.'

All the players pat the Dog, who then becomes the Farmer for the next round of the game.

Three Blind Mice

No. of players: 5 or more
Equipment: None
Complexity: ☆

One of the players is chosen to be the Farmer's Wife. The other players join hands to form a circle around the Farmer's Wife and dance round her, singing:

> 'Three blind mice, see how they run.
> They all run after the Farmer's Wife,
> Who cut off their tails with a carving knife.
> Did you ever see such a thing in your life
> As three blind mice?'

As the last word is sung the players scatter and run to the walls of the room, while the Farmer's Wife tries to catch one of them. A player is 'safe' once he touches a wall. The first player to be caught becomes the Farmer's Wife for the next round of the game.

Oranges and Lemons

No. of players: 6 or more
Equipment: None
Complexity: ☆

Two of the players are chosen to form an arch. To do this they stand facing each other, holding hands with their arms raised in the air. One of the players is 'Oranges' and the other is 'Lemons'.

The other players march round in a large circle, one behind another, continually passing under the arch. As they march they sing this traditional English nursery rhyme:

> 'Oranges and Lemons,
> Say the bells of St. Clement's.

You owe me five farthings,
Say the bells of St. Martin's.
When will you pay me?
Say the bells of Old Bailey.
When I grow rich,
Say the bells at Shoreditch.
Pray, when will that be?
Say the bells at Stepney.
I'm sure I don't know,
Says the great bell at Bow.
Here comes a candle to light you to bed,
Here comes a chopper to chop off your head.'

As the last line is sung the players forming the arch move their arms up and down, finally bringing them down to trap one of the players marching through the arch.

The game continues in this way until all the players have been trapped under the arch. As the players are trapped they are asked to choose Oranges or Lemons. They join a line on one side of the arch or the other, according to their choice, each player holding the waist of the player in front. The game then concludes with a tug-of-war between Oranges and Lemons.

Poor Pussy

No. of players: 4 or more
Equipment: None
Complexity: ☆

All the players sit in a circle. One player is then chosen to go into the middle to be the pussy cat. The pussy cat, on hands and knees, goes to each player in turn, purring and crying 'Meeow' as much like a cat as possible. Each player must stroke or pat pussy's head three times, each player saying 'Poor pussy, poor pussy'. The first player to smile or laugh takes the next turn at being the pussy cat.

Squeak, Piggy, Squeak

No. of players: 5 or more
Equipment: A blindfold and a cushion
Complexity: ☆

One player is chosen to be blindfolded and is given a cushion to hold. He is turned around three times and the other players sit down in a circle around him. The blindfolded player has to place the cushion on another player's lap and then sit on it. He calls out 'Squeak, Piggy, squeak' and the player he is sitting on must squeak like a little pig.

If the blindfolded player can name the player he is sitting on then they change places, otherwise the blindfolded player must find another lap to sit on.

Whenever there is a new blindfolded player the others swap seats before he tries to sit on their laps.

Pass the Parcel

No. of players: 4 or more
Equipment: A small present; gift-wrapping materials; a piano, or record-player or other source of music.
Complexity: ☆

In preparation for the game, the present is wrapped in ten layers (or thereabouts) of paper, each layer being fastened either with string or with adhesive tape.

The players sit in a circle, and while the music is playing they pass the parcel from hand to hand around the circle, as quickly as possible. The music is stopped abruptly at frequent intervals, and when this happens the player holding the parcel at that moment unwraps one layer of paper. The player who is lucky enough to unwrap the final layer wins the present.

Musical Chairs

No. of players: 4 or more
*Equipment: Chairs (one fewer than the number of players); a
piano, record-player or other source of music.*
Complexity: ✩

The chairs are lined up in the centre of the room, alternate chairs facing
opposite walls. The music is started, and while it is playing the children
march round and round the line of chairs, without touching them. When
the music stops, each child has to try to sit in a chair. The one who is left
without a chair is eliminated. One chair is removed and the game starts
again. This is repeated until in the last round there are two players and a
single chair – the first one to sit in the chair when the music stops is the
winner.

Musical Bumps

No. of players: 4 or more
Equipment: A piano, record-player or other source of music
Complexity: ✩

This is similar to *Musical Chairs*, except that the chairs are not required.
While the music is playing, the children skip up and down. When the
music stops, the children drop down to sit cross-legged on the floor. The
last one to do so is eliminated. This is repeated until only one player is
left.

Musical Islands

No. of players: 8 or more
*Equipment: Small mats or sheets of newspaper; a piano or
record-player or other source of music*
Complexity: ✩

The mats or sheets of newspaper are placed on the floor at various points around the room to form 'islands'. The players walk around while the music plays, and when it stops they rush to get on to an island. An island may be occupied by several players, but any player who cannot squeeze on to an island or who falls off is eliminated. The number of islands is gradually reduced, and the last player left in the game is the winner.

Musical Statues

No. of players: 4 or more
Equipment: A piano or record-player or other source of music
Complexity: ☆

While the music is playing the children must dance about the room moving continually. As soon as the music stops they must 'freeze' in whatever position they happen to be in at that moment and must remain as still as statues. Anyone who moves is out. The music is restarted and the children continue dancing. The game continues in this manner until only one player is left in, and that player is the winner.

Hunt the Thimble

No. of players: 3 or more
Equipment: A thimble (or other suitable small object)
Complexity: ☆

One player is chosen to 'hide' the thimble while all the other players are out of the room. The thimble should not really be hidden but should be placed in some inconspicuous spot where it will be visible to all the players though not immediately noticeable. The players then come back into the room and begin to hunt the thimble. Each player, as soon as he spots the thimble, sits down without saying anything and without drawing attention to its location. The last player to spot the thimble and sit down is the loser, and he hides the thimble for the next round.

Hot and Cold

No. of players: 3 or more
Equipment: A thimble (or other suitable small object)
Complexity: ☆

One player leaves the room while the other players hide the thimble. When he is called back into the room the other players help him in his search for the thimble by calling out 'Cold' or 'Very cold' as he moves further away from it, and 'Warm', 'Hot', 'Very hot' as he moves nearer to it. Each player has a turn at being the one who has to find the thimble.

Hunt the Slipper

No. of players: 8 or more
Equipment: A slipper or shoe
Complexity: ☆

The players sit in a circle on the floor with one player sitting in the middle with the slipper. The player in the middle hands the slipper to one of the players around the circle, then covers his eyes and recites this rhyme:

> 'Cobbler, cobbler, mend my shoe,
> Have it done by half past two.
> Cobbler, cobbler, tell me true,
> Which of you has got my shoe?'

While the player in the middle is reciting, the players around the circle pass the slipper from one to another behind their backs. Whoever is holding the slipper when the last word of the rhyme is uttered holds on to it, being careful to keep it out of sight. The player in the middle has two tries to guess who is holding the slipper. If he guesses correctly, the player holding the slipper goes into the middle for the next round.

Blind Man's Buff

No. of players: 4 or more
Equipment: A blindfold
Complexity: ✫

One player is chosen to be the Blind Man and is blindfolded. The other players lead him to the middle of the room, turn him round three times in each direction, and then leave him on his own.

The Blind Man tries to catch one of the other players, while they move about the room, calling to him and taunting him, approaching as near as they dare and dodging away again. A player who is touched by the Blind Man must immediately stand still. If, by touching and feeling, the Blind Man can say who it is he has caught then the captured player becomes the Blind Man for the next round of the game. If the Blind Man guesses wrongly the name of the captured player, then he must let him go and carry on trying to catching another player.

Blind Postman

No. of players: 8 or more
Equipment: A blindfold
Complexity: ✫

One player is chosen to be the postman and is blindfolded. The other players sit in a circle with the postman standing in the middle. Each of the seated players is given the name of a town. The postman calls out the names of two towns, and those two players have to exchange seats, while the postman attempts to occupy one of the temporarily vacant seats. Whoever loses his seat becomes the postman.

Cat and Mouse

No. of players: 8 or more
Equipment: A blindfold
Complexity: ☆

One player is chosen to be the cat and is blindfolded. Another player is chosen to be the mouse. The other players form a circle, with the cat and the mouse standing in the middle. The cat has to try to catch the mouse by following the sound of his voice. At any time the cat can stand still and call 'Meeow'. The mouse must then reply 'Squeak squeak' but can immediately run, creep or tiptoe to another part of the circle. When he is caught he becomes the cat for the next round and another player is chosen to be the mouse.

Hide and Seek

No. of players: Any number
Equipment: None
Complexity: ☆

A particular spot is chosen to be 'home'. The seeker stands there, covers his eyes, and counts up to fifty while the other players scatter and hide themselves in various parts of the house. When he has counted up to fifty, the seeker calls out 'Ready!' and goes off in search of the other players. The first player to be spotted and tagged by the seeker becomes the seeker for the next round. But any player who manages to get 'home' without being tagged is safe.

Potato Race

No. of players: 2 or more
Equipment: Three potatoes for each competitor; a cardboard box
Complexity: ✫

The cardboard box is placed at one end of the room; all the potatoes are placed in a pile at the other end. The players are lined up beside the box. They have to run to the other end of the room, pick up a potato, bring it back and drop it in the box. They repeat this procedure twice more, and the first player to drop three potatoes in the box is the winner.

Balloon Race

No. of players: 2 or more
Equipment: One balloon for each competitor
Complexity: ✫

The competitors stand at one end of the room, and each is given a balloon of a different colour. They race to the far end of the room and back again, taking their balloons with them. The only restriction is that the balloons may not be held – they must be moved along by being patted or kicked. Any player who holds his balloon is sent back to the start and has to begin all over again.

Blow Ball

No. of players: 2 or more
Equipment: One ping-pong ball and one straw for each competitor
Complexity: ✫

Starting at one end of the room, each of the competitors, on hands and knees and using a drinking straw, has to move a ping-pong ball to the other end of the room and back again by blowing through his straw. Any competitor who touches the ping-pong ball with the straw or with any part of his body is sent back to the start. The first player to complete the course successfully is the winner.

Nose Ball

No. of players: 2 or more
Equipment: One ping-pong ball per competitor
Complexity: ☆

This is similar to *Blow Ball*, except that the players have to push the ping-pong balls with their noses.

Ankle Race

No. of players: 2 or more
Equipment: None
Complexity: ☆

The competitors line up at one end of the room, each one crouching or bending down and grasping his ankles. They must race to the other end of the room and back again in this position. Any competitor who takes his hands away from his ankles is sent back to the start.

Plate and Feather Race

No. of players: 2 or more
Equipment: A paper plate and a feather for each competitor
Complexity: ☆

The competitors line up at one end of the room, and each is given a feather on a paper plate. Carrying their plates, they have to race to the other end of the room and back again. A competitor whose feather comes off his plate must stop to put it back again, but otherwise no competitor must touch the feather on his plate – anyone who does so is sent back to the start.

Newspaper Race

No. of players: 2 or more
Equipment: Two sheets of newspaper for each competitor
Complexity: ☆

The competitors, each with two sheets of newspaper, line up at one end of the room. They have to make their way to the other end of the room and back again, using their sheets of newspaper as stepping stones. Each player stands on one sheet, lays the other on the floor in front of him, steps on to it, picks up the first sheet and lays it on the floor in front of him, steps on to that, and so on. Any player who touches the floor with any part of his body is sent back to the starting point and has to begin all over again.

Back-to-Back Race

No. of players: 4 or more
Equipment: None
Complexity: ☆

The players compete in pairs, each pair standing back to back with their arms linked at the elbows. Starting at one end of the room, the linked pairs race to the other end and back again.

Three-Legged Race

No. of players: 4 or more
Equipment: A scarf for each pair of competitors
Complexity: ✰

The players compete in pairs. Each pair of players stand side by side, and a scarf is used to tie the right leg of one player to the left leg of the other. Starting at one end of the room, the pairs race to the other end of the room and back again.

Piggy-Back Race

No. of players: 4 or more
Equipment: None
Complexity: ✰

The players compete in pairs. One member of each pair climbs on to the other's back to be carried. Starting at one end of the room, the pairs of competitors race to the other end of the room. There the rider dismounts, and he has to carry his partner back to the starting-point.

Tortoise Race

No. of players: 2 or more
Equipment: None
Complexity: ✰

This is an unusual race, in that the aim is to be the last to finish. Starting at one end of the room, the competitors 'race' to the other end as slowly as possible. They must go in a straight line towards the other end of the room, and are not allowed to stop – they must continue moving, however slowly. The last to finish is the winner.

Two Minute Race

No. of players: 2 or more
Equipment: A watch with a second hand
Complexity: ★★

Before the game begins any clocks in the room are removed or covered up, and any wristwatches are confiscated. Starting at one end of the room, the players then 'race' to the opposite wall in exactly two minutes. The competitors can move as slowly as they like but they must never stop moving, and they have to use their own sense of timing to complete the course when they think two minutes have passed. The competitors are timed by an umpire who is provided with a watch with a second hand. The winner is the player who is nearest to the wall when the two minutes have passed.

Pass the Balloon

No. of players: 6 or more
Equipment: Two balloons
Complexity: ★

The players are divided into two teams, and the members of each team stand in line, one behind another. The leader of each team is given a balloon, and when the signal is given to start, he passes it over his head to the player behind, who passes it over his head to the player behind him, and so on down to the end of the line. When the player at the end of the line receives it, he runs round to the front of the line. The balloon is then passed back as before. This continues until the original leader receives the balloon at the end of the line and returns to his place at the front. The first team to finish wins the game.

Egg and Spoon Race

No. of players: 8 or more
Equipment: A spoon for each player; two ping-pong balls
Complexity: ☆

Hard-boiled eggs are traditionally used for this game. When playing at home, however, it is advisable to substitute ping-pong balls – they cause less mess if they are trodden into the carpet.

The players are divided into two teams, forming parallel lines. Each player is given a spoon which he holds in his mouth, and a ping-pong ball is placed in the spoon of the first player in each team. The first player has to transfer the ping-pong ball from his spoon to the spoon of the second player, and so on down the line. No player may use his hands to touch the ball. If it falls to the floor the player who dropped it must go down on hands and knees and scoop up the ball with the spoon still held in his mouth. The first team to transfer the ping-pong ball successfully to the player at the end of the line wins the game.

Simon Says

No. of players: 4 or more
Equipment: None
Complexity: ☆

One of the players is chosen to be the leader, and the other players space themselves out in front of him. The leader performs various actions (such as standing on one leg, patting his head, raising his left arm, bending down) and commands the other players to do the same. If he begins the command with the words 'Simon says' – e.g. 'Simon says, touch your toes' – then the other players must obey the command. If the command does not begin with the words 'Simon says' – e.g. 'Touch your toes' – then the other players must not perform that action. A player who makes a mistake or who hesitates for too long before doing what Simon says drops out of the game. The last player left in is the winner, and he becomes the leader for the next round.

Do This, Do That

No. of players: 4 or more
Equipment: None
Complexity: ☆

This game is similar to *Simon Says*. Whenever the leader performs some action and says 'Do this', the other players must copy him. But when he performs some action and says 'Do that', the other players must remain still.

On and Off

No. of players: 4 or more
Equipment: An old blanket
Complexity: ☆

An old blanket is spread out on the floor. When the leader calls 'Everybody off the blanket' the children stand on the blanket, and when the leader calls 'Everybody on the blanket' they all get off, always doing the opposite of what the leader tells them. Any player who makes a mistake is out, and the last player left in is the winner.

Card Throwing

No. of players: Any number
Equipment: A wastepaper bin and an old pack of cards
Complexity: ☆

Each contestant is given ten playing cards, which he attempts to flick into the wastepaper bin. The players should stand about eight feet from the bin but, of course, this distance may be varied depending on the ages of the players. The player getting most cards into the bin is the winner.

Ping-Pong Throwing

No. of players: Any number
Equipment: A wastepaper bin and five ping-pong balls
Complexity: ⋆

This is similar to the previous game except that each player in turn attempts to throw the five ping-pong balls into the bin. Balls that bounce out of the bin do not count in the score.

Coin on the Plate

No. of players: Any number
Equipment: A plate (preferably enamel or aluminium) and a supply of coins
Complexity: ⋆

The players, each of whom is provided with five coins, stand about six feet away from the plate. The player who manages to throw most coins so that they land on the plate – and don't bounce off – is the winner.

Wool Gathering

No. of players: Any number
Equipment: A chair and a ball of wool for each player
Complexity: ⋆

A ball of wool is entwined round the legs and back of each player's chair. When the word of command is given, each player has to wind his wool up into a neat ball again without rising from his seat. The first player to succeed is the winner.

Balloon Battle

No. of players: Any number
Equipment: A rolled-up newspaper and a balloon on a
string for each player
Complexity: ☆

Each player has his balloon tied to his ankle, and is armed with a rolled-up newspaper. While attempting to protect his own balloon, each player tries to burst as many of the other balloons as possible, using only his rolled-up newspaper. No balloon may be touched by hand. A player whose balloon is burst is eliminated, and the last player left in is the winner.

Goodies and Baddies

No. of players: Any number
Equipment: Two balloons
Complexity: ☆

The players are divided into two teams. One team, the Goodies, attempt to keep a balloon up in the air while the other team, the Baddies, attempt to burst it, using only their hands and feet – pins and other suchlike weapons of destruction are outlawed. When the balloon eventually has been burst, the teams swap roles and play with the second balloon.

Handshake

No. of players: 8 or more
Equipment: None
Complexity: ☆

One of the players is 'it'. The others stand in a circle, facing inwards, with their hands behind their backs. The player who is 'it' runs around the outside of the circle, slaps the hands of one of the players, and carries on running. The player whose hands were slapped runs around the circle in the opposite direction. When they meet they shake hands and then race back to the vacant space in the circle. The one who gets there last is 'it' for the next round.

Happy Travellers

No. of players: 6 or more
Equipment: A newspaper for each player
Complexity: ☆

The players sit in two rows, facing one another with their knees touching, and squashed together like passengers on a very crowded train. Each player has a folded newspaper which has been thoroughly muddled up – with pages in the wrong order, some being back to front and some upside down. On the word of command each player tries to arrange the pages of his newspaper into the correct order as quickly as possible. The first to succeed is the winner.

Dead Lions

No. of players: Any number
Equipment: None
Complexity: ☆

This is a very quiet game which makes an ideal interlude when the party becomes too boisterous.

The players lie face down on the floor and pretend to be dead lions. Any player who makes the slightest movement is eliminated, and the last player left in is the winner. The players who have been eliminated may help to spot movements made by the remaining dead lions, and they may 'encourage' the lions to move by taunting them or trying to make them laugh – but no touching is allowed.

Ghosts

No. of players: 8 or more
Equipment: An old sheet
Complexity: ☆

The players are divided into two teams. The first team leaves the room, and its members come back, one at a time, to stand in the doorway draped in the sheet and moaning and groaning like a ghost. The second team has to guess the identity of each member of the first team as they appear. The teams then change roles. Thus every player has a turn at being a ghost. The game is won by the team which correctly identifies most of the other team's ghosts.

13 CHILDREN'S CARD GAMES

Snap
Speed Snap
Old Maid
Le Vieux Garçon
Beggar my Neighbour
Donkey
Snip-Snap-Snorem
Happy Families
Fish
Go Boom
Cheat
I Doubt It
Slapjack
Menagerie
Animal Noises
War
Cuckoo
Pelmanism
My Ship Sails
Rolling Stone

Snap

No. of players: 2 or more
Equipment: Normal pack of 52 cards (or two packs shuffled together if there are more than 4 players).
Complexity: ☆

Special *Snap* cards may be bought for this game but it can be played just as well with ordinary playing cards.

All the cards are dealt out to the players, one card at a time and face down. Some players may get one card more than the others but this does not really matter. Each player forms his cards into a neat pile in front of him, face down, without looking at them. The player to the left of the dealer takes the top card from his pile and puts it face up on the table to start a new pile next to his face-down pile. The player to his left does likewise, and so on around the table. The cards played on to the face-up piles should be placed tidily so that only the top card of each face-up pile can be seen.

Whenever any player sees that the cards on top of any two face-up piles have the same value (e.g. two sevens or two queens) he calls 'Snap'. The first player to do so wins both piles and adds them to the bottom of his own face-down pile. Play then starts again with the player to the left of the last player turning over a card.

A player who has played all the cards from his face-down pile can still stay in the game as long as he has a face-up pile in front of him. He passes when it is his turn to play a card, but he may still call 'Snap' when he sees two cards of the same value, and thus may get a new face-down pile. Only when a player has neither a face-up pile nor a face-down pile is he out of the game.

If a player calls 'Snap' in error when there are not two cards of the same value showing, then he is penalised by having to give each of the other players a card from his face-down pile. These cards are added to the bottom of the other players' face-down piles.

The winner is the player who wins all the cards.

Variation 1
In this variation, if two or more players call 'Snap' and it cannot be decided who called first, the matching face-up piles are put together to form a face-up pile (called the 'pool') in the middle of the table. Play continues, and when the top card of any face-up pile matches the top card of the pool the first player to call 'Snap pool' wins the pool.

Variation 2
When a player has played all the cards from his face-down pile he is allowed to turn over his face-up pile to form a new face-down pile from which he may play cards.

Variation 3
Instead of having a separate face-up pile for each player, all the players turn over their cards on to one central face-up pile. Players call 'Snap' when the two top cards are of the same value. This makes the game less interesting, but it is easier for younger children.

Speed Snap

No. of players: 2 or more
Equipment: As for Snap
Complexity: ☆

This is the same as normal *Snap* except that all the players turn over a card at the same time, and play proceeds as briskly as possible. This makes *Speed Snap* a faster and more exciting game.

Old Maid

No. of players: 3 or more
Equipment: Normal pack of 52 cards
Complexity:

Special sets of *Old Maid* cards may be bought, but the game may equally well be played with an ordinary pack of cards from which one queen is removed. There are no winners in this game – only a loser. The object is to get rid of all one's cards by laying them on the table as matched pairs (e.g. two aces, two sevens etc.). One player will be left with an odd queen, thus losing the game.

The whole pack is dealt out to the players, one card at a time and face down. Some players may have one card more than the others, but this does not really matter. Each player picks up and examines his cards without letting them be seen by any of the other players. He discards, by placing face down on the table in front of him, any pairs of cards with the same value. If he has three cards of the same value he may only discard two of them and must keep the third, but if he has four of the same value he may discard them as two pairs.

When all the players have done this, the player to the left of the dealer fans out his cards and offers them face downwards to the next player on his left. The player to whom they are offered takes any one of them and puts it with his own cards. If it forms a pair with any card that he already holds he can then discard the pair. This player in turn then fans out his cards and offers them face downwards to the player on *his* left, who takes any one of them.

This continues around the table until all the players have managed to pair and discard all their cards – except for one player left holding the odd queen, who is the 'old maid'.

Le Vieux Garçon

No. of players: 3 or more
Equipment: Normal pack of 52 cards
Complexity: ☆

This French game is played in exactly the same manner as *Old Maid* except that it is played with a pack of cards from which the jack of hearts, jack of diamonds and jack of clubs have been removed. At the end of the game the loser is the player who is left holding the jack of spades – the *vieux garçon* or 'old boy'.

Beggar My Neighbour

No. of players: 2 to 6
Equipment: Normal pack of 52 cards
Complexity: ☆

This popular game, although it is very simple and requires no skill, can be very exciting.

The whole pack is dealt out to the players, one card at a time and face down. Some players may get one card more than the others but this does not really matter. Each player forms his cards into a neat pile, face down, without looking at them. The player to the left of the dealer begins the game by turning up the top card of his pile and placing it face up in the centre of the table. Each player in turn, going round to the left, similarly turns up the top card of his pile and places it face up on the central pile.

This continues until one player puts on the central pile an ace or a court card (king, queen or jack). When this happens the next player has to 'pay' him by playing a certain number of cards on to the central pile – four cards for an ace, three cards for a king, two cards for a queen, and one card for a jack. However, if one of the 'pay' cards happens to be an ace or a court card the payer stops paying and the next player has to pay *him* the appropriate number of cards. This continues around the table until a player pays the correct number of cards without turning up an ace or a court card. The player who played the last ace or court card wins the central pile and places it face down at the bottom of his own pile. The last player then starts a new round by playing the top card of his pile face up in the centre of the table and play continues as before.

A player who has played all his cards drops out of the game. The winner is the last player left in the game.

Donkey

No. of players: 3 to 13 (best with 5 or 6)
Equipment: Normal pack of 52 cards
Complexity: ☆

Donkey is a game for fast, furious fun. There are no winners, only a loser who is the 'donkey'.

From the pack of cards a number of sets are taken out, each set consisting of four cards of the same value. There should be one set for each player. The rest of the pack is put aside and is not used. For example, if there are five players the aces, twos, threes, fours and fives might be used.

The cards are shuffled thoroughly and dealt out face down to the players. The objective is to obtain four cards of the same value, or to avoid being last to react when another player has done so. Each player picks up his four cards and examines them, making sure that they are concealed from the other players. He chooses one card that he does not want and puts it face down on the table in front of him. All the players, at the same time, pass their face-down card to the next player on the left. Each player picks up the card he has been given and puts it in his hand with his other cards.

Again each player chooses a card he does not want (which may be the card he has just been given) and puts it face down on the table to be passed to the next player. The passing continues in this way, as quickly as possible, until one player has four cards of the same value in his hand. As soon as this happens he quickly places his cards face down on the table and puts his finger alongside his nose.

When the other players see what is happening they also must do the same as quickly as possible. The last player to put his finger to his nose is the 'donkey' for that round.

Further rounds are played until one player has been 'donkey' six times. He is the loser and as a penalty must 'hee haw' three times.

The best way of keeping score is to write down the names of the players on a sheet of paper and to write down one letter of the word 'donkey' by a player's name whenever he loses a round. The first player to have the word 'donkey' beside his name is the loser.

Variation
A number of counters (or buttons or matchsticks or whatever) are placed in the middle of the table. The number of counters must be one less than the number of players. When a player lays down his cards because he has a set of four he grabs a counter, and the other players must then do the same. The player who fails to grab a counter is the 'donkey' for that round.

Snip-Snap-Snorem

No. of players: 3 or more
Equipment: Normal pack of 52 cards
Complexity: ☆

The whole pack is dealt out face down to the player. Some players may get one more card than the others but this does not really matter. The players pick up their cards and look at them, without letting the other players see them.

The player to the left of the dealer starts the game by playing any card he chooses from his hand and placing it face up in the centre of the table. The next player to his left must play a card of the same value if he has one, placing it on top of the first card in the centre, and calling 'Snip'. If he has more than one card of the same value he plays only one of them. If he does not have a card of the same value he calls 'Pass'. It is then the turn of the next player on the left.

The game continues around the table in this way, each player playing a card of the same value as the first card if he can, or else calling 'Pass'. The player putting out the second card calls 'Snip', the player putting out the third card calls 'Snap', and the player putting out the fourth card calls 'Snorem'.

The player of the fourth card starts a new round by playing any card he chooses from his hand.

The winner is the first player to get rid of all his cards.

Variation 1
If a player has two or more cards of the same value then he must play them all in one turn. For example, if the first player plays a jack and the next player has two jacks he must play both of them at once, calling 'Snip Snap'.

Variation 2
Each of the players starts the game with an equal number of counters (or buttons or matchsticks or whatever). Whenever a player has to call 'Pass' he pays one counter into the kitty. The first player to get rid of all his cards wins all the counters in the kitty.

Happy Families

No. of players: 3 or more
Equipment: Normal pack of 52 cards (or 'Happy Families'
pack)
Complexity: ☆

This is a very popular game for young children. The whole pack is dealt out face down to the players. Some players may get one card more than the others but this does not really matter. Each player picks up and examines his cards and sorts them into 'families'. A family is four cards of the same value (e.g. four sixes or four queens). Throughout the game each player should take care to avoid letting other players see what cards he has in his hand.

The player to the left of the dealer begins the game by asking any other player for a particular card that he wants, to help complete a family. He may ask for any individual card he chooses provided that he already has at least one member of that family in his hand. If the player being asked has the card then it must be handed over to the player making the request, who again may ask any player for another particular card. He can go on doing this for as long as he continues to receive the cards he has asked for. When a player is asked for a card that he does not have then it becomes his turn to ask other players for the cards he wants.

Whenever a player collects all four members of a family he places the four cards face down on the table in front of him.

The game ends when all the cards have been collected into families, and the player who has collected the highest number of families is the winner.

Fish

No. of players: 2 or more
Equipment: Normal pack of 52 cards (or 'Happy Families'
pack)
Complexity: ☆

Fish is very similar to *Happy Families*, and like that game it may be played with an ordinary pack of cards or with a special 'Happy Families' pack.

Five cards are dealt out to each player, one at a time and face down. The rest of the pack is placed face down in the centre of the table and is known as the 'fish pile'. Each player picks up his cards and examines them. Throughout the game each player should take care that other players do not see what cards he has in his hand.

The player on the left of the dealer starts the game by asking any other player for any particular card he chooses – provided that he already has at least one card of the same value in his hand. If the player asked has the card then it must be handed over, and the first player may again ask any player for another card. He can continue doing this for as long as he receives the cards he has asked for.

When a player is asked for a card that he does not have then he says 'Fish' and the player making the request must take the top card from the fish pile. It then becomes the turn of the player saying 'Fish' to ask other players for the cards he wants. Whenever a player collects all four cards of a particular value he places them face down on the table in front of him.

The winner is the first player to get rid of all his cards. If two players finish at the same time, the one who has collected the most groups of four is the winner.

Go Boom

No. of players: 2 to 12
Equipment: Normal pack of 52 cards (or two packs if more than 6 players)
Complexity: ☆

The cards are shuffled and the dealer deals out the cards face down, dealing one card to each player in turn, and proceeding clockwise around the table until each player has been dealt seven cards. The remaining cards are placed face down in a neat pile (called the 'stock') in the centre of the table. Each player then picks up and examines his cards. The object of the game is to be the first player to get rid of all his cards.

The player to the left of the dealer starts the first round by choosing a card from his hand and placing it face up on the table beside the stock, thus forming the start of a new face-up pile. Then each player plays in turn, proceeding to the left around the table. Each player has to play a card of the same suit as the first card or, if he has no card of that suit in his hand, a card of the same value as the first card. For example, if the first card was the eight of hearts then he must play a heart or, if he has no hearts, an eight.

If a player has neither a card of the correct suit nor a card of the correct value in his hand then he must take a card from the top of the stock, and must carry on doing so until he picks a card that he can play. If all the cards of the stock have been taken he says 'Pass' and the turn passes to the next player.

The round ends when each player has played a card or has passed. The player who played the card of the highest value (ace counting high) starts the next round. If two or more players played equally high cards the first one to have played his card starts the next round.

The first player to get rid of all his cards is the winner. It is customary for the winner to yell 'Boom!' in as loud a voice as possible. (This might account for the name of the game.)

Variation
Go Boom may, if you like, be played for points. A series of games are played, and whenever a player 'goes boom' he scores points according to the total value of the cards left in the hands of the other players. An ace counts as one point, a two as two points and so on, court cards all counting as ten points. The first player to score 250 points, say, is the winner of the series.

Cheat

No. of players: 3 or more
Equipment: Normal pack of 52 cards
Complexity: ★

Cheat is an entertaining game that allows plenty of scope for lying and bluffing. It is best played as quickly as possible.

The cards are shuffled and the whole pack is dealt out to the players. Some players may get one card more than the others but this does not really matter. The object of the game is to get rid of all the cards in one's hand.

The player to the left of the dealer starts the game by choosing any card from his hand and placing it face down in the centre of the table. At the same time he announces its value. The next player on his left then plays a card face down on top of the first, announcing the next higher value. For example, if the first player said 'Nine', the second player must say 'Ten'. The card he plays may be a ten – he may be telling the truth. But on the other hand he may 'cheat' by playing a card of any other value.

So the game continues, each player in turn playing a card face down on to the centre pile and announcing the next value, the following calls being 'Jack', 'Queen', 'King', 'Ace', 'Two' etc. It is important that each player should make sure that none of the other players can see the value of the card he is playing.

Whenever a player has played his card any other player may challenge him by calling 'Cheat'. The card is then turned over so that all the players may see it. If the card actually is what the player announced it to be (i.e. he was telling the truth) then the challenger has to take all the cards from the centre of the table and add them to his hand. If the player *had* cheated, however, and the card is not what he had declared it to be then *he* has to add the cards from the centre of the table to *his* hand.

If several players all call 'Cheat' at more or less the same time, you may need an umpire to decide who called first and therefore has the right to be the challenger. But probably the best way to decide is to play by the rule that if two or more players call 'Cheat' at the same time the challenger is the one nearest to the left-hand side of the player being challenged.

After a challenge a new round starts with the player to the left of the challenged player playing and announcing any card he chooses from his hand.

The game ends when one player gets rid of all his cards, and that player is the winner.

The players who are most successful are usually those who can bluff by looking innocent when they are cheating and by looking guilty when they are playing truthfully.

I Doubt It

No. of players: 3 or more
Equipment: Normal pack of 52 cards
Complexity: ☆

I Doubt It is played in the same way as *Cheat*, except for the following differences:

(a) Instead of playing only one card at a time each player may play up to four cards at a time.
(b) The players announce the number of cards they are playing as well as their value (e.g. 'Three aces' or 'One three' or 'Four jacks' etc.).
(c) A player may 'cheat' not only by playing cards that are not of the value that he announces, but also by playing more cards than he announces.
(d) A challenge is issued by calling 'I doubt it'.

Slapjack

No. of players: 2 or more
Equipment: Normal pack of 52 cards (or two packs if there are more than 4 players)
Complexity: ☆

Slapjack is a simple game that may be enjoyed by very young children. It is most fun when played as quickly as possible.

The object of the game is to win all the cards by slapping the jacks when they appear. All the cards are dealt out to the players. It does not matter if some players get one card more than the others. Each player forms his cards into a neat pile face down in front of him without looking at them. The player to the left of the dealer starts the game by taking the top card of his pile and placing it face upwards in the centre of the table. The player on his left then takes the top card from his own pile and places it face upwards on top of the first player's card. Each player in turn around the table does the same, playing a card face up on top of the previous player's card.

Whenever a jack appears as the top card of the pile, the first player to slap his hand on top of it wins all the cards in the pile. He turns over the cards he has won and shuffles them into his own face-down pile. The player to his left then starts a new round by playing the top card of his pile face up in the centre. When more than one player slaps the jack the player whose hand is underneath wins the pile. If a player slaps a card that is not a jack he must give the top card of his pile to the player whose card he slapped.

A player who is left with no cards may stay in the game until the next jack is played. If he is the first to slap it he wins the pile and can carry on playing, otherwise he drops out of the game.

The winner is the player who wins all of the cards.

Menagerie

No. of players: 3 or more
Equipment: Normal pack of 52 cards (or preferably two packs if more than 4 are playing)
Complexity: ☆

This game, which is similar to *Snap*, is a great favourite with children. Before the game begins each player must be given the name of an animal – the longer the name the better. The fairest way to do this is to write some animal names on small pieces of paper which are then folded and mixed up, and to let each player pick one at random. Some suitable animal names are

RHINOCEROS	ANT-EATER	ORANG-UTANG
HIPPOPOTAMUS	CHIMPANZEE	FLITTERMOUSE
DROMEDARY	ARMADILLO	GRIZZLY BEAR
PORCUPINE	BUSHBABY	PLATYPUS

Each player must try to remember the animal names of the other players.

The cards are shuffled and are all dealt out to the players, one card at a time and face down. It does not matter if some players get one card more than the others. Each player forms his cards into a neat pile face down in front of him without looking at them. The player to the left of the dealer takes the top card from his pile and puts it face up on the table to start a new pile next to his face-down pile. The player on his left does the same, and so on around the table. The cards played on to the face-up piles should be placed neatly so that only the top card of each face-up pile can be seen. Whenever the top card of any player's face-up pile has the same value as the top card of another player's face-up pile, then each of these two players should, as quickly as possible, call out the other's animal name three times. The first to do so correctly wins the other's face-up pile and, turning it over, adds it to the bottom of his own face-down pile. The player to the left of the winner then starts a new round by turning up the top card of his pile, and so the game goes on.

A player who calls out an animal name by mistake (when there are no matching cards) must give his face-up pile to the player whose animal name he called out.

If a player has used all the cards in his face-down pile he turns over his face-up pile when it is his turn to play and continues playing from that. A player who has no cards left drops out of the game.

The winner is the player who wins all the cards.

Animal Noises

No. of players: 3 or more
Equipment: As for Menagerie
Complexity: ☆

Animal Noises is the same as *Menagerie* except that the players are given the names of animals (cat, dog, sheep, duck, donkey, cow etc.) whose noises may easily be imitated. When matching cards are seen the two players must each make the noise of the other's animal three times (e.g. 'Woof woof woof' or 'Baa baa baa').

War

No. of players: 2
Equipment: Normal pack of 52 cards
Complexity: ☆

War is a simple but satisfying game for which no skill whatever is required – the outcome is decided purely by chance.

One player deals out all the cards, one at a time and face down. Each player forms his cards into a neat pile face down in front of him, without looking at them. Each player then picks up the top card from his pile and the two cards are placed face upwards and side by side in the centre of the table.

If one card is of higher value than the other, the player who put out the higher card wins both of them and puts them, face down, at the bottom of his pile. Suits are not important – an ace is the highest value, followed by king, queen, jack, ten and so on down to two which is the lowest.

If both cards are of the same value, each player takes a card from the top of his pile and places it *face down* on top of his original card. He then plays one more card *face up* on top of that. If the two top cards are again equal, each player again plays a face-down card followed by a face-up card on top of the cards he has played previously. This goes on until one of the two top cards is higher than the other, and the player of the higher card wins all the cards in the centre of the table.

The game may be played until one player wins all the cards. But because the game may go on for a very long time when played this way, it may be decided that the winner is the player with the higher number of cards after the game has been played for some agreed length of time.

Cuckoo

No. of players: 3 or more
Equipment: Normal pack of 52 cards; 3 counters per player
Complexity: ☆

The object of this game (which also goes by the name of

Ranter-Go-Round) is to avoid being left with the lowest card. The cards rank in value from king (highest) to ace (lowest), suits being ignored. Each player is given three counters before the game begins. These are his 'lives' and when he has lost all three of them he is out of the game.

One card, face down, is dealt to each player. Each player picks up his card and looks at it, without letting it be seen by any of the other players. The player to the left of the dealer then decides whether he wants to keep his card or to exchange it. Naturally, if it is a high card he will want to keep it, but otherwise he puts it face down on the table and offers it to the next player on his left, saying 'Change'.

The player being offered the exchange may refuse it if his card is a king – he says 'King' and the first player must keep his own card. But if his card is not a king then he has no choice – he must accept the exchange. He puts his card face down on the table and each player picks up the other's card. But now it is his turn to decide whether to keep the card he has been given or to exchange it. If he so chooses he offers to exchange his card, in the manner just described, with the next player on his left. So the game goes on, once round the table, each player holding on to his card or offering to exchange it with the next player.

The dealer's turn comes last, and if he wants to exchange his card he does so by cutting the pack and taking the top card from the lower half. If the card the dealer takes from the pack is a king, he is the loser of the round and he loses a life. Otherwise the players all reveal their cards and the player with the lowest card loses a life. If two or more players tie for lowest card they all lose a life.

More rounds are played and each player drops out of the game when he has lost his last life. The winner is the last player left in the game.

Pelmanism

No. of players: 2 or more
Equipment: Normal pack of 52 cards
Complexity: ★

This game (also known as *Concentration*) is an excellent test of memory and of concentration. It can be enjoyed both by children and adults – and the younger players may often prove to be more skilful than their elders.

The pack is shuffled thoroughly and then all the cards are laid out, singly, face down on a large table (or on the floor). The cards may be laid out in rows or higgledy-piggledy, as long as no card is touching any other card.

Then each player in turn turns over any two cards so that all the players may see them. If the cards are of different values (e.g. a king and a seven) then he turns them face down again in their original positions and it is the next player's turn. But if the two cards are of the same value (e.g. two sixes) then the player wins them and puts them in a pile in front of him. He then has another turn and may continue as long as he turns over matching pairs. His turn ends when he turns over two cards that do not match.

Successful play depends on watching all the cards that are turned over and then replaced, and memorising their values and positions. For example, suppose the first player turned over a three and a seven and the second player turned over a king and a seven. The third player should immediately be able to turn over and win the pair of sevens – provided that he remembers where they are.

The game continues until all the cards have been won, and the player who has collected the highest number of cards is the winner.

My Ship Sails

No. of players: 4 to 7
Equipment: Normal pack of 52 cards
Complexity: ☆

My Ship Sails is a simple game but can be very exciting when played as quickly as possible.

The pack is shuffled and seven cards are dealt to each player, one card at a time and face down. The remaining cards are put to one side and are not used. Each player picks up his cards and sorts them into suits. Throughout the game each player should take care not to let any of the other players see the cards he has in his hand. The object of the game is to be the first player to collect seven cards of the same suit (i.e. seven hearts, seven diamonds, seven clubs or seven spades).

Each player selects from his hand one card that he does not want and places it face down on the table in front of him. All the players, at the same time, pass their face-down card to the next player on the left. Each player then picks up the card he has been passed and puts it in his hand with his other cards.

Again each player chooses a card to get rid of and the cards are passed on in the same way. This goes on until one player has managed to collect seven cards of the same suit. He calls out 'My ship sails' and wins the game.

Rolling Stone

No. of players: 4, 5 or 6
Equipment: Normal pack of 52 cards
Complexity: ✲

The object of the game is to be the first player to get rid of all his cards. Before the game starts, some cards must be removed from the pack so that there are just eight cards for each player. If there are six players all the twos should be removed; if there are five players all the twos, threes and fours should be removed; if there are four players all the twos, threes, fours, fives and sixes should be removed. The remaining cards are shuffled thoroughly and then dealt out one at a time, face down, so that each player receives eight cards. Each player picks up his hand and sorts it into suits.

The player to the left of the dealer chooses a card from his hand and plays it face up in the centre of the table. Each player in turn, proceeding round the table to the left, must place on top of it a card of the same suit if he can. If all the players put out a card of the same suit the pile of cards is put to one side and is not used for the rest of the game. The player who played the highest card (ace being high) then starts the next round by playing any card from his hand.

If at any time a player is unable to play a card of the suit that was led he must pick up all the cards that have already been played in that round and add them to his hand. He then starts a new round by playing a card of any other suit (he is not allowed to start with one of the cards he has just picked up).

The first player to get rid of all his cards is the winner.

INDEX